Spiritual Assassin

Wake Up the Warrior God Created You to be to Dismantle the Kingdom of Darkness

Printed in the United States of America

First Printing, 2020

ISBN: 978-0-578-66017-2

Published by DoQuoi Green Ministries

4780 Ashford Dunwoody Rd. Suite A #199

Atlanta, GA 30338

www.doquoigreen.org

Part I. Assassins' Battle Preparation

Introduction.....V

Chapter 1: The Two Opposing Governmental Structures.....1

Chapter 2: Preparing for the Fight.....14

Chapter 3: Understanding Your Responsibility.....25

Chapter 4: Understanding Your Rights vs. Demonic Legal Rights.....41

Chapter 5: The Battleground.....59

Chapter 6: The Weapon of Prayer.....72

Chapter 7: The Warfare Team.....87

Part II. On the Offensive: Assassins' Weaponry of Retaliation

Chapter 8: Putting Angels to Work in Warfare.....98

Chapter 9: Engaging the Enemy and Exposing Witchcraft.....111

Chapter 10: Demonic Plots and Patterns.....135

Chapter 11: How to War through Praise and Worship.....153

Chapter 12: The Blood Power Activated.....165

Chapter 13: Releasing the Destructive Power of the Fire of God.....174

Chapter 14: Calling Forth the Four Winds.....183

Chapter 15: Fight for Your Family: Warfare Over Your Bloodline…..192

Chapter 16: Your Divine Right to Healing: Confronting the Spirit of Infirmity…..207

Part III. On the Defensive: Assassins Closing Demonic Doors

Chapter 17: The Warfare Over Your Mind…..220

Chapter 18: The Weapon of Faith…..230

Chapter 19: Relationships: Destroying Covenant-Breaking and Sex Demons…..250

Chapter 20: Regaining Control of Spiritual Gates…..278

Chapter 21: Warfare Over Your Wealth…..288

Chapter 22: One of Satan's Top Secrets to Delayed Manifestation Exposed…..310

Part IV. Assassins' Strategy to Maintain the Victory

Chapter 23: The Need for Deliverance…..323

Chapter 24: Defending Against Demonic Retaliation…..342

Chapter 25: The Hostile Takeover…..350

Warfare Declarations…..363

Part I. Assassins' Battle Preparation

Introduction

You're not from the earth. You are from heaven. You originated in heaven inside of God. You're a spirit being with a soul and flesh. Although you are not from the earth, you have been sent to earth by God to bring His kingdom on earth, and the moment you became a seed and put on flesh in your mother's womb, you became a part of a war. It's a fierce and brutal war that Satan and his demons wage against us.

They try to get you and me to not fulfill our earthly mission given to us by God. They too are not from the earth. They were once with God, as you know. They were a part of the family of God and also originated in heaven, but because of their rebellion, they were banished to the earth. The crazy thing is they were on earth before us and really believe it belongs to them. They believe it's their domain, but they are sadly mistaken. The first thing God gave humans was dominion on earth. We were commanded to rule. Although you have the victory in heaven in spiritual warfare, you must manifest that victory on earth. Contrary to popular belief, it doesn't just automatically happen. It's a battle over territory. Where God has planted you, He expects you to flourish. He expects you to rule. The warfare comes into play when demons don't want to leave the territory you were assigned. So, you find yourself in a standoff. They won't leave if you ask them, but you must command them. Some will leave at your first command in Jesus's name, but there are others who are determined to engage you in a long battle. That's why persistence is critical. You must **Pray and War Until You See the Results.** You must be persistent and consistent not only in your pursuit of God, but you must be persistent and consistent in your counterattack against the enemy. You don't stop praying and warring until you see breakthrough! Spiritual warfare is not something to be afraid of, but it's something to be aware of because you're in it whether you know it or not. It's not enough to just fight, but you must know whom it is you're fighting against. The enemy studies you, so you need to have an effective strategy to fight them. A lot of Satan's camp will be exposed in this book to help you know who and what you're fighting against and how to combat their tactics.

At the writing of this book, my wife Donna and I have already helped walk hundreds of people through the deliverance and soul-healing process. I have trained and influenced thousands in strategic prayer and spiritual warfare. I'm not new to these topics. Through revelation of the Holy Spirit, I have been blessed to have been given some great insight on the topic of spiritual warfare, deliverance, and prayer. It's constantly evolving, and none of this can be done without the Holy Spirit. He teaches me new things and strategy all the time, and I am constantly in awe. Some say this is the dirty work, but I say this is all of our work as warriors of Christ. I'm excited to share some of my revelation, experience, and knowledge in this book. Some of what you read in this book may shock you, but as I tell everyone who goes through our deliverance and soul-healing process, stick with the process. Participate in your own deliverance, and you will definitely get there.

You must know that God has given you access to His power so that you can destroy what is trying to destroy you! Anything not of God is of Satan. Anything that rejects Christ is of Satan. It doesn't matter how nice and sweet it sounds; if it does not glorify God through Christ, it was sent by Satan. What makes the warfare so much heavier is that there are Christians who don't believe Satan is real or that demons even exist, although we hear about them all throughout Scripture.

We see it in Scripture through idol worship of false gods (which are demons) and demons manifesting themselves in people, sin, disobedience, rebellion, etc. Scripture talks about Satan, the antichrist, the dragon, etc. Keep in mind that Satan and the angels who rebelled with him are fallen angels who were cast down to the earth. Some roam around seeking whom to possess. Some are in chains in hell right now awaiting their final judgment. Some will be released before their final judgment. It is very real, which is why spiritual warfare is very real. Satan knows he is defeated, but he wants to cause hell in the lives of God's children. In the midst of it all, we have power over Satan and all who work for him. Hence, you are already victorious, but you must walk in your victory because the fight is still taking place on earth.

Smiles and nice words aren't always holy. If God through Christ is not the engine behind it, it's from Satan. We are in a war, and it's between good and evil, darkness and light. True freedom and peace come from God and are your rights as a child of God. You must exercise those rights and take back what's yours.

Satan is banking on you not knowing how to fight in the spirit so he can keep robbing you. It's time to learn how to war in the spirit. It begins and ends with prayer. However, you must also know what God's Word says. Even if you just have one or two verses that you have memorized, when you pray, pray that back to God. Your words are powerful, but when you speak God's Word over your life, it's far more powerful!

When you declare God's Word, it always accomplishes something in the earth. It never returns without accomplishing a goal. Satan and his demons know God's Word, so we should know it too and apply it. The Word of God is the constitution in God's government, and we need to study it. If you don't know what God's Word says about you, you are living below your potential. Study His Word.

When you combine prayer, God's Word, and spiritual warfare strategy, you become a spiritual assassin and Satan and his demons' biggest problem! You are a warrior, and warriors must know how to fight. You're God's child! The title alone won't do you any good in spiritual warfare, but you need to walk in the power that's behind the title.

A child of God in God's army who does not know how to fight in the spirit is a liability. God is ready to train you for warfare! It's one thing when you just don't know, but in the revival season we've already entered, there will be an awakening of God's people to understand who has been stealing from us and how to fight and command it to be given back. Some battles the Lord will fight for you, but most battles He will fight through you. You must make yourself available for Him to use you. This is why prayer is so vital. There are certain levels of God's power you cannot consistently access until you consistently pray.

Spiritual warfare isn't spooky. It's not scary, but it is confronting Satan and his demons on behalf of God to remind them that we run this yard! They are uninvited guests on our territory. They don't like us, and we don't like them. However, we're more powerful. We just need to know how to access the power.

We must understand that everything God creates, Satan tries to duplicate. Satan is not original. However, as Satan attempts to duplicate, he makes an evil and twisted version of what God created. **You are an original creation by God, and there was never and will never be another like you!**

Destructive cycles in our lives are caused by demons, and if they see any opening, they will influence others to connect with you to continue the cycle. It will continue until you are delivered and the cycle is broken. God has placed a sword in your hand, and you must learn to use it to fight what has been fighting you in the spirit!

You can no longer sit back and let the works of Satan control your life. Command every demon trying to ruin your life to leave. God has given you the power and authority to do so. You are a king or queen on earth, and you don't have to settle for crumbs because God has given you access to the entire palace. You have to fight for what's yours sometimes. You are not weak because God is not weak. Stop leaning on your feelings and start leaning on your faith!

Through many trials and errors and unfortunate defeats, I have learned how to win through the leading of the Holy Spirit when it comes to spiritual warfare. I have become a spiritual assassin. I eradicate, eliminate, erase, and utterly assassinate witches, warlocks, and sorcerers in the spirit who are on assignment to kill me, my family, and my destiny. That may make you uncomfortable when you're not used to it because you've been taught only to love your neighbor and those who persecute you. That is true; Christ commanded us to do so. Trust me, I understand because I was afraid to assassinate witches until my wife encouraged me to do so because of the intense warfare. When I became more aggressive, they knew I meant business. It doesn't mean Satan didn't send more troops, but they had to respect me in a different way because the casualties were piling up in the kingdom of darkness.

Scripture backs it up in Exodus 22:18: "You shall not permit a sorceress to live." Witches, warlocks, sorcerers, and demons on assignment to kill you aren't your neighbors. Demons are evil spirits, and witches, warlocks, and sorcerers are human agents who work for Satan. You have a legal right on the spiritual battlefield to shoot and kill. It's not done in the physical, but we handle it in the spirit realm through prayer and strategic warfare by using the spiritual weapons God has given us. There are casualties in warfare, and you should refuse to be one. However, our wicked enemies will become the casualties.

You were born into spiritual warfare, so it will make sense that you know how to fight the enemy in spiritual warfare. The enemy waged war against you before your mother gave birth to you. Thank God for protection and for teaching you how to fight back. You are very important in God's government, and that's what makes you such a threat to Satan's government. You have a right to be there because God placed you there. Don't allow scare tactics of the enemy make you fold. Walk in the power God gave you! God gave us a clear outline. It is outlined in His Word, and Christ showed us how to live it. Live like the world, and you become a demon's playground. Live like Christ, and you become a demon's biggest problem. When engaging demons in spiritual warfare, know that you will lose when you fight in feelings, but you always win when you fight in faith. Satan was an enemy of God before he was an enemy of yours. He's been around a long time. Follow God's rules, not your rules. It's a proven formula. Do it God's way.

Stop trying to fit into the world. Stop trying to look for the common because you will never be common if you're doing God's will. Jesus was not common. He was so uncommon that people were waiting for Him to show up and some of them still missed

Him because He was so uncommon. Stop looking for normal. A child of God walking in their power and authority will seem abnormal to the world, but you will produce results. It takes an extraordinary person to defy the ordinary because it's your job to bring God's extraordinary kingdom in this ordinary-acting world. The enemy wants you to think that you're crazy and will use people to make you think you are. You were sent on earth to do God's will, and if any demon gets in the way of that, you're expected to rebuke them and cast them aside.

Some overlooked Jesus on earth, but demons recognized Him immediately. Some overlook you, but demons recognize your power. You need to use it. You have gifts, and those gifts will be used by God if you surrender to Him. God qualified you before any demon attacked you, but no attack can completely stop you unless you choose to quit. Demons recognize who you are supposed to be in God before you do, and they come to steal what you don't know you have yet. You must pray. Too many are walking around saying they don't have much. You have the inheritance of God, and it's an eternity's worth. Go get it! You shouldn't go on with business as usual. You shouldn't take spiritual warfare lightly because you have an enemy who is literally trying to kill you, while Christ wants you to have life. You should look at the magnitude of the fight. Satan sent demons to kill us. Satan put a hit out on your life, but it's nothing to fear because what's trying to kill us is not more powerful than us when we are in Christ. This warfare is a battle between two kingdoms. God's kingdom has supreme power and authority. Satan's kingdom has some power, but its power is no match for the power in God's kingdom. The creation can never be greater than the creator. The bottom line in spiritual warfare is Satan doesn't want you to live for God, and God wants you to live more abundantly through Christ! If your light isn't shining in dark places, you're simply a spectator and not demonstrating the power you have in you to bring glory to God. You're not on earth to just take up space. There must be action. People are always waiting for their time. Your time is always now to do what God wants you to do right now.

There are some who are deceived and are convinced that Satan and his demons don't exist. Some are convinced that warfare is not needed and misled to believe all we need is to love God. God gave us work here, and that work comes with great responsibility. That work is also challenged by opposition. Come to grips with the fact that the enemy will oppose you. The enemy is not your biggest problem in warfare but backing down from them is. When demons invade your territory, it is your divine right and responsibility to make them leave in Jesus's name.

The goal is to save you time, heartaches, heartbreaks, and mistakes by not having to go through what I went through for as long as I went through it as you become the spiritual assassin God has called you to be. Everyone needs a mentor. The old saying goes, "When the student is ready, the mentor appears." I want to say thank you for taking time out to read this book. Thank you for investing in yourself. I am elated that the Holy Spirit led you to get a copy of this book. It is my prayer that you are ready for significant change in your life, and reading this book is one giant step forward on your journey toward winning in Christ on earth as you already have in heaven on a consistent basis.

Chapter 1: The Two Opposing Governmental Structures

In learning about spiritual warfare, you must first recognize three key points. First, there are only two sides in spiritual warfare. Also, there is a difference between prayer and spiritual warfare. And you must have a strategy in spiritual warfare.

Let's first consider that there are only two sides in spiritual warfare: **God's side and Satan's side.** Good vs. evil. (God's side wins.) There are two governments.

We must first understand that there are six key components that make up God's government.

1.) A King- God

2.) Kingdom or Territory- Heaven and earth, first, second, and third heaven

3.) Inhabitants- Angels/spirits in heaven/humans

4.) Rules/Constitution- Word of God. It's also the type of food in God's government. This is what we feed our spirit with.

5.) Language- Prayer. Prayer is also the currency of God's government and another way in which we feed our spirit. It's also our war cry in battle.

6.) Currency- Faith and Prayer

Satan also tried to duplicate what God did. Notice I said **tried.** His government is no match for God's government, but he is organized. His organized crimes unit aims to shut down God's government on earth, but it won't happen. There are six key components that make up Satan's government as well.

1.) A King- Satan

2.) Kingdom or Territory- Hell and territory he stole from Christians. His spiritual world under the sea, in the air, on the land.

3.) Inhabitants- Demons/souls in hell/human agents who work for him

4.) Rules/Constitution- Doctrine of Devils/kill, steal, destroy. It's also the type of food in Satan's government. They love human blood or blood sacrifices unto them.

5.) Language- Idol worship. Demonic worship is also the currency of Satan's government as it's how demonic transactions are made, and it is used by non-Christians and even some who call themselves Christians who intentionally invite demons in to possess them as a part of their worship. In this government, demons can also print their own money or give money to those who are employed in this system.

6.) Currency- Fear and blood

We know that we're in a war between good and evil, and we're on the good side. The battle is already won, but you still have to show up to receive the rewards of the victory. Demons and witches and warlocks have power, but our power is greater than their power because we have the power of the Holy Spirit. With that being said, they have power that they use against us in an attempt to weaken us. Demons may have power, but you have the power and authority to strip them of that power so they will be powerless in your life.

Demons can only steal where there is an opportunity for them to steal. You can break the legal rights any demon feels they have to steal. Some demons have robbed us with our eyes opened. However, it's time for you to strip the enemy of what they stripped from you! The enemy is being exposed in your life, and when they're exposed, use the power and authority given to you through Christ to cast them out. Power gives one the ability to do something. There is a force behind that power. The Holy Spirit is the power that allows you to do God's will and defeat demons at the same time. The Holy Spirit is the power, and He gives you the ability to walk in His power. Demons have the ability to cause chaos in our lives, but as followers of Christ, we have the ability to strip them of that ability.

God is calling His soldiers to the forefront, and backing down is not an option. Your training has brought you here. Your faith has brought you here. God is calling you to participate in revival to bring His kingdom on earth like the world has never seen it before. Greater glory is coming. It's time to bankrupt the works of the enemy in your life. The church has been living below its potential for too long. God's glory is coming to revive His people to wake up and rule on earth!

You've been called into a private meeting with God, and He is going to unlock things in you that you didn't imagine would happen so soon. Rapid shifts are taking place. Rapid acceleration. Things are moving rapidly in the spirit, and that means it is beginning to rapidly manifest in the natural. Demons know this, and that's why they have been practically working overtime. Don't be fooled by what you see because all the enemy is trying to do is to convince you that they're not already defeated. You've already won!

Spiritual warfare is real, and when the enemy messes with who and what belongs to you, you have an obligation to fight back in the spirit! God has equipped you for the warfare. The warfare is increasing because your responsibility and territory assigned to you has increased. Either way, use your power over the enemy. Notice that I said to use your power. You have power and authority over demons, but it only works when you actually use it.

Demons want you to be frustrated with what's going on so that you don't make them leave. You must command them to go in Jesus's name! You must be persistent until they go. They prey on our ignorance. They prey on our weaknesses. The power of the Holy Spirit in you is greater than any weakness the enemy tries to attack. You are in God's army, so you must know how to fight. If you sit around and let demons beat on you, they will. Wake up to the power of the Holy Spirit in you and beat on them.

Your threat level to Satan's kingdom has increased, and they're plotting against you. Send the blood of Jesus to destroy their plans. Demons know that you matter, so they want to do everything they can to get you off track. Every demonic plot against you is a response to God's divine plan for your life. Your response will spoil their plans. Don't shy away from your power. Your power has nothing to do with your earthly status, but it has everything to do with your kingdom status in God. It's time to wake up to your power. When you wake up to the power of God in you, you will stop being intimidated by the power of the enemy. Your power is greater!

You are a conqueror, and conquerors aren't manmade, they're God-made. You must take over in your God-assigned territory and be unapologetic about it. People are waiting for you to shift into the position God is calling you to because there are answers in you that they've been waiting on for a while.

There is something called the 10/40 window. A Christian missionary named Luis Bush coined the phrase in 1990. It's a rectangular area on the map going across Northern Africa and most of Asia from 10 degrees latitude north of the equator to 40 degrees latitude north of the equator. In that rectangular area is two-thirds of the world's population, or more than 4 billion people. Ninety percent are unevangelized and have never heard the gospel. Half of the world's least evangelized cities are in this window. It is often known as the "Resistant Belt." Many of the leaders of the countries in this window are opposed to Christian work in these areas. Roughly 85% of the people living in this window are the poorest of the poor in the world and 84% have the lowest quality of life. Islam, Buddhism, and Hinduism are the main religions there. So, we know that Satan has been given great access in this window, and the foundation has grown strong there. There are also demonic principalities that attempt to influence politics and have certain laws put in place to give demons more legal access.

We know we are overcomers and more than conquerors, but as glory carriers, we want to reclaim territory on earth for God's kingdom that Satan has taken hold of. All the earth is the Lord's, so if Satan has any territory, it is because we gave some of it away. We must reclaim territory that rightfully belongs to the kingdom of God. This is why we must be strategic and also know the areas we are called in. We all have assigned territories, and if we do our part, we will take back the territories assigned to us that Satan and his demons have set up demonic portals in. You can't afford to lose territory to the enemy. Fight back in the spirit and take back the territory that rightfully belongs to you.

Matthew 13:24-25: *Another parable He put forth to them, saying: "The kingdom of heaven is like a man who sowed good seed in his field; but while men slept, his enemy came and sowed tares among the wheat and went his way."*

Here, we find Jesus telling a story about someone who sowed good seeds, but the enemy came and sowed weeds to grow when the crops began to grow. This example shows us one tactic of the enemy in warfare. For starters, Satan and his demons want to catch us sleeping. In other words, they want to sow bad seeds when we aren't looking, or they try to trick us. Those who operate in occult practices of witchcraft, which include sorcery, divination, etc., and other evil spirits attempt to cast spells and curses and plant negative seeds during this time while most sleep. This is why the enemy tries to attack us in our sleep and tries to enter through our dreams through the demon known as Mare. We hear the term nightMare, but there are demonic forces who cause them. "Mare" is an actual demon. This is why it is important to pray before you go to sleep.

The term occult refers to those who seek or operate in hidden or secret knowledge pertaining to things like magic, mystical, voodoo, astrology, tarot cards, psychics, necromancy (supposedly communicating with the dead, but it's really demons posing as the deceased), etc. It's a big deal to keep a secret how they operate unless you're a part of it. It's like a secret society and the aims may vary, but it's all influenced by Satan's kingdom.

Many of you feel like you have done well by others and try to live a peaceful life, but it seems like trouble always seems to find you. It's not so much about what you've done, but what has been done while you were sowing good seeds. Don't be discouraged because we see here that Jesus let us know that the enemy will attempt to sow bad seeds. When we recognize it in our lives, we now know how to attack it in spiritual warfare. You must open your mouth and speak crop failure to every seed that demons have sowed in or around your life. Declare that it will not take root!

Satan and his demons have attempted to sow seeds in your life. They can go way back to your ancestors. They could be in relationships, friendships, job, finances, health, etc. Once you recognize something that you know is not from God or of God in your life, you must pray for revelation to locate the seed in the spirit. Whenever there are reoccurring problems or attacks in specific areas of your life, it can be traced back to a seed planted by Satan. Some of you can go back to your childhood and see some of the things you had to overcome then because Satan and his demons felt they had rights to you through your family bloodline. If you are to be married, Satan doesn't want you married. If you're married, he doesn't want you happily married. He wants to keep you broke, depressed, sad, lonely, and to steal any and every blessing sent by God for you.

6

As spiritual agents of Christ, it's our duty to investigate what is going on. We investigate by seeking God and getting revelation from the Holy Spirit. Demonic agents of Satan's goals are to stop you from seeing the hand they have played in your life. Satan and his demons hate to be exposed because they are automatically weakened. Satan is frightened by revelation you receive from the Holy Spirit because he knows it gives you more ammunition to use. For every attack from Satan and his workers, you are equipped with a far more powerful counterattack. You just have to tap into your power!

This passage lets us know that there is an enemy trying to work against us. We all have been and will be attacked by Satan, his demons, and human agents, but we all have the power to overcome through the blood of Jesus. We win.

1 Peter 5:8-9 gives us even more insight into this battle:

Be sober, be vigilant; because your adversary the devil walks about like a roaring lion, seeking whom he may devour. Resist him, steadfast in the faith, knowing that the same sufferings are experienced by your brotherhood in the world.

We know that Satan and his demons go about the earth looking for whom they may devour. Demons are looking for any opening possible through sin and disobedience, whether from you or from your parents or those before you. They are looking to gain access to you through you hooking up with the wrong people. They will jump on the wave of negative words spoken to you. This is why you must rebuke and cast down the seed of negative words spoken to you so it does not take root because words attach to something. Keep your eyes open through prayer, and God will expose the devil and the traps that have been set in your life. If Satan is going about like a roaring lion, he's looking to tear us apart, but he knows he can only attack in one of two ways: if God allows it, or if we or someone in our bloodline allows it through sin, disobedience, ungodly covenants, etc. Satan must still be governed by the laws of the spirit realm (which I will discuss in detail in chapter 4). Technically, when God allows it, it's really a legal right the enemy tries to use anyway. God can use what the enemy tries to do to us to bring shame to the enemy. This can happen often because the enemy often goes too far.

We are told to resist the devil and to be strong in our faith. Resisting doesn't mean running, but it means to stand your ground. Resisting is to oppose the enemy. It means you don't back down. Attacks may come, but we have already overcome. We see from verse 9 that we all will experience tough times from attacks, but we must keep the faith because our faith in God will give us strength to fight through and break through. Tell the devil and his crew to leave in Jesus's name. God sent you to earth to rule, and you must evict the enemy from your life. Satan and the workers in his kingdom are looking for territory to take. They are looking for families and households to take. This is another reason why God told us to rule on earth. You would fight to protect those you love in the natural, but more importantly, you must fight to protect them and yourself in the spirit!

Secondly, **there is a difference between prayer and spiritual warfare.**

Prayer is your communication with God. You are literally communing with God and maintaining and building your relationship with Him. There is so much to God. We are always learning more and more. We have the opportunity to go deeper and deeper into the knowledge of Him. Prayer is your currency used to make spiritual transactions from heaven to earth.

Prayer is how you bring God's kingdom on earth as it is in heaven. Prayer is also your war cry. Prayer and spiritual warfare must go hand and hand. Spiritual warfare is a spiritual war between God's army and Satan's army. So, you must be armed spiritually through prayer and God's Word, which strengthens your spirit to be able to enter into spiritual warfare. If you go into spiritual warfare without having already formed a habit of praying unto God, it's like going into a war without strategy, guidance, or full protection.

Along with prayer, you still need the Holy Spirit to lead you and guide you in the midst of warfare. You are able to engage the devil and his demons in spiritual warfare because you are coming in the name of Jesus Christ. You are covered in the blood of Jesus. You have warring angels also fighting on your behalf. So, it's a team effort. This is when you began to literally war with your words and the Word of God. You command what has been attacking you or someone else to leave. You plead the blood of Jesus. You rebuke demons, cast them out, etc. You can easily go from warfare back into prayer to God. God doesn't just want you to ask Him to deliver you, but He wants to use you to go and fight what has been tormenting you.

2 Corinthians 10:3-6: *For though we walk in the flesh, we do not war according to the flesh. For the weapons of our warfare are not carnal but mighty in God for pulling down strongholds, casting down arguments and every high thing that exalts itself against the knowledge of God, bringing every thought into captivity to the obedience of Christ, and being ready to punish all disobedience when your obedience is fulfilled.*

Here we find the apostle Paul defending his ministry. There were those who were attempting to discredit his ministry and the gospel he preached. Opposition will come when you are doing the right thing, but you already have the victory. This is another example showing us that it is not a flesh fight, but a spiritual one. Our weapons are not of the world because worldly weapons cannot accomplish anything in a war in the spiritual realm. The weapons of our warfare are not carnal, but mighty. There is more revelation on this passage. It's not only talking about how our weapons are not fleshly, but the weapons also referred to here in this passage are angels. The heavenly host. They are mighty and pull down strongholds. You have an entire army fighting with and for you. We can utilize this heavenly army as a weapon and send them to fight on our behalf. Of course, these angels who fight for us are spirit. We can send them as a weapon in our toolbelt to fight on our behalf.

A demonic stronghold is an incorrect thought pattern. It can be a simple seed the enemy plants in our mind and we believe it, even though it's a lie. However, based on our flesh/feelings, we may believe it for a period of time until we correct that thought pattern with the truth of God's Word. So, we must cast down that stronghold. You must renounce it and cast it down in the spirit. A stronghold in general is referred to as a castle, fortress, or anything that is fortified. In this passage, it was figuratively speaking of a fortified wall of defense that was based on arguments and reasoning philosophers and teachers used to attempt to discredit the Word of God. This was a spiritual issue. With our spiritual weapons, we can pull down those strongholds.

This passage paints a picture of how the enemy will attempt to build a stronghold, wall, etc., around you and hide behind it while attempting to use it as a defense or offense against followers of Christ. So, we are to tear down these walls and anything that tries to exalt itself above God or goes against God's will. Any thought pattern contrary to God's will is Satan's attempt to exalt himself above the truth of God. You must cast it down in Jesus's name. You must tear down walls set up by the enemy through prayer, study of God's Word, praise and worship, and obedience. You have the ability to demolish the strongholds, take thoughts captive, and punish disobedience in the spirit. The way you punish disobedience is simply through obedience. You are royalty of God sent from heaven to rule on earth on His behalf. Take your place! This is very important to understand when it comes to deliverance: Not only must we be delivered from anything that has held us in bondage, but we are expected to also be able to deliver others through the power of Christ at work in our lives.

There are many weapons we can use in spiritual warfare, including our spiritual gifts. However, I have included seven key weapons. We will get deeper into weapons later in the book.

1.) **The Name of Jesus/Blood of Jesus**
2.) **The Word of God**

3.) **Prayer/Fasting**

4.) **Angels**

5.) **Praise and Worship**

6.) **Power of Your Words**

7.) **Love** (showing love of Christ to your enemies)

Finally, there must be a strategy in spiritual warfare.

2 Chronicles 20:17-22: *"'You will not need to fight in this battle. Position yourselves, stand still and see the salvation of the LORD, who is with you, O Judah and Jerusalem!' Do not fear or be dismayed; tomorrow go out against them, for the LORD is with you." And Jehoshaphat bowed his head with his face to the ground, and all Judah and the inhabitants of Jerusalem bowed before the LORD, worshiping the LORD. Then the Levites of the children of the Kohathites and of the children of the Korahites stood up to praise the LORD God of Israel with voices loud and high.*
So they rose early in the morning and went out into the Wilderness of Tekoa; and as they went out, Jehoshaphat stood and said, "Hear me, O Judah and you inhabitants of Jerusalem: Believe in the LORD your God, and you shall be established; believe His prophets, and you shall prosper." And when he had consulted with the people, he appointed those who should sing to the LORD, and who should praise the beauty of holiness, as they went out before the army and were saying:

"Praise the LORD,

For His mercy endures forever."

Now when they began to sing and to praise, the LORD set ambushes against the people of Ammon, Moab, and Mount Seir, who had come against Judah; and they were defeated.

Jehoshaphat was king of Judah at the time, and he prayed to God because the enemy army was going to attack. He fasted and prayed to God and ordered a fast for the entire city. The Lord told Jehoshaphat a few verses prior that the battle was not his, but it was the Lord's. The Lord said that they would not have to fight this battle. This shows that there are some battles that can only be won in the spirit. Truthfully, every battle is first won or lost in the spirit.

Their praise confused the enemy, and Judah won the battle. Your praise is a powerful weapon. Even when we look surrounded and like we are defeated, we must know that we have already won. Our praise to God also wins battles. We can praise Him knowing the victory has already been won regardless of what it looks like. **Give God praise even when it looks hopeless because praise has a proven record of producing results.**

Notice that for this particular battle, the strategy changed. All they were to do was stand in position. We should never run ahead of God in battle. There are some battles where we don't even have to get on the field. Although we are in the battle, the strategy may change, and we must adapt. Had they gone and fought in this battle, they would have suffered damage and lost the battle because it was not God's instructions. Obedience is key. Not just obedience when you feel like obeying, but I'm talking about immediate obedience.

We must always be ready to change roles or strategy in different seasons. Your role and assignment may change in different seasons. You should never get too comfortable with doing just one thing because God is the God of a new thing! God is always adding onto your tool belt. You should be able to advance in ranks over the course of your life. If you are in battle and fighting in the wrong position, you are open to higher levels of attack than you are equipped to deal with. As you advance, your position and responsibilities will change. This is why we must stay in communication with our commander-in-chief, God.

Strategy is so important because you must know when to fight with your words, when to fight with your actions, when to fight with your praise, etc. God's given you many weapons, and one advantage you have in spiritual warfare is the enemy doesn't know which one you'll use at any given time! It's just like a surprise attack. They think you're going to use the last weapon and then God switches it up.

Strategy is critical because it gives you a distinct advantage over the enemy. The enemy cannot get revelation; only the redeemed children of God can. So, demons try to get intel from us based off our revelation. The good news is that as you employ the strategies given to you from heaven, you will always be one step ahead of the enemy. The attack may come, but it will eventually fall flat because it will only elevate you and shame the enemy. As you progress through this book, I want you to be mad at the enemy. However, now you will be even more equipped to do something about it.

Chapter 2: Preparing for the Fight

Before you engage the enemy in warfare, you must go in knowing that you have already won! It is a certain mind-set that you must have. You're not going in hoping that you will win, but you are going in knowing you have already won.

You are a soldier enlisted in the army of God, and your role is very important for the overall mission. What you do matters. Satan and his demons will certainly try everything they can to get you to drop out, but you must persevere. The only way a child of God can lose to Satan is if the child of God does not accept the fact that he or she has already won. You win.

God does not enlist losers into His kingdom army. He only enlists winners, and you are a winner because you are in Christ. You must understand this because it requires you to speak a winner's language, not a language of one who is defeated. The language spoken in God's army is faith, and one who doesn't speak this language doesn't have access to the spoils from the victory.

As a member of God's kingdom army, you must have discipline because trying to do it your way instead of God's way will lead to disaster. This is very important as it goes back to strategy. Following God's strategy is the best way to consistently win in spiritual warfare. You don't know everything or have everything, but when you have the Holy Spirit living in you, you now have access to everything. Therefore, your victories are limitless. For every battle you enter into in the spirit realm, God has a winning strategy for you to follow.

Spiritual warfare isn't for the fearful because there's no fear in Christ. You're fighting in His name and His power, and that scares the enemy. One part of preparing for the fight is in making sure that you remove anything that opposes God. Fear, doubt, stress, worry, etc., oppose God. Those are enemies of God. When you walk in fear and doubt, you are opposing God because they are enemies of God. Therefore, you must activate your faith in God! You certainly don't want to engage in spiritual warfare and turn against God in war by allowing fear and doubt to push your faith aside. It's impossible to fight Satan and his demons without faith in God through Christ because you cannot access any power from God without faith. Spiritual warfare is not a game. It is a real war that you are in whether you signed up for it or not. So, it's up to you if you will take the necessary steps to prepare for the fight or go into the fight and surrender to the enemy. You don't have to be a prisoner of war. God gave you the power and authority to enter into spiritual warfare and make the enemy run.

If you want to measure strength, look at who your strength relies on. If it's in people, you're weak. If it's in Christ, you're strong. Some people focus on the wrong things, and it's often based on what they see with their physical eyes rather than what they see through the lens of the spirit. In spiritual warfare, you can't go by what you see or hear in the physical, but you must go by what God said and what you see in the spirit.
There is such a thing as being weak in the flesh, but there is no such thing as being weak in Christ. This is why we must be in Him. If you step out of Christ, you step out of power/authority and lower your rank without the covering that comes with the level you were on.

You've come through too much getting to this level to go back to eating from the table God lifted you from because you think this level is hard! The weight may seem heavy, but you are more than capable of handling it. You're not in warfare just for yourself, but for your family and many others God will assign to you.
There is a war that Satan and his demons have waged against God's kingdom, but although they started the fight, we will finish it. You just need to get on the field and fight. You must know that you have power over Satan, and your power is at its highest when you make room for the Holy Spirit to take full control. When you do that, it is a certainty that you will be entrusted with even more. God trusts you with more because you are able to do more!

There are at least three key principles when preparing for spiritual warfare:

1.) Be Dressed for Spiritual Warfare

2.) Have the Right Mind-set for Spiritual Warfare

3.) Study the Blueprint

1.) Be Dressed for Spiritual Warfare

Ephesians 6:10-18 (emphasis mine): *Finally, my brethren, be strong in the Lord and in the power of His might. Put on the whole armor of God, that you may be able to stand against the wiles of the devil.* ***For we do not wrestle against flesh and blood, but against principalities, against powers, against the rulers of the darkness of this age, against spiritual hosts of wickedness in the heavenly places.*** *Therefore take up the whole armor of God, that you may be able to withstand in the evil day, and having done all, to stand. Stand therefore, having girded your waist with truth, having put on the breastplate of righteousness, and having shod your feet with the preparation of the gospel of peace; above all, taking the shield of faith with which you will be able to quench all the fiery darts of the wicked one. And take the helmet of salvation, and the sword of the Spirit, which is the word of God; praying always with all prayer and supplication in the Spirit, being watchful to this end with all perseverance and supplication for all the saints.*

When we accept Christ as our Lord and Savior, we enlist into the army of God. In this army, we must make sure that we are fully armed so that we will be able to withstand the tricks and tactics of Satan. It is very important that we have the full armor or we will be wide open for an easy attack. You must be clothed with Christ if you want to be clothed with power to overcome the enemy!
Notice that it said to be strong in the Lord and in the power of His might. This is a reminder that we are never fighting alone. When you're in Christ, God won't leave you alone because His Spirit lives in you. It's impossible to fight in the spirit with the flesh.

Lean on God's power and there will be no other power that will be able to stop you from doing what God empowered you to do.

Again, we know that the battle is not a fleshly battle. There are angelic principalities and powers in God's kingdom, but the names in verse 12 are referring to demons. Everything God creates, Satan attempts to duplicate. I will break down powers and principalities in chapter 8.

Armor of God

With the armor of God, five pieces of the armor are defensive weapons and one is offensive.

1.) **Belt of Truth**- The belt or girdle kept every part of the armor in place. Just like the girdle kept everything in place, standing on the truth of God's word keeps us in place. It keeps us balanced. We cannot be swayed by false doctrine, and when the enemy tries to twist truth, we are braced up in truth.

2.) **Breastplate of Righteousness**- The breastplate covered the body from the neck down to the thighs. It had two parts. It covered the front and the back and protected the vital organs. We must keep the faith and operate in love. Evil done to us should not make us give evil back, but evil can never overpower love. The enemy will try to pierce our hearts and cause us to act out of our flesh, but the breastplate of righteousness helps protect us not only from the enemy, but from ourselves at times.

3.) **Feet Shod with the Preparation of the Gospel of Peace-** Soldiers wore what was known as "greaves" or bronze boots to protect the feet from rocks and other things that could cut the feet. Our feet must be shod in the sense that we are prepared to spread the gospel of Jesus Christ. Our feet must be ready for whatever marching orders we receive and to move swiftly as needed. We must be prepared at all times because there is no time to prepare when the attack comes. Even if we walk on shaky ground, our feet are firmly planted in God's Word.

4.) Shield of Faith- The shield was carried by the soldier to protect against arrows and swords. The shield also protected other parts of the armor. A soldier could lift the shield to cover his entire body. Our faith serves as a shield. When our faith is firmly planted in God, nothing will be able to move us. Our faith will be able to defend against everything the enemy tries to throw at us. No matter what the enemy tries, we are grounded in our faith that God will protect and deliver.

5.) Helmet of Salvation- The helmet defended against blows from the enemy to the head. When we put on the helmet of salvation, our soul is protected. We are putting on Christ and believe that when the battles are done here, we will have eternal life through Christ Jesus. No matter what blows the enemy gives us, we will remain firm in our salvation, knowing that we also have a reward in heaven.

6.) Sword of the Spirit- This is our offensive weapon. It is the Word of God. Sometimes the enemy will attack, and we can counterattack with the Word. Sometimes, we are to go right at the enemy and attack. This is why it is so important to continue to be a student of God's Word and understand your position in battle. I love warring against the enemy by using God's Word.

Romans 13:12-14: *The night is far spent, the day is at hand. Therefore let us cast off the works of darkness, and let us put on the armor of light. Let us walk properly, as in the day, not in revelry and drunkenness, not in lewdness and lust, not in strife and envy. But put on the Lord Jesus Christ, and make no provision for the flesh, to fulfill its lusts.*

Here, we find the apostle Paul talking about putting on Christ or being clothed with Christ. In order to do that, we must remove the works of darkness, which can only manifest sin. Works of darkness are what Satan tries to manifest by preying on our flesh. Notice in verse 12 that Paul talks about putting on the armor of light. So, we see that light doesn't automatically come. Christ is that light, and that is also a type of armor against the works of the enemy. As children of God, we are the light of the world, so we must shine our lights. Your life is a light, and the life you live for Christ will be the same light that will help others see when they're on a dark path. The only way for the light to shine is through Christ. The only way for your light to shine is to let Christ shine through you. That light makes darkness leave. We put on Christ through our obedience and faithfulness. We put on Christ through prayer and His Word.

Verse 14 talks about making no provision for the flesh. In other words, we are either feeding our flesh or our spirit. When we cater to our fleshly desires, we are making provisions for it, which will only result in sin. You're either feeding your flesh or your spirit. Feed your spirit because it's the only one that can produce good fruit. It's not talking about the necessities of food and appearance, but it's talking about the lustful and other ungodly desires of the flesh.

You must be unclothed of things that are contrary to God and be clothed with Christ! If we put on the Lord Jesus Christ, that means it's possible to take Him off. We do this through sin and disobedience. If you don't have the right clothes on in spiritual warfare, you will leave naked and wounded. This is why the blood of Jesus is important, as it allows us to go to God in prayer for ourselves and ask for forgiveness. After being back in good standing through repentance, we once again must remember to be clothed with Christ through prayer and obedience to God's Word and instructions.

You fulfill the lusts of the flesh when you chase things, but you fulfill your spirit when you chase God, who will make things chase you. When you enter spiritual warfare, you have the authority of

Christ to command any demon to get off your personal and spiritual property.

2.) Have the Right Mind-set for Spiritual Warfare

Ephesians 2:4-6 (emphasis mine): *But God, who is rich in mercy, because of His great love with which He loved us, even when we were dead in trespasses, made us alive together with Christ (by grace you have been saved),* ***and raised us up together, and made us sit together in the heavenly places in Christ Jesus.***

Our identity is Christ, and we rule on earth. **Earth is simply our physical office space where we make spiritual business transactions on behalf of God.** We are saved by the grace of God, not any good of our own. We must make sure we stay in our seat of authority in Christ. **If you leave your seat, you are giving demons permission to rule on your behalf.** I assure you that they won't be attempting to make you look or feel good. We no longer belong to ourselves. We were literally bought with a price when Jesus died in our place for our sins. So, how does God accomplish His will on earth? He does so through us! The enemy is always trying to bait us to get off our throne. **Don't bite the bait of the enemy, but stay on your throne.**

We were raised up together with Christ. Christ was resurrected from the dead, and we were resurrected from our sins. We are connected to Christ. He ascended back to heaven on the right hand of God, and our life is seated with Him. That's why He is also our Advocate. He can intercede with God on our behalf. You must have a mind-set shift. There are demons in your God-given territory who will only leave when you walk in your authority and command them to leave.

It's an honor and a privilege to be able to sit with Christ. Look at the key word "together." It was used a total of three times in this passage. That shows you the importance of our covenant with God through Christ. We're never alone unless we choose to not put on Christ. You are royalty, and it's about time for you to enjoy your reign on earth through the power of Christ in you. You can bring kingdom power to the earth. This is why you must put on Christ: when you do, wherever you show up, Christ will show up because you are being led by the Spirit. Your kingdom power can be most activated when you are in the place God has planted you. Get in alignment through prayer. You have the divine right and authority of Christ to make any demon leave your life or the life of anyone else you come in contact with. Use what God gave you.

Heavenly Places- Heavenly places are not just in heaven. You can't help it but to be great because you came from the greatest place, which is heaven. We must be born again to be accepted again as children of God. When you roll out of bed and your feet hit the ground, you are in a heavenly place. When you go to work or the store, you are in a heavenly place because the spirit of Christ is in you. Therefore, what is happening around you does not determine where you really are because you're in a heavenly place. You have the power to create and change the atmosphere because of the power and authority of Christ in you. Speak crop failure to every seed Satan has sown in your mind in an attempt to get you to think below your seat of authority in Christ. You insult the power of the Holy Spirit in you when you plead with the enemy to stop. **You don't negotiate with demons; you cast them out!**

We need our minds to be renewed to think like Christ. We must first realize that the kingdom of God is within us. We find it in Scripture.

Luke 17:20-21 (emphasis mine): *Now when He was asked by the Pharisees when the kingdom of God would come, He answered them and said, "The kingdom of God does not come with observation; nor will they say, 'See here!' or 'See there!' For indeed, the kingdom of God is within you."*

All the power and authority that we need here on earth to carry out God's will are already in us. However, we must keep tapping into the power source for the power to flow through us. We can relinquish that power and lose full access to it through disobedience, sin, etc. Repentance is important. When the Holy

Spirit is leading you, you have the ability to think like Christ in any situation. It will change your perspective.

You don't have to look up to the sky because the kingdom of God is already here. You must have the mind-set of a warrior in spiritual warfare! Fear should never cross your mind because the only option is victory. Even if you physically feel fear, don't bow to it. The answers are already in you. We just have to unlock them through prayer, the Word, and relationship with God. Earth is an extension of God's government. What we do here determines if we get back to heaven. Although we originated in heaven, and it's where our citizenship is (Philippians 3:20), God didn't give us a round-trip ticket. He gave us a one-way ticket to earth, and we must do our part here so that we can obtain a one-way ticket back to heaven.

Some spend their entire lives looking for an answer in other people when God placed it in them all along, but they never bothered to ask. This is again why prayer is important before entering warfare because you need instructions first on how to attack and revelation on exactly what's trying to attack you. Prayer unto God must be your go-to resource to unlock what He placed within you. Again, the kingdom of God is a kingdom of power. It is a kingdom that is unlike any other kingdom. You are armed and dangerous as a child of God, and it's time to start using your weapons of power against the enemy. It's not enough to just talk about the power—it's time to walk in your power! If you're afraid to fight demons, it means you're in the flesh. There's no power that can overpower the power of the Holy Spirit in you. We have the power of the Holy Spirit and authority of Christ.

Power-the ability to perform something

Authority-permission or right granted by God through Christ to act on the behalf of God through His power in you

Power is the strength to command something. Authority is the right to do so. You may have the power to perform something, but if you have not the authority, you are out of order. We need the power and the permission in order to carry out God's will. He gives us the power to do it and the right to use His name. We use the power and authority to cast out demons. **The authority is like a bench warrant for their arrest, and the power is the ability to use the force necessary to pull demons out when they put up a fight or try to plead their case.** You have the authority because you are sent in the name of Jesus Christ. We have the right to be here in our territory and those demons do not. They are trespassing illegally. We have the power because the Holy Spirit stayed on earth with us and in us.

3.) Study the Blueprint

Isaiah 55:10-11 (emphasis mine): *"For as the rain comes down, and the snow from heaven,*
And do not return there,
But water the earth,
And make it bring forth and bud,
That it may give seed to the sower
And bread to the eater,
So shall My word be that goes forth from My mouth;
It shall not return to Me void,
But it shall accomplish what I please,
And it shall prosper in the thing for which I sent it."

The Word of God is our blueprint to follow. Christ is also our blueprint. He showed us how to effectively carry out the will of God on earth as a spirit being with a physical body as He was when He was on earth and as we are. The Lord made it clear to us that just as rain and snow come down and do not return back to the clouds—they water the earth and produce crops—the same thing applies to what God speaks. God's words do not return unto Him. They accomplish what God wills, and wherever His word is sent, it produces fruit. You must study God's Word so that you can use it for your growth, the growth of others, and in spiritual warfare against the enemy.

So, when God's word is sent to you, not only will you prosper, but whomever (or wherever) you speak those words to will also prosper. So, the pressure is taken off of you. Some things will manifest through your words, and other times, they're manifested through your actions. Either way, you cannot afford to be silent because you were sent here to be a light. God sent you to shine a light. Don't always look to fit in because sometimes the message God gives you will take people out of their comfort zones. You are armed for the fight, but as you move forward, you must know your responsibility. God gave you a great responsibility on earth, and that is to bring His kingdom on earth.

Chapter 3: Understanding Your Responsibility

Too often, when it comes to spiritual warfare or when it seems like something is too big or that someone else is so much greater, some people tend to think less of themselves. Sometimes you may fall into the trap of looking at yourself as you see you or how Satan wants you to see you. When you're in Christ, nothing and no one is bigger or better than you. It only becomes a challenge when you start thinking about your physical limitations, strengths, and weaknesses. This is why our mind must be renewed in Christ. We all have weaknesses in the flesh, but there is no such thing as a weakness in Christ, and that's where you are seated. You must take your seat. The enemy can sense fear because they threw the bait hoping you would bite. Fear is a poor excuse not to have faith because faith is not in a person, but it's in God through Christ. It's impossible to lose with Christ!

Therefore, if it's impossible to lose with Christ, what are you holding onto? What you're holding onto is flesh, and it must be thrown aside. One big mistake as a Christian is to believe that the real you is in your flesh. The real you is in the spirit and hidden in Christ! You must wake up to the real you. God never created flesh to be able to make sense of the spirit. He simply created flesh as a vehicle to transport your power around. This is important when dealing with spiritual warfare because if you get into a spiritual fight with your flesh, you will get wounded and badly wounded. You far outrank any demon, and when you understand that, you truly won't be afraid to fight in the spirit for what belongs to you. As a Christ follower, God wants you to go from a place of talking about His power to actually walking in and demonstrating His power on earth. You already have the ability to do so because when you accept Christ, you are in Christ and you can use His authority and the power of the Holy Spirit.

It only becomes a challenge to accept this reality because, for too long, too much of the church has raised co-dependent Christians to feel that they must always depend on someone who supposedly has more power or authority than them, which is not the case. As followers of Christ, we all have access to the same Father, Son, and Holy Spirit. We all have the same access to the power and authority. The only difference is that we all have different gifts, functions, and responsibilities. It's only through Christ that we have this access. The church has talked about the power, studied the power, flirted with the power, but this is a generation that will demonstrate the power. God is talking to you!

This is kingdom dominion time, and that dominion is for the children of God to rule on earth as the kings and queens we are. The church must walk in power and not just say cute words or talk a good game because in spiritual warfare, you either bring it or stay home! The cute programs are nice, the fellowship is nice, but when it's all said and done, there needs to be demonstration of power. There needs to be healing the sick, casting out demons, raising the dead, setting the captives free, shifting the atmosphere, etc. Yes, you have the power and authority in you to do all of that. The Holy Spirit didn't give you gifts just so you can say you have something. He gave it to you so He can demonstrate His power through you.

Shifting the atmosphere isn't just changing the mood in a place. It's literally evicting demons by bringing the power and authority of Christ! Since you're seated in Christ and have the power of the Holy Spirit living in you, when you show up, Christ shows up and shifts the atmosphere. The reason it may not happen all the time is because perhaps it's a day we didn't wake up to our power and authority. It is a daily process. We know that Scripture tells us that "to whom much is given, much is required" (Luke 12:48). There's no greater responsibility you will ever have than demonstrating the authority of Christ and power of the Holy Spirit on the earth. Much has been given to you because all things are in God through Christ, and you have the right to use His authority. Resurrection power lives in you, as the Holy Spirit is the power. It has been given to you, and much is required. The much is in doing. You're not waiting on God, but God's waiting on you to let Him use you to bring His kingdom on earth as it is in heaven. It's your job! That's also what you're doing in spiritual warfare. In spiritual warfare, you're evicting what Satan's kingdom has set up, and you're establishing God's kingdom on earth as it is in heaven. God is opening our eyes to who we really are. You can't effectively engage in spiritual warfare without first knowing your spiritual rights, and we will get into that in the next chapter. There are things that you've sat back and watched others do because you thought they were more anointed. God is saying you're just as anointed.

You're anointed to do what God called you to do because He gave you the responsibility that comes with it and expects you to do it. No excuses. We all have specific assignments. However, there are some things we all are to do. We all have the responsibility to tell others about Christ. We all have the responsibility to bring light into darkness. We all have a responsibility to cast out demons, heal the sick, etc. The power and authority are already in you to do it, but the problem is you thought the job was for someone else. You have a responsibility to evict any works of Satan from your life as well as anywhere or any person God sends you to. You have the power and authority. You are not weak. You are a dangerous weapon in spiritual warfare because all power and authority from God lives in you. You will be the best you when you wake up to and accept the power and authority living in you through Christ.

There are three key responsibilities you will have in spiritual warfare:

1.) **You're responsible for uprooting anything Satan's kingdom has established and establish God's kingdom in its place.**

2.) **You're responsible for the lives of others.**

3.) **You must have faith.**

Responsibility to Uproot

You're responsible for uprooting anything Satan's kingdom has established and to establish God's kingdom in its place.

Matthew 10:1: *And when He had called His twelve disciples to Him, He gave them power over unclean spirits, to cast them out, and to heal all kinds of sickness and all kinds of disease.*

This takes us back to the basics. This is Christianity 101. Some feathers might be ruffled here for those who have a religious mind-set or those leaders who want all the power but don't want the congregants to be able to walk in the same level of power. So, I'm not talking to the flesh because flesh will not grasp it. I'm talking to your spirit. The power and authority described in this verse is the type of power and authority we're supposed to walk in early in our walk with Christ. Yes, this is basic Christianity. This was intended to be the beginners' level. As we grow, we're supposed to see more people healed and delivered through our obedience to God through Christ. Yes, old tradition has kept many of us bound for years, and I'm speaking of myself, too. If I knew what I know now ten years ago, I can't imagine how many more lives could have been impacted through the power and authority of Christ in me. Thank God that He redeems the time. Imagine how many lives you're going to impact after you fully get this revelation. It's time to go and do what God called you to do.

You must first realize that the first thing Jesus gave to His disciples was power over unclean spirits, to cast them out, and to heal all kinds of sickness and disease. He didn't say some, but all. This is another reminder that the first thing Christ gave us was power. That power is the Holy Spirit. He gave you power over demonic spirits. He gave you power to heal all sickness and diseases because of the power at work in you. He didn't say some, but all. There's no problem bigger than another because everything Satan tries looks small to Christ; you're in Christ, so it should look small to you.

Notice that Jesus called His disciples to Him, and upon them responding to Him, He gave them the power. This was before His death, burial, and resurrection. Now, we get the authority first to use Jesus's name once we accept Him, and then we get the power, which is the Holy Spirit. Whenever you see sickness, disease, sin, or anything that opposes God, it's a seed sown by Satan. You have the power to do something about it. Not only do you have the power and authority to do something about it, but you have a responsibility to do something about it.

You have assigned territory, and God gave you the responsibility to shine your light on any darkness that tries to hang around it. With the help of the Holy Spirit and warring angels, you are also an enforcer in the areas God assigns to you. You are expected to replace darkness with light. You are expected to literally shift the atmosphere. You are expected to bring order where there is disorder. The responsibility God gave you may seem like a tall task for you, but the results are on God; the obedience is on you. Do your part. This power and authority are not something God suggested that we walk in, but it is what He commanded.
Let's take a look at another example of how what you do in spiritual warfare shakes up things around you.

Acts 9:36-42: *At Joppa there was a certain disciple named Tabitha, which is translated Dorcas. This woman was full of good works and charitable deeds which she did. But it happened in those days that she became sick and died. When they had washed her, they laid her in an upper room. And since Lydda was near Joppa, and the disciples had heard that Peter was there, they sent two men to him, imploring him not to delay in coming to them. Then Peter arose and went with them. When he had come, they brought him to the upper room. And all the widows stood by him weeping, showing the tunics and garments which Dorcas had made while she was with them. But Peter put them all out, and knelt down and prayed. And turning to the body he said, "Tabitha, arise." And she opened her eyes, and when she saw Peter she sat up. Then he gave her his hand and lifted her up; and when he had called the saints* *and widows, he presented her alive. And it became known throughout all Joppa, and many believed on the Lord.*

We find here a disciple named Tabitha. We know Jesus began with the original twelve disciples, but once we accept Christ, we are also disciples of Christ. Tabitha did many great deeds, but she became sick and died. We see that Peter's faith came in contact with the Holy Spirit in him and Tabitha was raised from the dead. Peter activated his power and authority. While others are tied up in their feelings, God expects you to get tied up in your faith. People were weeping and had already considered her dead. It doesn't say they called Peter to raise her from the dead, but they called because he was close by and was one of their leaders. They had even already washed her body and practically were beginning to prepare her for the burial process. Peter did not believe the report even when he physically saw she was dead. He looked in the spirit and knew the power and authority he had. So, he prayed and then turned to her and told her to arise. He commanded her body to get in alignment with God. His faith was all that was needed, even though everyone else thought it was over. Where something is dead that is supposed to be alive, God gave you the power and authority to bring it back to life.

The interesting thing about it is that they didn't need Peter to raise Tabitha from the dead because those in the room who had accepted Christ had the same power and authority as Peter, but they had not fully accepted it. You don't need someone else to come in and do what God has already called and qualified you to do. Peter chose to walk in His power and authority, and you have that same choice. He had nothing to lose because Tabitha was already dead. It wasn't just that he had radical faith, but he chose not to accept the report because he knew he had power and authority living in him. Raising Tabitha from the dead didn't require any more faith than healing someone from a sickness because the same power and authority are what bring it about.

Notice that after she was raised from the dead, the word of this miracle spread quickly, and many believed in God. The miracles, signs, and wonders that God will use you to do will point others back to Him. This was an uncommon miracle, not because it wasn't possible, but because there wasn't faith enough to believe God to do it. However, Peter had faith. What God is doing in your life is not common, so you need to stop trying to make it common. Accept that He is doing a new thing. You must begin to accept that who you are in Christ is totally different from who you are in the flesh. In Christ, you rule on earth! In Christ, you can command sickness, pain, stress, depression, and any attack of the enemy to go away, and it must obey because they must obey Christ. No matter how much of a fight it puts up, we don't back down.

So, what happens if they don't go away at first? Keep fighting. Some demons are stubborn, but you must keep fighting and enforce your victory no matter how big the fight seems. Demons don't obey you, but they obey the authority of Christ that comes with you. Start using your authority and command them to leave. Whatever Satan has established or tried to get you to accept, you must overturn it by bringing God's kingdom. Many have called something from Satan God's will just because it's been a part of their life for so long. God gave you power to change it. No matter how long it's been around, if it's not of God, it must go. You have the power and authority to make sure that happens.

Responsibility for Others

You are also responsible for the lives of others.

Acts 12:5, 11-17 (emphasis mine): *Peter was therefore kept in prison, but constant prayer was offered to God for him by the church...*

And when Peter had come to himself, he said, "Now I know for certain that the Lord has sent His angel, and has delivered me from the hand of Herod and from all the expectation of the Jewish people."

So, when he had considered this, he came to the house of Mary, the mother of John whose surname was Mark, where many were gathered together praying. And as Peter knocked at the door of the gate, a girl named Rhoda came to answer. When she recognized Peter's voice, because of her gladness she did not open the gate, but ran in and announced that Peter stood before the gate. But they said to her, "You are beside yourself!" Yet she kept insisting that it was so. So they said, "It is his angel."

Now Peter continued knocking; and when they opened the door and saw him, they were astonished. But motioning to them with his hand to keep silent, he declared to them how the Lord had brought him out of the prison. And he said, "Go, tell these things to James and to the brethren." And he departed and went to another place.

Here we see the power of corporate prayer. Corporate prayer is the prayers of more than one person collectively. The church continued to pray and engage in spiritual warfare for Peter while he was in prison, and the Lord sent an angel to rescue him. He was wrongfully put in prison to begin with. However, the people did not feel like it was only Peter's issue. They took the issue on and confronted the enemy. Some people think it's just about them, but God gave you responsibility for others as well. Your faith may be the only faith someone has to work with, but the results of your faith will change them. When one is weak, the other is strong. There are some people who will be in bondage from the enemy, but God will use you to set them free!

The only issue here is that the church almost missed the answered prayer, which was right at the door. Rhoda was so excited that she saw Peter at the door, she didn't open the gate but ran to tell everyone else. They thought she had lost her mind and thought she was seeing an angel. Peter kept knocking, and they finally opened it up and were amazed. This increased their faith because they were praying to God, but apparently, they did not think He would move that fast. God specializes in overnight miracles, and He is going to use you as a vessel to bring about miracles.

The answer to your prayers may be knocking at your door, but you may be praying and so focused on what you are praying about you may not see that God already answered it. It just may not be in the exact way you expected. The church didn't expect Peter to physically be rescued by an angel. They were probably praying that Peter would be released, but God exceeded their expectations. Don't box God in when you pray. Expect the miraculous! Expect a great surprise!

Responsibility to Have Faith

Luke 17:5-6 (emphasis mine): *And the apostles said to the Lord, "Increase our faith." So the Lord said, "If you have faith as a mustard seed, you can say to this mulberry tree, 'Be pulled up by the roots and be planted in the sea,' and it would obey you."*

This is evidence that our faith can and must be increased. Faith is an undefeated heavyweight fighter and has proven time and time again that it will knock out any opposition sent by the enemy. God placed the seed of faith in you, and it can grow. If you need more faith, ask God to increase it. We all need more faith, and you won't get it by thinking, but you will get it by praying. He wants you to ask for more. Jesus gave an example in this passage of what faith can do. Your faith is a mountain mover because God said it is. So, if God said it, all you need to do is believe it! Faith doesn't get tied up in all the questions and what ifs. Faith just goes and gets the answer. Faith doesn't need to debate because it will settle the matter by producing the results in due time.

Faith is never rushed and never panics. Flesh may do it, but faith is cool and calm because its confidence is in God through Christ. Faith combined with the power of your words can accomplish something in the spirit in one minute that would take years to do in the physical. Your faith is able to go into heaven and bring back what you're believing God for. Faith cannot fail because of its DNA. Faith is a spiritual seed given to you by God, and you can and should ask for more because it will be needed. Your faith is literally a weapon. It's such a necessary weapon that God is not pleased with you if you don't use it. It's important to remember that you are spirit with spiritual power, and our Father in heaven is spirit with all power. Your faith already believes what God said. It's just waiting on you to send it to go and get what God already said you can have. Faith is not concerned with what your flesh thinks or feels. Faith is directly tied to God, and you should be, too.

Our faith is like a seed that is sown, and it grows and grows over time. This passage shows us that things in the world must obey our words by God's law. Our body will obey us through faith. Faith is one of the main access points to the supernatural. When your faith is attached to the power of God's Word, manifestation must take place in your life. Your flesh may see disappointment, but your faith doesn't understand disappointment because it only knows miracles and manifestation. This is why we need to ask God to help our unbelief. We must command the spirit of fear and doubt to leave through faith, and those spirits must obey you.

Again, I reiterate, if it doesn't happen right away, stay in faith and command demons daily to leave until they're gone. You must remain persistent. Faith is persistent and doesn't stop until it reaches its target. So, you just need to keep it activated in your life. Obstacles must obey you in the spirit when you have consistent faith. Your flesh may have been disappointed, but your faith has never been disappointed by God. Faith is not a loser, and as you keep faith in Christ, you simply cannot lose. Keep working your faith until it produces. Faith comes with the guarantee that it will produce. Keep in mind that more and more of faith is being built up in you. Faith is your ticket to the abundant life Christ promised. God wants our faith to go to an entire new dimension.

Faith is always a requirement if you expect anything from God. Not only is faith always a requirement, but in this season, your faith will have to be at an all-time high. Some of the responsibilities God trusts you with will be bigger than what your mind can comprehend. Faith doesn't need your mind's input, but it needs your spirit's input! Your spirit always goes all in for God. Your mind can get you in trouble because it can entertain things contrary to God's will. It will use logic for something supernatural.

Logic and faith never enter the same room. They never see eye to eye. You may feel like you're outnumbered, coming up short, or that you're competing with too many other people who are doing something similar to what God is telling you to do, but you need faith. It doesn't matter if you feel like the vision God gave is what many are doing. When you have faith in what He said, there is no competition! It may appear that way, but that's because you're looking through the lens of the flesh instead of the lens of faith. There is always room at the table because when God places the vision in you, He always makes room.

Anyone can use natural things to get natural things. That doesn't require faith. However, faith is not natural. Faith is supernatural. Faith can produce things in the spirit and in the natural. Faith in God gives you the ability to fast forward things in the natural because faith supersedes natural time. Faith won't just open doors, faith in God is the door! Walk through the doors of faith and all the impossibilities become possible. Faith literally transforms you. Faith takes you from functioning on the world's clock to functioning on God's clock. If you want to walk in God's divine time, you just need to walk in faith.

You were created to operate in faith. The flesh was never supposed to have power. You've given your flesh too much credit. Your spirit is supposed to rule over your flesh. Stop taking orders from the servant. Walk in the spirit. When we leave earth and are in Christ, flesh goes back to the dirt, but our spirit goes back to God. Start following your spirit. The flesh was only made to be a vehicle to legally carry your spirit around on earth. That's why Jesus needed a physical body to legally walk the earth.

When in your feelings, faith is hard and doubt is easy. When in the spirit, doubt is hard and faith is easy! Doubt has never entered heaven. You came from heaven, so doubt should never enter you. Yes, we all will face challenges in the natural. They're natural challenges. We will feel the impacts of them naturally. That's the human condition. That's why we have a soul that has a mind, will, emotions, appetites, etc.

We've heard the term "crazy faith," meaning you're believing God for something big and trusting Him no matter what. However, all faith is crazy to the natural. All of God's children have exercised crazy faith. Any time you believe God for something, it's crazy to your flesh. Man-based faith will never sustain you. It will never pierce through heaven. Man-based faith can easily be snatched away by the enemy en route to heaven. Man-based faith is based more on intellect and reason. Just because it makes common sense doesn't mean it makes God sense. Faith has been known to be radical. Man-based faith is based more on feelings and is not true faith at all. Faith is not a feeling, but it is a lifestyle. If you trust God in only some things instead of all, that means that other things are based on feelings and natural facts. If you trust God and then doubt God, flesh is coming into play. You must have faith. We can find the definition of faith in Scripture.

Hebrews 11:1, 6: *Now faith is the substance of things hoped for, the evidence of things not seen...But without faith it is impossible to please Him, for he who comes to God must believe that He is, and that He is a rewarder of those who diligently seek Him.*

This passage gives us the definition of faith. Faith is the support, groundwork, or confidence of the things we hope for. This verse deals with the natural and the spiritual. The first half talks about hope. You only need hope in the physical, not in the spiritual. The second part of the passage, and also the second aspect of faith, is that it is evidence for something we cannot see. Notice that it says faith is evidence. How can something we cannot see become evidence? Faith is the evidence that must be produced in the supernatural realm in order for it to manifest in the natural. Faith is your down payment for spiritual transactions from heaven. In order to get anything from heaven, faith is the ticket that's required to gain access. Faith is not something you can physically get. It must be imparted. It must be spiritually transmitted. The faith realm does not operate in the physical realm. It is purely spiritual. This is why prayer is vital. This is why the study of God's Word is vital. Faith is not hard to find. You just have to trust God. If you need more faith, all you have to do is ask! I say it often: faith in

God is saying, "Lord, I trust you in everything, over everything, no matter what."

Verse 6 lets us know that we cannot please God without faith. Before we even come to God in prayer, we must believe that God is able to answer it. No matter how good we are, we cannot please God without faith. Faith is our prerequisite. Your faith in God is tied to facts because God is the truth. We must believe that He hears us. Our faith is increased through prayer and God's Word. Prayer is our language and currency in God's government. Doubt is a foreign language to heaven. Walk in faith because heaven speaks the language of faith. Emphasis is often placed on the first part of the passage in verse 6, but the last part is just as important. It's a promise of God. God is a rewarder of those who diligently seek Him. The more you seek God, the more He will release to you because He promised to reward those who diligently seek Him. God promised that if you diligently seek Him, He will reward you. It's a proven formula for success. That's a promise of God, and He doesn't go back on His promises.

When you have a lifestyle of faith, you trust God in everything. Building faith takes prayer and practice. The more you declare God's Word and pray, the less room that doubt will have to get to you. When you're in faith, it allows you to live in part of heaven while on earth. Heaven has no limitations. Heaven knows no lack, doubt, sickness, etc. Faith seeks out a challenge and thrives in the impossible. The faith realm is beyond your natural senses. It's beyond what your mind was intended to grasp. It's spiritually discerned. When you're in the spirit, faith makes sense, not doubt. Healing makes sense, not hurt. Miracles make sense, not disaster. Prosperity makes sense, not lack. Strength makes sense, not weakness. Courage makes sense, not fear. You came out of God, so you were spirit long before you had flesh. Get back to who you really are and that's spirit! It's the job of your faith to activate things on earth sent from heaven. So, you must employ faith because it comes with lifetime benefits.

Some people won't understand your faith. Some won't understand what God is doing, but they don't have to. Don't take it personally. Don't get mad with them. God showed it to you. He gave you the vision. Don't lower your rank by stepping out of faith to entertain someone's doubt about anything in your life. Don't get into a flesh battle about your faith. Faith in God comes with a 100% guarantee, which is that it always produces results. The enemy may wage a war, but you will know how to effectively fight back.

Your faith gives the Holy Spirit permission to perform miracles in your life and in the lives of others. This is why your faith is so important. Your bold faith in Christ can push others into having more faith. You should never feel weird for trusting God the way you do, no matter how impossible it may seem. Faith doesn't need to show up when it looks possible, but faith is a far better companion to what appears impossible. Your faith is so powerful that even if someone else doesn't have the faith, your faith can carry them. This is one reason why Satan and his demons want you to live outside of faith. Satan wants you live outside of faith, and God wants you to live inside faith.

Faith doesn't actually begin in your mind, but it begins in your spirit, and it's up to your soul to believe it or not. Your spirit doesn't need help having faith in God because it has all faith in God, but it's your soul that must get on board. Again, faith has a natural and spiritual component. It originates in the spirit, but it must overtake our soul so that our soul believes. Without our soul believing it, we cannot please God. The soul either obeys the spirit or the flesh. Feelings are obedient to the flesh, but faith is obedient to God. So, this is why we're to walk in the spirit, which is simply not submitting to the sinful desires of the flesh or any other thing that goes against God's will. Faith already has a made-up mind that God will work it out. All you need to do is make up your mind to have faith. Fear and doubt try to steal what your faith has produced, but you can snatch it back the moment you shift back into faith.

Living in faith takes practice and prayer because your soul must be disciplined to where it no longer accepts what your flesh has to offer. Demons can only access your flesh in an attempt to corrupt or contaminate your soul, but they can't touch your spirit. The soul is so important because the choices it makes can determine if our spirit will be sent back to heaven or sent to hell. Therefore, the soul plays a vital role. Faith can change your entire life if you're bold enough to actually live in faith. Faith wants to take you places you've never been before, and all you have to do is accept the invitation. It's easy from the perspective of your spirit, but it can seem complex from the perspective of your soul and flesh.

Your soul is the seat of your mind, will, emotions, and appetites. This is why demons try to get into your mind, and why God said we need to have the mind of Christ. This is why demons try to prey on your emotions in an attempt to get you to act off of feelings instead of faith. Christ showed us that it's possible to have emotions but still live in faith. Emotions can go up and down, but faith is consistent! Jesus was on the cross and felt pain and agony. He was in tears and His emotions went up and down. He was in so much pain that He felt God had forsaken Him in that moment, but He knew that was flesh talking, and He shifted back into the spirit. His faith never wavered. Even when He prayed for God to take Him another route, He shifted back into the spirit and said, "Not my will, but your will be done!" You have feelings that will talk, but don't allow your feelings to talk louder than your faith.

If you can just get that faith is a part of who you are really supposed to be in God, you'll stop believing things that oppose your faith. God said we can't please Him without faith, and He's not going to say something that's difficult for us to do. Faith is not something we create, but it was in us once we accepted Christ. It's a living organism that can and should grow in us. Faith is alive, and that's why we can receive faith in our lives and allow it to grow. The more it grows, the more it produces. It's one of the things God gave us to be able to make spiritual transactions. Faith is a natural producer of a harvest, so if it is not producing enough in your life, ask God to increase your faith.

Faith is not a mind-set, but it is a spirit that must change your mind-set. Your mind-set can't create faith, but faith creates your mind-set. If it was simply about mind-set, you wouldn't need faith. Remember that your natural mind is in your soul, but your spiritual mind is in the spirit. That's why Romans 12:2 tells us that we must be transformed by the renewing of our mind. Faith in God makes room for the impossible to become possible in your life. Faith was not placed in you to create results sometimes, but it was placed in you to create results all the time. We've lived so long in between our faith and our feelings that sometimes both can seem just as strong. Faith wants to overtake you in every area of your life so that it can do the job God placed it in you to do. God is looking for your faith, not your feelings, because faith is relentless and won't stop until it brings back what God has for you. It should be clearer to you that faith is truly the currency of God's government and a key component in prayer and spiritual warfare.

Chapter 4: Understanding Your Rights vs. Demonic Legal Rights

Satan is a legalist. He knows the laws of God very well and could not care less if we are ignorant of the laws governing the spirit realm. He will use any law available to try to gain an advantage. A legal right is Satan's tool he uses to steal from us legally. Have you ever heard of a legal robbery? Well, in the spirit realm, it is possible. It happens every day. It's our job to make that robbery illegal and bring those demons to trial. As a child of God, you must know that you have a God-given right to rule on earth. You don't get to rule because of how great you are, but you get to rule because of how great your Father in heaven is. You get to rule because of the authority of Christ and power of the Holy Spirit that you have in you. You have the authority to strip demons of any legal rights they had to gain access to your life.

A legal right is a way in which demons can gain legal access to your life and blessings based on the laws in the spirit realm. The legal right could be through sin, word curses, soul wounds, soul ties, being connected with the wrong people, etc. It's any access point in which the enemy can legally gain access to you. Sometimes it's not based on anything you did or did not do. It could be through your bloodline and something that your ancestors did. However, the responsibility is now on you to be that interruption in your bloodline. There is no attack by the enemy that you don't have power and authority to overcome.

There are laws in the spirit realm, and the enemy is well versed in all of them. They look for every technicality possible in an attempt to put God's children in bondage on earth. Demons know they can legally steal from us if they have a legal right. You must cancel every legal right they have to gain access to you and to what is rightfully yours. They hope to get you to a place where you think it's God not releasing something when, really, they stole it. They hope you will get mad with God, which buys them more time to continue to steal. The enemy has legally stolen too much from you, and now is the time for you to take back by force in the spirit what rightfully belongs to you.

Warfare takes endurance. It's rarely just a one-time thing because the enemy is relentless. If demons are relentless at seeking ways to attack you, you need to be relentless at seeking God. The enemy has used legal rights to keep so much of the body of Christ in bondage for long periods of time, but the more you know, the more you will be able to pass on to others. The dominant thought you have that's not of God is most often a place the enemy has a legal right to attack. You can break it. God told us to rule here on earth, so He expects you to move so He can move through you. We all must learn to rule the way God intended for us to rule. You have legal rights to all God has released to you, and you must exercise those rights by defending your territory against the enemy! Deliverance is very important because if one is not delivered, they are living in some form of bondage. Demons can be cast out, but if they have a legal right, they can easily come back and make a home in the life of a child of God. They understand legal rights. So, we must understand legal rights. Salvation is not enough. That's the beginning of Christianity. Salvation secures our eternal dwelling place, but God still expects us to live an abundant life on earth. The enemy wants to prevent both, but they will take what they can get. Contrary to popular belief, you can be in good standing with God but still in some form of bondage because of a legal right the enemy has to you. Cancel the legal right. Keep warring in the spirit until you see the change. Just like in legal cases, even if a person was convicted, attorneys still work hard to appeal.

We are in a turf war. It's a battle over territory. You can't lose because God said you already won, but you still must defend what's yours in the spirit to live the abundant life Christ promised. We must still show up because the victory is not automatic. Demons really believe it's their territory because they were on earth before us, but it's really ours because it belongs to God, and He wants us to reclaim the territory for His kingdom. God could easily do it Himself, but He chose to use us. So, it's time for you to rule. You're invading earth to establish God's kingdom on earth.

Don't allow a demon to bully you in territory God said is yours. God did not ask you to rule and have dominion on earth, but He commanded you to! You must take authority where God has assigned you. Yes, the enemy will attack, but those attacks will never prosper in your life as a child of God. An attack of the enemy doesn't give you an excuse to roll over. It's just a reminder that you need to take over.

You cannot effectively engage the enemy in spiritual warfare if you don't know your rights. You can't engage the enemy in warfare if you don't recognize and accept your power and authority. God gave you territory to have dominion in, and He expects you to handle business on His behalf. If Satan strikes, you must strike back. You don't just defend, but you play offense, too. We already know that the enemy is trying to steal, kill, and destroy us. So, we may as well be prepared. Sometimes you don't need to wait for demons to attack you, but you must attack them in the spirit if you see their work in your territory.

When you accept the fact that you have the authority of Jesus and power of the Holy Spirit, you'll realize that you were created to rule. Yes, I said you were created to rule. Accept it already! Yes, you have flesh, which makes you sometimes lean toward the human condition. However, you are far greater than flesh. Your flesh goes back to the ground when you die, but your spirit goes back to God when you die in Christ. You may be a mere human in the flesh, but you are a force to be reckoned with in the spirit.

You have a right to an abundant life on earth because you're seated in Christ and all things are in Him. You must stop accepting whatever is thrown at you. It doesn't matter how long you've been in the situation; if it's from Satan, you have the right, the power, and the authority to change it!

Spiritual warfare is a battle over territory, but you must realize that the territory belongs to you because it belongs to God. You are not some weak creation God sent to earth. You are literally a king or queen on earth sent by God. Do the will of God here and you will get to upgrade your current crown. You must have a renewed mind to recognize that you are truly royalty. It's not just something nice to say to make you feel special. It's the truth. If you don't know it, then you can't know your rights. Accept the fact that you're literally royalty. It's only when you think independently of Christ that you see things like flesh sees them.

You will win consistently in spiritual warfare when you use the right set of eyes. Don't use eyes of flesh; use the eyes of faith! This guarantees the victory that has already been won. Flesh is just a punching bag in spiritual warfare. Flesh has been known to do one thing, and that's mess things up. Get in the spirit to get things right. It is a daily process, but if you discipline yourself through God's Word, prayer, and worship, you will surely make it.

Having peace is your right, and you have the right to evict anything that disturbs it from your life. There are many things that God has already promised. This is why it's so important to remain in Christ. If you step out of Christ, you step out of life because He is your life.

God is not looking for fear because fear is an enemy of God. Fear brings Him no glory! God is looking for faith, and He should find it in you. There is never a time to walk in fear. If you walk in fear, you automatically know that you stepped way below your rank. Step back in Christ where fear cannot exist. This is the only place in which you can engage in spiritual warfare. You have to fight. Some things will not change until you effectively fight them. It's not in your own strength, of course, but it's in the power of the Holy Spirit and authority of Jesus Christ that is in you. You live in the world only to bring God's kingdom on earth. Praising Him alone will never be an excuse not to do the work He sent you to do. This is what the enemy wants you to stop doing. Satan isn't as concerned about you worshipping God. He's more concerned with trying to stop you from carrying out the will of God. You are too powerful to bargain with the enemy. Make the enemy wish they never messed with you! When you understand your kingdom rights, you will never live below your rank again.

Luke 11:24-26: *"When an unclean spirit goes out of a man, he goes through dry places, seeking rest; and finding none, he says, 'I will return to my house from which I came.' And when he comes, he finds it swept and put in order. Then he goes and takes with him* *seven other spirits more wicked than himself, and they enter and dwell there; and the last state of that man is worse than the first. "*

We see from this passage one way that demons operate. They are persistent. They don't like taking no for an answer. So, we must be persistent. If demons don't like backing down after a no, children of God should certainly not back down from a no! Don't accept a no when God said yes. The demonic stronghold must first be torn down out of your life. It begins and ends with prayer. That stronghold began with a legal right to build. Don't give the enemy a license to build walls in your life. Obey God and reject anything the enemy uses to throw at you. They try to get you to bite the bait so they can gain another legal access. The demonic forces that are stealing from you and trying to keep you in bondage must be stripped of the legal rights they feel they have to you and then you must cast out the demon. We must also remember that the foundation being destroyed is key so that they don't have room to come back. When you speak against these demonic spirits, things happen in the spirit.

A demon who was evicted from your life will try to come back later, so you need to replace the space it took up with God's Word. Deliverance is the first step, but after deliverance, your mind must be renewed in Christ. To be delivered but not have a renewed mind is like living in a half-built house. You need the mind of Christ to live like Christ lived! That half-built house has a lot of openings with all types of access for unwanted guests. You must open up your mouth and command the evil spirits to leave. This is again why prayer must become a lifestyle because it will help you war in the spirit. You must say that you are destroying every demonic foundation. You have the power and authority from God to overcome the enemy. The more you pray and submit to God, the more the Holy Spirit will have control and will lead you and guide you on what to do, where to go, etc. Once delivered, a demonic spirit can only return and stay if there is an open door. They must have a legal right to gain access. Keep the door shut through prayer and obedience! They may attack from the outside, but they will have no room to attack from the inside because you will be a clean vessel.

In spiritual warfare, demons are intruders, and it's our job to kick them out of our lives and the lives of those who are around us. Sometimes it could simply be the ruling spirit Satan assigned over your region that feels it has legal rights to you based on what was done in the region, but that's why you're there. You're there to help reestablish order.

In this passage, the spirit that was cast out realized it could not get back in. However, the foundation was still there. The demon still saw an area of opportunity. So, it went to go and get higher ranking or more evil or powerful spirits than itself to come so they could enter the man. So, that means the demonic foundation was not destroyed or there was an opportunity to rebuild. You should pray on a daily basis that every demonic foundation that has been set up in or around your life be destroyed in Jesus's name! Victory has already been won in heaven, and we maintain that victory on earth by staying connected to heaven by faith. Spiritual warfare requires persistence, and although it's a war we have already won, as soldiers we still have to show up for battle.

You aren't warring just for yourself, but others will benefit. It matters that you pray because there are others who benefit from your prayers because you are praying in the area they live in. You may have never called your neighbors' names, but they can benefit because you prayed and warred in that area. Demons will look for a way to influence you like in the past, but this time they will see that your offense and defense are better than ever. The old you denied your true power in Christ, but the new you will walk in your true power in Christ. Let's identify your rights.

3 Key Rights You Have in Spiritual Warfare

1.) The Right to Use the Authority of Christ and Power of the Holy Spirit

2.) The Right to God's Will

3.) The Right to Rule in Your Territory

As you can see, these rights are no small matter. These rights seem like common knowledge. However, there is a difference in knowing about them, talking about them, and actually being about them. You have many rights in God's kingdom, but those rights can only be realized fully in your life when you know them and exercise them. Demons understand the legalities of heaven, and they know their rights. They don't really have rights per se, but through the legalities of God's laws, they know how to work the system. They know what they can and can't do based on the law. The rights they have are rights to gain legal access to us based on certain things like personal sin, generational sin, trauma, word curses, etc. The list is extensive, but we can overturn demonic legal rights. We will get into that later in the book.

So, you need to know your rights because demons know how to use the law to their advantage. Our ignorance of it doesn't make them back off. So, we must exercise our rights. On earth, you can have the right to vote, but that right only truly holds value in your life when you actually apply it. You have rights to all power and all authority over all works of the enemy, but they only hold value in your life when you know them and use them. See, it's not enough to just know it; are you using it?

The Right to Use the Authority of Christ and Power of the Holy Spirit

John 17:20-24: *"I do not pray for these alone, but also for those who will believe in Me through their word; that they all may be one, as You, Father, are in Me, and I in You; that they also may be one in Us, that the world may believe that You sent Me. And the glory which You gave Me I have given them, that they may be one*

47

just as We are one: I in them, and You in Me; that they may be
made perfect in one, and that the world may know that You have
sent Me, and have loved them as You have loved Me.

"Father, I desire that they also whom You gave Me may be with
Me where I am, that they may behold My glory which You have
given Me; for You loved Me before the foundation of the world."

In this passage, Jesus was praying, and we see that there are two instances where He mentioned that the glory God gave to Him, Jesus gave to us. Christ is in us, and we are in Christ. Christ is in God, and God is in Christ. Although they are two individuals, they are still one in spirit. He also said that He desired that we may be where He is. When you accept Christ, you have the authority to use His name against the enemy, and in that moment, you literally arrest any demon.

God's glory can also mean being attached to His kingly rule. When you have Christ, heaven's rules apply, and heaven's rules say that there are no limitations. Therefore, you cannot be denied on earth. God's glory can also be revealed, seen, or something that appears. Sometimes it is also seen as the physical manifestation of His being. We were created in His image, so if we are in Christ and Christ in us, then we are the physical manifestation of God's glory in the earth. That makes you a glory carrier who is attached to God's kingly rule. Hence, you are entitled to rule on earth. This also means that what is His is ours, and He distributes it among His children. So truthfully, we have the greatest inheritance anyone could have, which is God. To inherit God means we inherit all good things.

Knowing this is powerful, so we must also be careful. To walk in this fullness is amazing, but Satan once walked in it and gained so much pride because of the power and authority until he thought he was God. God is the supreme King, and we are the little kings or queens who can only function because of Him through Christ. To have the glory of God, the world will have to acknowledge the power and authority. Some may still reject it, but they won't be able to deny the demonstration of power that took place. They won't be able to deny that there is something very special about you. They won't be able to deny the miracles, signs, and wonders. They won't be able to deny what belongs to you. You either take your seat of authority as a child of God or have your seat taken! It is only through the power and authority from God through Christ that we can do His will. You have been given the authority of Christ, and it comes with responsibility. You're expected to use it anytime you see darkness. Anything not of God opposes God and is an enemy of God. You are expected to use your authority.

There is another passage in Scripture that shines a light on this power and authority that you have.

Acts 1:4-8: *And being assembled together with them, He commanded them not to depart from Jerusalem, but to wait for the Promise of the Father, "which," He said, "you have heard from Me; for John truly baptized with water, but you shall be baptized with the Holy Spirit not many days from now." Therefore, when they had come together, they asked Him, saying, "Lord, will You at this time restore the kingdom to Israel?" And He said to them, "It is not for you to know times or seasons which the Father has put in His own authority. But you shall receive power when the Holy Spirit has come upon you; and you shall be witnesses to Me in Jerusalem, and in all Judea and Samaria, and to the end of the earth."*

We see in this passage an account of when Jesus was resurrected (by the Holy Spirit). He appeared to the apostles and was among them over a period of forty days before He was taken back up to heaven. Notice what Jesus said, "But you shall receive POWER when the Holy Spirit has come upon you!" (emphasis mine). They already had some power because the Holy Spirit was doing the work around them, but now the Holy Spirit would come upon them as He is now upon us who accept Christ. God's seal of approval on our life is the Holy Spirit. When you get Christ, you get the Holy Spirit and access to all power. Nothing can overpower the power of the Holy Spirit in you. If the enemy is beating on you, you must allow the Holy Spirit to beat on them. It's actually quite easy and simple. Stop thinking about it, and start praying about it. You must let the Holy Spirit go to work in your life by decreasing what you think and looking at what God says.

Look at what Jesus said would happen after they received the power. They would be witnesses of Christ to the end of the earth. In other words, they would bring God's kingdom on earth, and the only way possible for that to be done was through the POWER of the Holy Spirit at work in them.

The same thing applies to us today. If you have a power shortage, I assure you there's nothing wrong with the power; it's just a temporary disconnection from the Holy Spirit. You just need to check your connection. This is why Scripture talks about not grieving the Holy Spirit or quenching the Spirit. He wants to work in and through you, but you must give Him opportunities to do the work because He won't force Himself on you.

There are various factors that can impact the flow of the Holy Spirit. Wounds in our soul and sin can impact the flow of His power. Not spending the necessary amount of time in prayer, worship, or God's Word can impact the flow of the power of the Holy Spirit in you. The Holy Spirit comes with accepting Christ, but He must be invited in your life to do His great works through you. It's tragic to be a Christian with all power living in you only to think that you have little power or that you're unqualified to carry it. Since I mentioned feeling unqualified, I think we need to dive into that a bit deeper. You are actually overqualified to be on earth. You are literally the DNA of God, Christ rules in us, the Holy Spirit is in us, God's kingdom is in us, and we carry God's glory. One of these qualifiers is enough to dominate on earth, but you have all. That makes you overqualified to be on earth. You have more than enough to get the job done.

This goes back to divine alignment. Prayers of faith keep you in divine alignment. God's will should become your will. There is nothing you can come up with that will be better than the will of

God. The problem is that because certain things haven't happened, too many in the church have made the excuse about it being God's will. It's never God's will for you to lack, be sick, struggle, etc. Stop calling Satan's will the will of God! Christ came to prosper you. As you keep the faith through prayer and war against the enemy, God will bring you out of what Satan took you into. Don't fall for the tricks of the enemy. Don't listen to the lies of demons. You are great in God, and the world will be forced to witness your greatness. You are righteous in God. You don't have to just be righteous some days, but if you keep living in Christ, He makes you righteous all days. I'm really trying to get you to accept your power, understand your power, and execute your power on earth. We see in Scripture that you are righteous in Christ.

Romans 1:16-17 (emphasis mine): *For I am not ashamed of the gospel of Christ, for it is the power of God to salvation for everyone who believes, for the Jew first and also for the Greek. For in it the righteousness of God is revealed from faith to faith; as it is written,* ***"The just shall live by faith."***

Apostle Paul knew the power of the gospel of Jesus Christ. He knew that through it, God's power was revealed to everyone who accepted, believed, and obeyed the message of Christ. It was first presented to the Jews and then to everyone else.
The righteousness of God is revealed through Jesus Christ and placed upon us when we accept Him. When you're righteous, it means to be innocent and conformed to the will of God. In other words, to be in right standing with God. One sure way to get here is through faith. The word "just" in verse 17 is the same word for righteous. So, faith in God through Christ is one way to stay in righteousness. Faith is the very thing that followers of Christ must live by. Faith allows you to make transactions from heaven to earth!

Faith in God through Christ helps you live the righteous life Christ came for you to have. If our faith is shaky, our results from heaven will be shaky. Faith doesn't dismiss you from the fight, but it gets you access to all the weapons you need to win the fight. As a child of God, you are bold in the spirit. This is why you can be one way by nature, but when the Holy Spirit works through you, you become bold. You don't become another person when you operate in the spirit, but you become who you really are when you're in the spirit!

We are all given a measure of faith, and it's up to us to build it and increase it. As we go from one level of faith to another, God's righteousness and power are revealed to us. A child of God does not live by feelings, but we live by faith. Your feelings remind you of who you are in the flesh, but your faith reminds you of who you are in Christ.

It is a privilege to carry God's name because that name comes with unmatched power! Carry His name with the confidence that comes with it. We go from faith to faith, so it reminds us that faith grows. Your faith is growing, and the more it grows, the more of Christ you will see in your life. This is where your authority is. The more Christ is reigning and ruling in and through us, the more authority we will operate in on earth.

Let's take it another step further. You're not just righteous, but you are to be holy.

1 Peter 1:15-16 (emphasis mine): *But as He who called you is holy, you also be holy in all your conduct, because it is written,* ***"Be holy, for I am holy."***

Apostle Peter is talking about the importance of holiness. We are to be holy in our character and how we live life because we represent God. As a child of God, you are to be holy because God is holy. He gave us all we need to live the life He intended for us to live. Holiness is a lifestyle. You're holy when Christ is in you and you're in Christ. What happens on the inside will manifest on the outside! You are not filthy rags. That saying came from Isaiah 64:6, which talked about us being unclean and our righteousness being like filthy rags and our sins taking us away. That was talking about who we are in the flesh, not who we are in God. That was also before Christ's sacrifice. It was before grace. Saying you're filthy rags now is false humility because it's glorifying the flesh. When you're in Christ, you are to be holy in God through Christ! So, you must change your language and speak the Word of God. You are not filthy rags, but as you live by faith, you are holy because God is holy! You can't walk in the blessing of God fully if you don't have a renewed mind. If it feels uncomfortable or if it feels like you're sinning against God because you say that you're holy in God through Christ or that you're righteous in God through Christ, then you need to pray for a renewed mind and keep feeding your spirit with God's Word. Say it out loud right now: "I am holy in Christ! I am righteous through Christ." Now say, "I am holy, and I am righteous!" Get used to saying it, and get used to living it, because Christ should reign and rule in you!

The Right to God's Will

Matthew 26:26-28 (emphasis mine): *And as they were eating, Jesus took bread, blessed and broke it, and gave it to the disciples and said, "Take, eat; this is My body." Then He took the cup, and gave thanks, and gave it to them, saying, "Drink from it, all of you.* ***For this is My blood of the new covenant****, which is shed for many for the remission of sins."*

In these verses, Jesus instituted the Lord's Supper, which we call Communion. When we partake in it, the bread represents Christ's body that was broken for our right to divine healing and the red juice/wine represents the blood He shed for the remission of our sins. He died in our place to get us back in right relationship with God. This was the new covenant. The passage contains every aspect of God's will for our lives because of Christ's sacrifice. God originally established the covenant with Abraham and all his descendants (including us). The covenant was that God would always be our God. Jesus restored the covenant that Satan tried to destroy through sin, and now we have the new covenant, which we now access through accepting Christ for being the sin offering in our place.

So, we must first realize that we are in covenant with God. We must also understand what covenant means in Scripture. Oftentimes, the belief is that it is a binding contract between two people who agree to do specific things. However, that's not necessarily the case.

Although humans made covenants with other humans, it was different when God made a covenant with humans. Humans had the type of covenant that was a negotiated agreement. However, God's covenant in the Old Testament that He made with humans was made up of benefits that would be given by one person to another. God's covenant with us is a one-party guarantee to another. It's an arrangement in which the superior party (God) presents the covenant to an inferior party (humans), and we choose to accept or reject it. However, we can't take anything away or add anything to it.

Accept God's will in your life, not Satan's. Satan wants you to think it's God's will for you to be sick or lacking. The devil is a liar. God made a guarantee to us. It was not a negotiated contract. God's will for your life comes with many guarantees, and if you do it, there is absolutely no good thing He will withhold from you. According to Strong's Concordance, the Hebrew word for covenant is "berith" (pronounced beh-reeth). The Greek word is "diatheke" (pronounced dee-ah-thai-k). The new covenant Jesus spoke of was like a last will and testament of things left to us (inheritance). It also often refers to a pledge or arrangement that is a one-sided promise. So, God made the terms; we just choose to accept it or not. We choose if we will accept Christ and walk in faith or not. God gave us a simple choice to either choose Christ and walk by faith or choose to walk by flesh. Follow Christ and answers will follow you.

So, our covenant with God through Christ is a promise. We have an inheritance. Spiritually, according to biblestudytools.com, inheritance means "to receive an irrevocable gift with an emphasis on the special relationship between the benefactor and the recipients." Our inheritance is irrevocable, which means it cannot be changed, reversed, revoked, etc. So, there is nothing any person, demon, or thing can do to change it. This inheritance is based on the relationship between you and God. So, in warfare, you need to understand that we are in covenant with God through Christ. You're with the winning team. In knowing this, you must make demons in your territory uncomfortable and force them out because your rewards from God do not belong to them. **It is never God's will for you to live below your position in heaven. Your position is to be seated in Christ, so take your seat.** Your God-given, assigned territory is part of your inheritance, and it's your divine right to have it. Not only do we have the right to God's will, but we are supposed to do more than Christ did on earth.

John 14:12 (emphasis mine): *"Most assuredly, I say to you, he who believes in Me, **the works that I do he will do also; and greater works than these he will do, because I go to My Father."***

Jesus made it clear to the disciples, and it applies to us today: the works Jesus Himself did on earth, we will do, and we will do even greater works on earth if we believe in Him. Jesus had to overcome demonic opposition and He conquered every one, and He will continue to conquer them through you. Notice that He said that we will do it. We're living way below our position in Christ if we aren't doing the works on earth that Christ did because He said we will do greater! Just do it. If we submit to Him, we will do what Jesus did on earth and even more because He was on earth a shorter time than most of us have been or will be. We will also do greater works because the Holy Spirit is at work in us. Part of the work Jesus did on earth was overthrowing demonic systems, and that's part of your job description as well.

What Christ started, we are to finish on earth through His authority and power of the Holy Spirit at work in us. It's expected as children of God to do great works on earth, and you're qualified because Christ qualified you. No demon, witch, warlock, or sorcerer should be able to push you aside. You have been pushed around long enough. God's kingdom invades earth because we are a part of His kingdom. If you want Satan and his demons to back off, use your power and authority. The key is persistence. Every demon will not go away quietly! You must develop the habit of fighting in the spirit until you get the results you're satisfied with. You must gain endurance in spiritual warfare because you aren't just putting out fires in your life, but also in the lives of others.

Every time God uses you to do His will is a great work you just accomplished on earth. That alone makes you successful. The best you is still to come because every time God shows up in your life, it is better than the last time, and that's daily. Your life is a bright light that is meant to shine in dark places to expose the enemy.

The Right to Rule in Your Territory

Revelation 5:8-10: *Now when He had taken the scroll, the four living creatures and the twenty-four elders fell down before the Lamb, each having a harp, and golden bowls full of incense, which are the prayers of the saints. And they sang a new song, saying:*
"You are worthy to take the scroll,
And to open its seals;
For You were slain,
And have redeemed us to God by Your blood
Out of every tribe and tongue and people and nation,
And have made us kings and priests to our God;
And we shall reign on the earth."

This was part of the vision revealed to John the apostle. Because of Jesus's death on the cross in place of our sins, we are redeemed and have the opportunity to rule and reign on earth through Christ. Hence, we are kings and priests. We are kings because we can rule and have dominion on earth. We reign on earth because of Christ in us. This alone makes you the living manifestation of Christ in the earth, as He works through you. It's your responsibility as a ruler on earth from God's kingdom to enforce order in your assigned territory.

God has not left His throne, but He uses us to carry out His will in the earth. Why? Because we are His children, and we are entitled to what comes with being His children. Your reign on earth for God will be a great one because your obedience to God ruins the plans of Satan! We are also priests because we can go to the throne of God and pray for ourselves and for others.

We are expected to reign on earth. As the revival is here, the renewed church, the kingdom church, will once again gain the attention of the world in many arenas. God's glory will manifest in such a way that many will not be able to deny His power. Many will be converted. Many will be healed and delivered. Many will be renewed and transformed, and you will have something to do with that. If you are willing, God will use you to transform people and places around you for His glory! Jesus didn't die for you to fit in, but He died so you could rule on earth. God's Kingdom does not fit in, but it stands out. You are a standout. You have territory because it was given to you by God. Not to mention it all belongs to God.

Psalm 24:1 says, *"The earth is the Lord's and all its fullness, The world and those who dwell therein."*

The fact that the entire globe belongs to God lets us know that as His children, we have an inheritance. So, that means we have territory assigned to us to possess and rule and have dominion in, not so that we are glorified, but so that God is glorified in the earth. It's part of your job to remind demons that nothing belongs to them, and you show them by taking back anything they stole. This basic principle helps us understand why Satan tries to fight us for territory that belongs to us because he has no inheritance. So, he tries to kill, steal, and destroy what rightfully belongs to us. So, it's a battle over territory. If it even seems like the enemy is trying to mess with what's yours, you are expected to use your power and authority to put them in their place!

We see it in Scripture and in war during our time. When an army invades another territory and they win, they have jurisdiction and control over the territory they conquered. The enemy has been waging war against us, but now it's time we wage war against the enemy and rightfully take our seat of authority. It becomes very difficult for demons to steal from you or continue to steal at a high rate when you are in your seat of authority and are aware of what's going on around you.

Chapter 5: The Battleground

We all must engage in spiritual warfare, and the more you accept the power and authority given to you, the greater your advantage will be. It helps to understand the battleground. It helps to be aware of what is going on around you so you're rarely caught by surprise. God gave you territory to manage on His behalf, and it's your responsibility to defend it against any attack of the enemy.
We already know the enemy will try to steal, kill, and destroy. So, our spirits, which are the real us, should be prepared. Your flesh may be caught off guard when the enemy attacks, but your spirit was born ready! It is important to understand your role in the battle so you aren't distracted. When you understand and do your role in God's kingdom, it becomes difficult for the enemy to place fear in you because you know you're covered. Therefore, fear is simply a lie that Satan wants you to believe. Fear is an enemy that attempts to get you to live below your rank in God by stepping outside of your faith in God. There's no place for fear on the battleground in spiritual warfare. It may show up, but we don't have to give in to it. Rest in your faith in God that He knows what He's doing through you. You're entitled to fight for what's rightfully yours because it rightfully belongs to God. Yes, we are in war, but it's a war we've already won. God wants you to get to the mind-set of living life from the perspective of It's Already Done! Just walk forward in Christ to activate it. Things look different from this perspective because you're no longer asking God to do what He already said He did.

When you ask God for something that He already said He gave you, there's nothing else He needs to do. You just need to receive it. It looks like a lack of communication on the battlefield in spiritual warfare when you ask for things you already have. You don't have to ask for power because you already have limitless power in you in the Holy Spirit. You don't have to ask for healing because Jesus already died for your healing. You don't have to ask to prosper because God already said that He desires that you prosper. You need to receive what God already said you have and attack the enemy in spiritual warfare when what you see contradicts what God said.

Fear is a lack of acknowledging the power and authority that God placed in you. When you really trust God's Word, fear won't stay around. You have the upper hand on the battleground. You may not be able to control everything that happens around you, but you can control what you do about it. You also have the ability to change the course of events. You have been given the power to change atmospheres.

Demons may attack you on your territory, but when you exercise your power and authority, they must stand down. You must fight back. You must be reminded that this is a spiritual thing, not a physical one. You've invested far too much energy in dealing with things in your flesh. The results will only be produced when you handle them in the spirit!

Spiritual warfare is a fight that you're guaranteed to win if you accept and utilize the power and authority God gave you. Sometimes it becomes hard to accept that reality because you have been led to believe that if something has been going on for so long that it's God's will. God won't contradict His will to justify our excuses to not do what He said we can do, considering the fact that He said we only need a small seed of faith to move any mountain. His will stands.

Most Christians don't have a faith problem. The problem is not feeling worthy to actually receive what God said you're worthy to have. This goes back to having a mind-set shift. You are too powerful to live below your potential by stooping down to the enemy's level. You're seated in Christ, so live in Christ! One of the biggest tricks of Satan is to try to get you to believe that you're not who God said you were before you were even born. You must trust God. When you realize that your life is not about you, but it's about Christ living through you, nothing will ever pose a threat to you.

This is the confidence that you need on the battleground. Sure, things will seem hard at times, but it is only hard according to your flesh. Every problem that comes your way in life has an expiration date because no problem can ever survive in the spirit realm when you're in Christ! The battleground is a place that you have expertise in. Even if you're in new territory and don't know anyone where you are, you still have the same power and authority. If you're looking for answers, you still have the same power and authority. Your mind must be renewed. Any thought or idea independent of God is a thought or idea that opposes God. God is not telling you to recreate the blueprint, but He's telling you to let Him work the blueprint through you. It's already been laid out for you to follow. Revelation from the Holy Spirit comes to give you a greater understanding of God's blueprint for your life and others' lives. What you're facing is not something your spirit hasn't seen before because you came out of God. Therefore, you have what you need to overcome. Therefore, spiritual warfare is a battle you've seen before, and you have all the power and authority you need to ensure victory.

We now need to understand where we live and how it operates, as it is where the battle occurs. You have been living here on earth all these years, so it will help to know more about it and why your role is so important. We must gain a better understanding of the word heaven and how it is used in Scripture. Earth is an extension of heaven. We hear the word heaven, and oftentimes, the first thing we think about is heaven where God is. When we talk about the heavens, we should look at it in a sense of it being spheres, dimensions, levels, hierarchy, etc. The highest heaven, of course, is where God's throne is.

The Three Heavens

There are three heavens: first heaven, second heaven, and third heaven. The concept is similar to how God instructed Moses to build the tabernacle which had three parts: Outer Court, Holy Place, Holy of Holies. Even Noah's ark had three levels (Gen. 6:16).

Deuteronomy 10:14: *Indeed heaven and the highest heavens belong to the LORD your God, also the earth with all that is in it.*

This passage gives us a clue that there is more than one heaven or dimension or hierarchy of heaven. The ultimate place we desire to get to is the highest heaven where God is. Satan tries to get you to come off your seat of authority in Christ, but when you know how important your position is, you'll stay focused.

The heavens belong to God. That means they don't belong to Satan. Satan and his workers are trying to steal our inheritance because they have none of their own. However, we aren't sharing with them.

First Heaven

The first heaven is earth. This is where humans reside. This also includes the earth and the atmosphere that surrounds it. The saying "heaven on earth" has some validity. We are to have dominion on earth. We are 100% spirit beings who happen to have flesh. As discussed, spirit can only get in the earth realm with a physical body. We are to bring God's kingdom to earth. When Jesus came, He invaded the earth and preached about the kingdom of God. Demons roam around earth trying to take our territory, and they recognize when we show up. Satan is also trying to establish his kingdom on earth, but we invade it for God's glory! The battleground only becomes a battleground in spiritual warfare because Satan wants from us what he knows he rightfully can't have. You must fight back.

Genesis 1:26-28 (emphasis mine): *Then God said, "Let Us make man in Our image, according to Our likeness; let them have dominion over the fish of the sea, over the **birds of the air**, and over the cattle, over all the earth and over every creeping thing that creeps on the earth." So God created man in His own image; in the image of God He created him; male and female He created them. Then God blessed them, and God said to them, "Be fruitful and multiply; fill the earth and subdue it; have dominion over the* *fish of the sea, over the **birds of the air**, and over every living thing that moves on the earth."*

We see that God gave humans dominion on earth, including over the birds of the air. We understand that these are English words. The Hebrew translation for "air" in verse 26, according to Strong's Concordance, is "Shamayim" (pronounced shä-mah'-yim), which means "heaven." So, it really would say, "over the birds of the heaven." These birds of heaven or the sky are part of the first heaven. The first heaven includes the earth and the atmosphere surrounding it.

God gave you dominion on earth, and that means that no demon has the right to imprison you because you are to imprison them. We also know that God gave Adam and Eve dominion before He blessed them. Not only do you have dominion, but you also have God's blessing. Don't ever allow a situation you experience make you forget that you are blessed by God through Christ.

Matthew 6:26: *Look at the birds of the air, for they neither sow nor reap nor gather into barns; yet your heavenly Father feeds them. Are you not of more value than they?*

Now we see a New Testament example. Jesus was talking to the crowd that was listening to Him. He let us know that the birds of the heaven do not sow or reap, but our heavenly Father feeds them. The word for "air" in the Strong's Concordance Greek translation of the New Testament is "Ouranos" (pronounced oo-rah-nos), which also means "heaven." This again refers to the sky, which is a part of the earth's atmosphere. We also know that it is talking about the first heaven on earth because Jesus said right after He mentioned birds of the heaven that our heavenly Father feeds them. So, we know Jesus is not referring to the same heaven here, but a different place because we can see the birds here. Our heavenly Father God is in the third heaven.

God takes care of the birds in the first heaven on earth, and they don't sow or reap. We are more valuable than birds. Believe God for what He said! He said He will provide, so don't allow fear to rob you of the truth in your faith. Demons will try to fight us with fear on the battleground in hopes we doubt what God said. Fear is an ugly enemy that tries to make you doubt the truth in God and the power in you. It's an enemy, and you must fight against it.

James 5:17-18: *Elijah was a man with a nature like ours, and he prayed earnestly that it would not rain; and it did not rain on the land for three years and six months. And he prayed again, and the heaven gave rain, and the earth produced its fruit.*

The heaven here is still the first heaven. This is the earth's atmosphere, and the clouds give rain. Elijah prayed to God, and we know God is in the third heaven. He prayed to God to manifest rain in the first heaven. Notice that it says that Elijah was a man like us. He was human like us and prayed to God to send the answer to his prayers on earth.

God responded to his request, and it did not rain for three years and six months. He was in relationship with God, and he walked in the power and authority of God, which is the same power and authority that we have today. He was able to use the power and authority to get it to rain. He was able to do this before Christ came and the promise of the Holy Spirit was given. So, imagine how much more we can do now because of what Christ did for us. When conditions are not suitable for you, you have full access to heaven to pray that God manifests on earth what's already done in heaven.

Elijah prayed for no rain, and it didn't rain. Elijah prayed for rain, and it rained. There are some areas that have dried up in your life, but you have access to all God has to bring them back to life!

James 1:16-17 (emphasis mine): *Do not be deceived, my beloved brethren. Every good gift and every perfect gift is from above, and comes down **from the Father of lights**, with whom there is no variation or shadow of turning.*

We already understand that Scripture tells us that we are the light of the world. Now, we see that God is the Father of lights. He's our father, and we are lights. Hence, He is the Father of all lights, which not only includes us, but also sun, moon, stars, angels, etc.

There are some things that people call good because they want them badly, but it doesn't mean they're good for them. God gives good gifts that last. Every good gift is from God, and He gives it to you to spoil you in ways He hasn't spoiled you before!

There is no variation or shadow of turning with God. This means that unlike the sun that can go down or be covered by clouds, God does not change. He always shines. He is the Light of all lights, King of kings, Lord of lords. God is not moving from His throne in the third heaven, so we must walk in our kingship and let our lights shine here on earth in the first heaven. Although this is not our original home, it's where we were sent to do the will of God.

So, it's expected that you rule and reign on earth through the power that works in you. The battleground is actually an area where you are expected to have influence. You are a king or queen, and God is over us all. Get used to this responsibility. Get used to carrying all this power. It's to make others around you better. It's to bring God's kingdom on earth. God gave you power so that you can demonstrate to the world that Christ is the only way.

It doesn't require much more convincing when you demonstrate the power of God to support the Word of God! This is necessary on the battleground. It's a fight for territory and a fight for souls.

Genesis 3:8, 23-24: *And they heard the sound of the LORD God walking in the garden in the cool of the day, and Adam and his wife hid themselves from the presence of the LORD God among the trees of the garden....therefore the LORD God sent him out of the garden of Eden to till the ground from which he was taken. So He drove out the man; and He placed cherubim at the east of the* *garden of Eden, and a flaming sword which turned every way, to guard the way to the tree of life.*

Adam and Eve were on earth in the Garden of Eden, and they heard God walking. They hid themselves because they knew they had sinned against God by eating from the tree in the middle of the garden. The tree gave them knowledge of good and evil. The Garden of Eden was on earth, and God planted it on earth. According to Brown-Driver-Briggs Hebrew Lexicon, Eden means "pleasure." So, it was the Garden of Pleasure. It was a place where man was in perfect relationship with God.

We see that God even walked in the Garden of Eden. However, because of sin, Adam and Eve were kicked out of the garden and sent to till the ground from which they were taken on the earth. God even had some cherubim angels guard it, as well as a flaming sword so that Adam and Eve were not tempted to try to come back. The fact that God brought angels to the garden to guard it shows how much of paradise and heaven it really was.

After Adam and Eve were kicked out, some things changed. After the flood came to destroy the earth, except Noah and his family, things changed. That fellowship with God was not as close as it should have been. This is why Jesus had to come to get it right for us. Nonetheless, we see how earth was always a heaven.

If you feel you've lost your place in God, it's never hard to find your place again. It's as simple as walking away from guilt and running to God. The enemy gets free shots on us when we are on the battleground and are afraid to go back to God because of something we've done. You're either running from God or running to God. No matter what has happened, you should always find yourself running to God. If you don't accept your power and authority from God to rule, you're saying you want to be ruled by someone other than God. You don't want that to happen.

Second Heaven

Daniel 10:12-13 (emphasis mine): *Then he said to me, "Do not fear, Daniel, for from the first day that you set your heart to*

66

*understand, and to humble yourself before your God, your words were heard; and I have come because of your words. **But the prince of the kingdom of Persia withstood me twenty-one days; and behold, Michael, one of the chief princes, came to help me**, for I had been left alone there with the kings of Persia."*

We see here that Daniel had prayed, and it took twenty-one days for the answer to be delivered because spiritual warfare was going on in the second heaven. Once Satan and the angels who fell with him were kicked out of heaven (third heaven), they had no access to God's throne. They typically reside in the second heaven. The demonic principalities Satan assigned over Persia were trying to prevent God's angel Gabriel from delivering the answer to Daniel's prayer. As Gabriel came from the third heaven, he had to pass through the second heaven, and that's where he ran into the opposition. However, God's angel Michael came to help Gabriel fight against the demonic principality so that Gabriel could get free to get to Daniel. This again is why prayer and engaging in spiritual warfare is so important. Every battle won or lost in the spirit realm or the second heaven is first won or lost here on earth in the first heaven. Our prayer life is critical. It passes from the first heaven, through the second heaven, and reaches the third heaven.

The battle that was going on couldn't be seen physically because it was happening in the spirit. However, Daniel's prayers from the first heaven caused a lot of activity to take place in the second heaven. So, while you're here in the first heaven, there is always activity going on in the second heaven, and you can influence it. You have a role to play. Earth is a physical realm, but it is still governed by the spirit realm. Technically, earth also has a spiritual component as well. We are spirit beings operating on earth. Angels are spirits who also operate on earth. Demons are spirits who operate on earth. It's another reminder that you are spirit living in flesh.

Your prayer life is too vital and too much is influenced by your prayers for you to play around with it! You don't have to see it all, but I assure you, as we see in this passage, activity is going on in the second heaven. So, the first heaven and the second heaven are battlegrounds, and you can influence both. You have dominion here, but you also have dominion in the second heaven because you're seated in Christ. However, that dominion, of course, is exercised through Christ and carried out by the heavenly host (warring angels). We can't literally get up to the second heaven and fight against principalities. However, if they cause problems in our territory on earth, we have every right and all the power and authority to engage them in our territory. You don't just randomly go and fight a principality because there are laws in the spirit realm. It's about jurisdiction. However, if they engage you, you have every right to engage them back. The only real problem you have as a child of God is allowing problems to stay. You've been given power and authority over every problem.

Third Heaven

This is where God Himself dwells. This is where His throne is. This is our first home. This is where we came from because we are spirit. This is where we go when we die in Christ and go to heaven. This is ultimately where we want to get back to, but that all depends on if we carry out God's will for our lives here on earth in the first heaven. This is also where God's angels dwell. Some of these angels have specific assignments, which is why they leave the third heaven and operate in the second and first heaven. For example, we know that we have guardian angels who protect us as well as deliver answers to us. Courier/messenger angels deliver answers to us. Gabriel is the chief over the courier angels.

2 Corinthians 12:1-4: *It is doubtless not profitable for me to boast. I will come to visions and revelations of the Lord: I know a man in Christ who fourteen years ago—whether in the body I do not know, or whether out of the body I do not know, God knows—such a one was caught up to the third heaven. And I know such a man—whether in the body or out of the body I do not know, God knows—how he was caught up into Paradise and heard inexpressible words, which it is not lawful for a man to utter.*

Apostle Paul was speaking of himself. He had received so many revelations, but he did not want to come across as one who boasted in his close relationship and fellowship with God. Apostle Paul had a vision of the third heaven. It was so powerful what he saw and heard in the spirit in the vision he had of the third heaven: the words were inexpressible, and he was not even permitted to utter it. There are great things that God will reveal to you that words will never be able to describe, but He will show you because of His love for you! So, whatever Paul saw, he was not even allowed to write it down. It's another mystery of God. Some things the Holy Spirit will reveal to us are not in Scripture, but the key to measure them by is that God will never go against His Word. He won't show us something or have us to do something that contradicts His Word. It's an honor and a privilege as well as a necessity to get revelation from God. Satan is jealous of us because he can't get revelation.

Isaiah 6:1-7 (emphasis mine): *In the year that King Uzziah died,* ***I saw the Lord sitting on a throne,*** *high and lifted up, and the train of **His robe filled the temple**. Above it stood seraphim; each one had six wings: with two he covered his face, with two he covered his feet, and with two he flew. And one cried to another and said:*
"Holy, holy, holy is the LORD of hosts;
The whole earth is full of His glory!"

And the posts of the door were shaken by the voice of him who cried out, and the house was filled with smoke.

So I said:
"Woe is me, for I am undone!
Because I am a man of unclean lips,
And I dwell in the midst of a people of unclean lips;
For my eyes have seen the King,
The LORD of hosts."

Then one of the seraphim flew to me, having in his hand a live coal which he had taken with the tongs from the altar. And he touched my mouth with it, and said:
"Behold, this has touched your lips;
Your iniquity is taken away,
And your sin purged."

The prophet Isaiah had a vision of the third heaven. We know this because he was able to see God sitting on the throne. He also saw the seraphim angels. Seraphim are the highest-ranking angels as they surround God's throne. They are the attendants to God's throne and have the most perfect knowledge of God. They are always singing, "Holy, holy, holy is the Lord of hosts." Isaiah was able to see all of this.

He had the vision around the time Uzziah, a king of Judah, had died. He uses that historical point to signify the year he had the vision. Isaiah recognized that he was in the presence of God and felt unclean and that he was not even fit to speak. However, a seraph took a coal from the altar and touched his lips with it, and it was symbolic that he had been purged of his sins. This then put him in a position to be able to answer God when He spoke to him and gave him the next assignment during this vision.

Revelation 4:1-4: *After these things I looked, and behold, a door standing open in heaven. And the first voice which I heard was like a trumpet speaking with me, saying, "Come up here, and I will show you things which must take place after this." Immediately I was in the Spirit; and behold, a throne set in heaven, and One sat on the throne. And He who sat there was like a jasper and a sardius stone in appearance; and there was a rainbow around the throne, in appearance like an emerald. Around the throne were twenty-four thrones, and on the thrones I saw twenty-four elders sitting, clothed in white robes; and they had crowns of gold on their heads.*

John had a revelation of the third heaven. Again, he saw God's throne. We see that he only saw it after he was in the spirit. It's impossible to see spiritual things and be in the flesh. Only spirit can see spirit. We gain more information from this revelation because now we see twenty-four thrones surrounding God's throne. These thrones are believed to represent the entire church. Some thought it was the twelve tribes of Israel and the twelve apostles. However, from those who have had some revelation of heaven, it has been revealed that the twenty-four elders around the throne are actually created beings that have been with God forever. It was the three (Father, Son, and Holy Spirit), and then they made the four living creatures and then the twenty-four elders. The elders are not on the throne as much because they're walking around heaven serving others.

Apostle John saw an open door in heaven. If there are open doors in heaven, there are open doors on earth, and we just need to walk through them. God is not shutting you out. He's inviting you to come closer to Him because there are things He will show you that you've never seen before. There is nothing to worry about on the battleground. You just need to do the good work of a soldier. God gave you territory. You are expected to rule and have dominion regardless of the attacks of the enemy because you have what you need to win in spiritual warfare. This is just more training to help you in battle.

Chapter 6: The Weapon of Prayer

Prayer is critical in spiritual warfare. Prayer is not an option for you to do when you feel like it. Prayer is a mandate from God. God didn't suggest that we pray; He commanded us to pray. Prayer and spiritual warfare go hand in hand. Prayer is not something God needs, but it is what we need. It is what strengthens us. You should not begin to think you will be effective concerning any matter in the spirit without prayer. I'm talking about a relentless pursuit of God in prayer. The good news is that every time you pray in faith, spiritual deposits are being made whether you hear an answer right away or not. I assure you that the answers will become clear as you move forward from day to day. God won't keep us in the dark because there is no darkness in Him. God wants you so relentless that you will not stop warring until you see breakthrough. There's a significant difference between praying and having a prayer life. God expects you to maintain a life of prayer. It gives you life. You need to have a habit of prayer to maintain the stamina needed in spiritual warfare.

Prayer helps you get your flesh out of the way to prevent it from creating unnecessary problems! Satan and his demons love nothing more than for you to engage in spiritual warfare in your flesh because they know it's an easy win for them. Flesh has never won a spiritual battle, but Jesus has never lost a spiritual battle. Get with Jesus! Prayer helps you get connected with Jesus because it gets your flesh in check and wakes your spirit up. Every prayer you pray unto God is like sending an email to heaven. You just need to wait for God to send a direct reply. God is reminding us, as He always will, of the importance of a prayer life. Prayer keeps you fresh for battle, and it makes sure you are prepared for whatever may come your way. Prayer is work, and you will be able to do it much more as you put in the work. When you don't have a prayer life, it's like telling God that you don't need the blood of Jesus to cover you! We know that the blood of Jesus cleanses us from our sins. Jesus made the sacrifice for you to grow closer to God, not to spend less time with God. When you don't pray, it's like not showing up to court. Satan and those working with him will keep showing up to bring accusations against you, so you don't want to give them an edge. Yes, Christ is our legal defense, but it looks pretty bad for the defendant to not show up to court. Prayer is not an option: it is your duty to pray as a soldier in God's army.

Prayer is phoning home back to heaven. Every time you pray, it reunites you with your first home, and your first home is called heaven. It should also be your last home! It's often said, don't just pray when you need something. However, prayer actually is about what you need because it's exactly what you need. It's easy to get in and out of the routine of consistent prayer, but prayer requires discipline. Prayer gives you discipline. Prayer is what prepares you for your victory in spiritual warfare! Yes, you have the power of the Holy Spirit. Yes, you have the authority of Jesus Christ. Yes, you have power over all works of the enemy. However, if you want to consistently see the power of God demonstrated in your life, you should consistently pray because prayer recharges your battery. The Holy Spirit doesn't need to be recharged, but we do. Since we carry Him around as followers of Christ, we must keep making room for Him. That places some responsibility on us. The Holy Spirit will heal, deliver, raise the dead, etc., through you, but you must ensure that you are making room for Him to do so. Making room for the Holy Spirit to heal, deliver, and raise the dead through you is a daily process that begins and ends with prayer. So, don't get caught up in thinking you can't do any of those things. That's an easy answer. You can't, but the Holy Spirit can through you! The Holy Spirit will do His job through you when you do your job by giving Him the opportunity to work through you. Prayer is a great way to do that.

You should not take prayer lightly because Satan doesn't. That's why he does everything he can to keep you from praying to God. Don't allow what you see to make you so frustrated that you don't pray. Prayer is what can change it. Satan knows that a key secret to your success is in prayer. That's why he aims to frustrate you to make you think prayer isn't working.
Prayer isn't boring. It's only boring if you don't have anything to talk to God about. Look at the world and you'll find much to pray

about. You should make it your business to consistently pray because prayer helps you effectively handle God's business.

Mark 13:35-37 (emphasis mine): *"Watch therefore, for you do not know when the master of the house is coming—in **the evening, at midnight, at the crowing of the rooster, or in the morning**—lest, coming suddenly, he find you sleeping. And what I say to you, I say to all: Watch!"*

Jesus was talking to the disciples about the end of the age. This passage refers to when the end of time may come. We see in verse 35 the breakdown of the four night watches. In this passage, the evening represents the first watch (6 p.m.-9 p.m.), midnight is the second watch (9 p.m.-12 a.m.), the third watch is the crowing of the rooster (12 a.m.-3 a.m.), and the fourth watch is the morning (3 a.m.-6 a.m.). These four watches in Scripture are where we get our night watches from.

The third watch is where a lot of spiritual activity and spiritual warfare occurs. It is also known as the "witching hour" because the enemy tries to sow seeds while many are asleep. My wife and I are very familiar with this watch, and it is familiar with us because we have prayed and warred countless hours on this watch during battles. We started at doing one hour, but we have consistently prayed in the past all three hours during this watch and also do prayer calls and services to pray during third watch. When I got introduced to midnight prayers many years ago, I started out on the third watch. That's where some of my early training came from, as the Holy Spirit revealed a lot to me on the third watch. Even during my college days, God would prompt me to pray during the midnight hour. I remember one instance where I was outside in the rain praying on the third watch before I even knew it was a watch.

My wife and I warred on the third watch leading up to our wedding. We had so much demonic opposition from finances to venue issues. Yes, I know many have had wedding preparation horror stories, but we knew for certain it was a spiritual attack because of our union. We would go to the venue location and war at midnight. One particular night, we went with some family to the original venue location (we ended up getting a venue about a mile or so from the original location), and it was pouring rain. We prayed and warred, and the venue down the street became available because a storm came through and flooded the place. So they shut down and opened back up for our wedding. Our wedding was the first event after the storm.

We got breakthrough in our finances just in time. We secured the caterer two days before. We got the photographer the night before and the videographer the day of the wedding. Essentially, everything was officially planned in three days. Not to mention Donna's wedding ring had to be sent somewhere to be resized and it literally arrived on the day of the wedding. God is faithful, and had we not prayed and warred on the third watch, those things would not have happened on our wedding day. Prayer watches matter.

We don't know when Christ shall return, but He said that because of this we must watch because He may come suddenly and find us sleeping. In other words, we must pray and be sure that we are living a life pleasing to God and are obedient to His will because we never know when He may return, and we don't want to be found unprepared.

God gave you responsibility in the territory He gave you, and He expects you to cover your territory in prayer. You must do your job because it is vital in God's kingdom. Accept the responsibility God trusts you with, and don't wait around for someone else to do tomorrow what God has called you to do today.

Prayer Watches

There are eight watches in the Bible. There are four in the day and four at night. In Scripture, watchmen would relieve each other to cover a different watch of the night. They were on post to watch out for an enemy who may have tried to approach the camp. We too are watchmen through our prayers and need to be on post. We know the enemy comes to kill, steal, and destroy, so we must be on the lookout through prayer, not just for ourselves but for others. The body of Christ is supposed to be one mighty, unified army. I've outlined the night watches, and these are the day watches.

Day Watches

First Watch: 6 a.m.-9 a.m. (9 a.m. is also referred to as the "third hour" in Scripture.)

Second Watch: 9 a.m.-12 p.m. (12 p.m. is also referred to as the "sixth hour.")

Third Watch: 12 p.m.-3 p.m. (3 p.m. is also referred to as the "ninth hour.")

Fourth Watch: 3 p.m.-6 p.m. (6 p.m. would be the "twelfth hour.")

Principles of Prayer

There are a few principles of prayer that we should be aware of.

You Must Pray for Yourself

Luke 18:1: *Then He spoke a parable to them that men always ought to pray and not lose heart.*

Jesus was speaking to the disciples, and this was and is a direct command to us as well that we should always pray and not lose heart in our praying. In other words, when you are facing tough times or when it seems like your prayers are not being answered, don't stop praying. If you quit praying, you're quitting on yourself and the people you didn't know were depending on your prayers. Prayer causes things to happen in the spirit, and you are spirit! The power of prayer is that it is a seed. No matter what, that seed will take root. Let's say you prayed and warred for someone's physical manifestation of healing and they passed away. That seed of prayer will not fall to the ground; it will impact a family member or friend connected to that person because the seed of a prayer of faith unto God must produce. So, your prayers of faith never fall to the ground.

He didn't say we ought to sometimes pray, but we should always pray. That's a lifestyle. Every time you pray, heaven responds. You're giving heaven permission to act on earth. Prayer helps give you a boldness that you didn't have before to face the enemy head-on in spiritual warfare. He knew the types of challenges Satan, his demons, and witches would throw at us because they were thrown at Him. However, we should not give up. Every time you pray, you are letting the devil know that you will not quit. Your persistence in prayer will create consistent results! We were instructed in Colossians 4:2, "Continue earnestly in prayer, being vigilant in it with thanksgiving."

Apostle Paul made it abundantly clear that we should continue in prayer, devote ourselves to prayer, and persevere in prayer. The only way to continue in prayer is to have a life of prayer. Prayer to God shouldn't just be something you do, but it should be a part of you. Devoting yourself to prayer is a lifestyle. Don't pray in your feelings, but pray in faith! Prayer is to be a regular and daily part of our lives. It's a process to get into the presence of God.

We must also be watchful, meaning you are attentive and your mind is in the right place. It's easy to begin to pray while your mind is thinking about other things. God wants your undivided attention. Yes, as you go throughout the day, you can be talking to God while doing things, but be sure to have intimacy and quiet time with God uninterrupted.

And of course, we always give thanks to God. Always thank God for what He's already done for you because He will always do more for you to be thankful for. There is some weight God never intended for you to carry. We are to place our burdens on Him. The only way to pick up your burdens and place your burdens on God is through prayer. If you give your heavy load over to God,

He will sustain you. He promised it, so He will do it. You cannot effectively carry out God's will if you don't pray.

You Must Pray for Others

1 Timothy 2:1-3: *Therefore I exhort first of all that supplications, prayers, intercessions, and giving of thanks be made for all men, for kings and all who are in authority, that we may lead a quiet and peaceable life in all godliness and reverence. For this is good and acceptable in the sight of God our Savior.*

Apostle Paul wrote this letter to his spiritual son Timothy. He made sure that he addressed prayer and that it should be made for everyone, including those in leadership and who have authority. It's not hard to please God. You just need to do what He expects you to do, and He even gave you the strength and power to be able to do it. We see that prayer is the formula to living a quiet and peaceable life in godliness. This does not mean that the enemy won't attack you, but it means an attack won't take your peace or impact who you are in God. Not only is prayer necessary, but it is good and acceptable in the sight of God.

From this passage, we see **four types of prayers:**

1.) **Supplications-** Other words used for supplication are petitions, requests, or entreaties. A supplication is when you are making your requests to God. This is what we do when we ask God for something.

2.) **Prayers of Faith, Agreement, and Dedication-** When we pray, it should be a prayer of faith. It does us no good to pray to God and not believe that He hears us or not believe that He can or will do it.

A prayer of agreement is when you come into agreement with someone else to pray about a certain thing. There is power in numbers. The more people praying together about one thing, the more results we may see if it's in God's will. We see many things in Scripture that are already God's will, like healing and deliverance.

A prayer of dedication is when we commit ourselves completely to the will of God. It is praying to God that He gives us the strength to carry out His will, even when it seems too hard.

3.) Intercession- Intercession is when you pray and stand in the gap on behalf of someone else. You plead for them through prayer on their behalf. It's essentially praying to God as if you were that person you are praying for. Jesus interceded for us when He was on the cross and died for us. He literally took our place. The Holy Spirit intercedes on our behalf today, according to the will of God. Intercession is very powerful, and it requires persistence. When you intercede, supplications are also often made because we are asking God to do something in the life of another.

4.) Thanksgiving- This is thanking God for all that He has done and for all that He is. It involves praise and worship. It's acknowledging God for His nature and all that He is, not just what He is able to do for us. This should be a part of all of our prayers.

You can see how all of these types of prayers can overlap together to make up one prayer. However, it's good to understand it because God is a God of order. If we understand His order, we will see results. The more we mature in Him, the more He expects from us.

You Must Pray With Others

Acts 1:13-14: *And when they had entered, they went up into the upper room where they were staying: Peter, James, John, and Andrew; Philip and Thomas; Bartholomew and Matthew; James the son of Alphaeus and Simon the Zealot; and Judas the son of James. These all continued with one accord in prayer and supplication, with the women and Mary the mother of Jesus, and with His brothers.*

Here we find the disciples along with many others, totaling about 120 people, gathered together on one accord to pray. This was before the Holy Spirit fell upon them. Corporate prayer is very important. It's more than one person bombarding heaven with prayer at one time. There truly is power in numbers.

Matthew 18:19-20: *"Again I say to you that if two of you agree on earth concerning anything that they ask, it will be done for them by My Father in heaven. For where two or three are gathered together in My name, I am there in the midst of them."*

Jesus showed us the importance of praying with others in agreement. Where two or three are gathered together in Jesus's name, He will be in the midst of them. This is why it's good to have at least one person who you can pray with and who can come in agreement with you that the will of God is done in your life.

You Should Pray More Than Once in a Day

Daniel 6:10: *Now when Daniel knew that the writing was signed, he went home. And in his upper room, with his windows open toward Jerusalem, he knelt down on his knees three times that day, and prayed and gave thanks before his God, as was his custom since early days.*

Here we find Daniel going to prayer after a law was made that no one was allowed to pray or make any petitions to any god or man for thirty days except to the king. This did not stop Daniel because he would not worship a man or a false god. Prayer gives you the courage to face the enemy no matter how big the challenge seems because prayer is tied to your faith in God. So, as usual, Daniel prayed three times a day (morning, noon, night). We don't have to follow that exact schedule. The key is that we are in constant communication with God. Some may pray longer in the morning before the day starts or longer at night when the day ends. Either way, our days should always start and end in prayer with something in the middle.

Prayer is a part of your spiritual exercise because it keeps you fit for spiritual warfare. Because Daniel prayed and went against the decree, he was thrown in the lions' den, but it was through prayer that God sent an angel to shut the lions' mouths, and no harm came upon Daniel. Notice that Daniel's prayer reached heaven while he found himself in spiritual warfare. Then, the angel fought on his behalf. Sometimes all you have to do is pray to God, and God will send an angel to fight the battle on your behalf.

Luke 5:15-16: *However, the report went around concerning Him all the more; and great multitudes came together to hear, and to be healed by Him of their infirmities. So He Himself often withdrew into the wilderness and prayed.*

Here we find Jesus as the ultimate example. Jesus was very busy teaching, healing, casting out demons, and performing miracles. However, notice that Jesus OFTEN went away from everyone into a quiet place to pray to God. Jesus is the example we are to follow. If Jesus made time to pray on earth, there is no excuse for us not to make time to pray. No one is busier than Jesus was. So, we must make time with God a priority. Notice that prayer was necessary for even Jesus to continue doing what He did on the journey.

The report went all over about what Jesus was doing in the lives of others. When you have a consistent prayer life, it will show because the Holy Spirit will have many opportunities to demonstrate His power in your life. You can't fully operate in the power of God if you don't follow His system, and His system requires prayer and devotion to Him. Prayer is your petition to God to do on earth what He has already done in heaven. Spiritual warfare is not just something you do, but it's what you're in. It's a war between God's army and Satan's army. God's army has already won! We just have to enforce that victory on earth.

1 Kings 18:41-46: *Then Elijah said to Ahab, "Go up, eat and drink; for there is the sound of abundance of rain." So Ahab went up to eat and drink. And Elijah went up to the top of Carmel; then* *he bowed down on the ground, and put his face between his knees, and said to his servant, "Go up now, look toward the sea."*

So he went up and looked, and said, "There is nothing." And seven times he said, "Go again."

Then it came to pass the seventh time, that he said, "There is a cloud, as small as a man's hand, rising out of the sea!" So he said, "Go up, say to Ahab, 'Prepare your chariot, and go down before the rain stops you.'"

Now it happened in the meantime that the sky became black with clouds and wind, and there was a heavy rain. So Ahab rode away and went to Jezreel. Then the hand of the LORD came upon Elijah; and he girded up his loins and ran ahead of Ahab to the entrance of Jezreel.

Here we find the prophet Elijah after he had had all of the false prophets of Baal killed. Elijah had been informed by God that rain would come. However, it did not come right away. It's not that Elijah did not hear from God or that he was crazy, but God gave him a head's up before the rain came. So, Elijah prayed seven times, and the rain finally came. This took persistence. You must learn to keep praying until you see the manifestation of your prayers on earth. Persistency and consistency are key!

Everyone may not see it just yet and may not see it like you see it. There are some things that you hear before you see. Elijah heard in the spirit that the rain was coming before he or his servant could physically see it. You must be persistent in prayer to the point that you will keep contacting heaven until change comes. There are some things you can't receive until you pray them down from heaven, but some things have been sent and you must snatch them from hell.

Again, prayer is your license to be a spiritual assassin against the enemy, and every time you pray, you renew your license. He will not allow the righteous to be moved. Righteousness is simply being in right standing with God. You may be shaken along the way, but you will remain in God's hand. When you put your trust all the way in God through Jesus, you won't be moved because you're planted on a solid foundation. If you're ignorant of what God has already said about you, it becomes difficult to know and receive what He has for you. You should be so persistent in prayer that you are confident that you will get results. Only those who are immature in God quit praying because they feel they aren't being heard. God always hears you, and every prayer you pray will come with a soon-enough answer. God usually sends the answer right when you pray, but remember that it must pass through the second heaven where the warfare really takes place. You must fight! Also, some answers are released in pieces so we can digest it all. When we pray and get into God's glory, there are answers to answers. There are questions that have not been asked with answers to them that God releases. We may not know what to ask, but thank God that He knows what answers we need even if we don't ask. So, the Holy Spirit reveals all of that to us based on how much we are ready to digest.

You Must Pray in Faith

Mark 11:22-24: *So Jesus answered and said to them, "Have faith in God. For assuredly, I say to you, whoever says to this mountain, 'Be removed and be cast into the sea,' and does not doubt in his heart, but believes that those things he says will be done, he will have whatever he says. Therefore I say to you, whatever things you ask when you pray, believe that you receive them, and you will have them."*

It does us no good to pray for something and not really believe we will receive it. This does not mean that everything you pray for you will receive. Some people pray out of their flesh and just want things for selfish reasons or want things that are not in God's will. The key is that if you pray and war as needed for something in God's will, you are guaranteed to receive it. However, God loves us so much that when we are obedient, He gives us more than what we asked for, and it will be better than what we asked for. We must still have faith that God will grant us our requests. We know we cannot please Him if we have no faith.

Think about it from another perspective. If you have a child who wants something and keeps asking you, but you know it's not the best thing for them, you won't give it to them, even though they are persistent. However, when you see that they finally get the point, you will give them something better than what they asked for. Perhaps they ask for something that you plan to give them, but it's not time. When you believe they are ready to receive it, you will surprise them with what they asked for plus some bonuses. God operates in a similar manner but far greater because He is our heavenly Father. It is impossible for us to want more for ourselves than God wants for us. That's a wonderful thing and why it is so important to be persistent in prayer.

Consistency in prayer and the Word of God are our most powerful weapons, but they are also the two weapons the body of Christ are most inconsistent in. Excuses are made such as, "I don't really understand the Bible," or "It's boring." Some say, "I don't really know what to say to God, or I try to pray, but it doesn't seem to work." On the other hand, there are some seasoned Christians who have gotten into a routine that is redundant and stale. One thing is for certain: we all must pray. We don't pray just for things, but it's through prayer that so much is discovered. It is through prayer that you can fully understand your purpose. When God gives us more as Christians, we shouldn't pray less, but we should pray more. This is because it will take prayer to sustain you on your level of success.

We will be able to see the importance of prayer and how our lives depend on it when we see it as a responsibility and not a choice. Prayer is required of us. We can no longer flirt with God in prayer, but we must truly saturate our life with prayer. Prayer to God is an open invitation to heaven to invade the earth on our behalf. It is the greatest power tool we will have. We must learn how to use it.

There is a fight over you. This is why you must engage the enemy in spiritual warfare. The way Satan and his demons were evicted from heaven is the same way they'll be evicted from your life as you walk in power and authority. Satan attempts to bring accusations against us, but because of Jesus's sacrifice, we who believe in Jesus are saved by His blood. Demons will attack, but you can be proactive and send the blood of Jesus to go into Satan's camp to destroy the plan they have against you. So, all Satan can do is to attempt to deceive us and get us to not carry out God's will on the earth. Satan brings accusations against us day and night. After this war, he will no longer be able to do that. This is another reminder of why prayer and warfare are important. Satan is showing up to court all the time; we need to show up as well through prayer.

The difference now is that because of Christ's sacrifice, He is our Advocate. It doesn't matter what accusations Satan brings against us because Romans 8:33-34 states: "Who shall bring a charge against God's elect? It is God who justifies. Who is he who condemns? It is Christ who died, and furthermore is also risen, who is even at the right hand of God, who also makes intercession for us."

According to Strong's Concordance, the Greek term in verse 33 is the judicial term "enkaleo," which means to bring a charge against. Satan tries to bring charges against us in the court of God, but Christ is our Defense. Satan is not like God, and he cannot be everywhere at once. He simply tried to duplicate what God did. God is in heaven, but He does the work through us and His angels. Satan is set up in hell and on earth, but he tries to influence people and has his demons to do the majority of his work. Yet, he still roams the earth.

We have a responsibility to pray. I'm not talking about praying just to say you prayed or praying for five minutes out of twenty-four hours and thinking that you prayed. Prayer is supposed to take some of your time because God requires your time no matter how busy you are or how much responsibility you have. Prayer is a part of our responsibility. Time with God should be our top priority and responsibility. Prayer is a powerful weapon in spiritual warfare. It's your first and last line of defense.

Chapter 7: The Warfare Team

There is a guarantee as a child of God that you are never alone in spiritual warfare. No matter how much pressure you may feel you're under or how heavy the task, you're never alone in any battle. You have all of heaven on your side when you enter spiritual warfare. All you need to do is make a prayer call. No matter how much the enemy throws at you, you must recognize that you have far more power on your side! What's even more amazing is that all of the power you need to win in warfare is already in you. The power of the Holy Spirit is nothing the enemy wants to run up on, so you ought to let the Holy Spirit literally have His way. So, you must give the Holy Spirit something to work with, and that's by doing. When you go about doing God's will, the Holy Spirit will go about demonstrating His power through you. This requires some action on our part. Being a child of God comes with responsibility, and God trusts you with it. There's no demon from hell that can stand up to Christ, and the good news as a Christian is that your seat is in Christ. Take your seat! It's not a matter of if the enemy will show up because we already know that they will. We just need to stay prayed up and studied up for the attacks. Satan, demons, witches, warlocks, and sorcerers are always forming weapons against us, but you ought to trust God when He said the weapons won't prosper against you. Satan shouldn't be prospering in your life because you don't belong to him. You belong to God, and God will prosper in your life. It's not God's will for you to lose because we don't lose. It's never your season of suffering because God opposes the suffering of His children. Satan sends his demons in an attempt to afflict us, but we must keep fighting with our heavenly resources.

If the enemy is spiritually attacking someone in your territory, it's your job to help them fight back in the spirit because you bring light. It is your business because it's God's business. You will find no place in Scripture where Jesus walked by someone in need. We are supposed to be like Christ, and since we are in Him and He's doing the work through us, we should be doing the same. We should be doing even greater works than Jesus because He said we should.

You have the upper hand in every spiritual battle you face! You just need to ask God to change your mind-set and open your eyes to see it. Ask Him to help you see it like He sees it. You just need to follow the directions of God. There is strategy for every single battle you will face. You're supposed to win because when you're in Christ, you have already won. Accept your victory regardless of what it looks like now. You just need to continue to fight through it and use all that God gave you. God never said the enemy wouldn't attack, but He promised that you would have everything you need to overcome it and win. God's army is the only army that can confidently celebrate a victory in battle while the battle is still going on because it's already done. The only thing you can do is forfeit a victory by being disobedient or doing it your way instead of God's way. It has never been and will never be God's will for you to live a defeated life. Jesus died so you could be free! Don't get me wrong; there are some battles that are just fierce and you may have gotten wounded for various reasons, but the good news is you have already won, and you will win on earth as long as you keep showing up in battle. The key is to keep showing up no matter what.

God has not and will not ever raise up an army of cowards. The enemy may pick a fight, but you will be sure to finish it. Don't roll over. Don't take the abuse of the enemy and hide in the corner begging for mercy. God's children don't beg the enemy to stop beating on us, but we fight back with the power God placed in us and beat on them. Don't let demons bully you, but you bully them because they don't get to play on your turf. You should not be afraid because you have the most powerful army there is on your side.

Demons don't own anything on this earth. They only have temporary residence here because they stole it. God's children need to reoccupy it! We already know that the enemy wants to steal, kill, and destroy. So, it should come as no shock. We just need to make sure we fight back. God wants His children to reclaim our position on this earth by allowing Him to reign on earth through us. So, get your opinions out of the way. Stop reading what it looks like according to your flesh and start reading God's report. It's a completely different outlook. Don't entertain the devil—overthrow his works! You are able to do that because of your warfare team.

Your warfare team consists of five key players:

1.) God
2.) Jesus
3.) Holy Spirit
4.) Heavenly host
5.) Brothers and sisters in Christ

Any one of the five key players is enough by themselves. Satan is no match for any of the first four. For the fifth key player, Satan and his demons are no match when we are in Christ. Satan, his demons, and his human agents do have power, but they don't have power over any of the five key players on the warfare team.

Warfare Team Player: God

Exodus 13:20-22: *So they took their journey from Succoth and camped in Etham at the edge of the wilderness. And the LORD went before them by day in a pillar of cloud to lead the way, and by night in a pillar of fire to give them light, so as to go by day and night. He did not take away the pillar of cloud by day or the pillar of fire by night from before the people.*

The children of Israel were being led out of slavery in Egypt. The Lord led them during the day as they followed the pillar of cloud and by night as they followed the pillar of fire. God protected them from the enemy army of the Egyptians. God's glory can stay with you as long as you keep seeking Him for it! This was God's actual presence and His divine protection for the Israelites. This is where we get the term Shekinah Glory. God's glory will take you from living naturally to living supernaturally. Although "Shekinah" is not found in Scripture, it was first found in the Targum. The Targum is the Aramaic translation or paraphrase of the Old Testament in Scripture. They used the term Shekinah to describe God. According to biblestudytools.com, it means "that which dwells." Hence, we get the Shekinah Glory, which is the Glory of God. It's God's presence. God doesn't want to simply visit you, but He wants to dwell with you.

So, God's presence guided the Israelites during the day and the night. He dwelled among the people. God's glory is His literal presence on a person, in a place, or situation. He did not leave them during this time, and He will not leave you. His entire glory can fill the whole earth, so imagine how powerful it is when His glory shows up right where you are. God's not looking to take His glory, but He is looking to give it to His people if you're willing to receive it all.

Warfare Team Player: Jesus

Matthew 28:18-20: *And Jesus came and spoke to them, saying, "All authority has been given to Me in heaven and on earth. Go therefore and make disciples of all the nations, baptizing them in the name of the Father and of the Son and of the Holy Spirit, teaching them to observe all things that I have commanded you; and lo, I am with you always, even to the end of the age." Amen.*

Here we find Jesus after His resurrection. He was speaking to the eleven disciples because Judas committed suicide after he betrayed Jesus. Here we see that Jesus said all authority has been given to Him. We're seated in Christ, so we have all authority because it's His authority! This is another reason why you win in spiritual warfare. Demons must obey the authority of Christ. This is why Christ wants to live through us on earth. We had dominion on earth and lost it because of sin, and Jesus redeemed us so we can have dominion again and to ensure we have the victory. He will do the work through us if we use His authority. It's not our authority, but it's His authority. There is authority in the name of Jesus, and it will stop any demon in its track in your life. Using the name of Jesus is a privilege, and the authority that comes with His name is activated through your faith in Him.

Notice after Jesus told the disciples that all authority was given unto Him in heaven and earth, He gave them instructions to go and make more disciples and to teach others all that Jesus taught them. It's easy to find your main purpose. Part of our main calling is to GO and make disciples of Christ and teach them what Christ taught. It's in the Word. Also notice that He did not send us alone. He said that He will be with us to the end of the age. That means forever. So, there is no excuse. Fear is never an excuse. There is no reason not to do what Christ commanded because He promised to be with you and to work through you.

When Jesus said He is with us always, He literally means He is with us and in us and we are in Him because we're seated in Christ. We came out of God and are literally the breath of God, and now we are seated in Christ because He is the only way to get to God the Father. Being in Christ gives you full access to the throne of God. Our seat of authority is in Christ, and we use His authority on earth. This is why Him having all authority on earth as well was so important. We need that authority to use on earth, and since He went back to heaven, He sent the reinforcement of the Holy Spirit, which is the power to do the work. Let's take a look at another passage.

Philippians 2:9-11: *Therefore God also has highly exalted Him and given Him the name which is above every name, that at the name of Jesus every knee should bow, of those in heaven, and of those on earth, and of those under the earth, and that every tongue should confess that Jesus Christ is Lord, to the glory of God the Father.*

This passage makes it clear that God exalted Jesus and gave Him the name all will submit to. Having Jesus on your warfare team is also enough by Himself. Even though there are those who reject Christ and rebel against Christ, like Satan, everyone will have to bow to Jesus when it's all said and done. Demons may have rebelled against God, but they know they must obey Christ's authority. This is why many of them will run when you bring Christ with you. Satan and his demons reject Christ, but they still know His authority and have to back off when Christ shows up in you. This is why it's such a focus on dying to our flesh because it's a daily process. The more we die to our flesh by denying it from doing whatever it wants to do, the more Christ reigns in us. The flesh gets in the way when it wants to do something against God's will. The flesh gets in the way when it makes you not want to pray or fast. Satan knows that his only way of truly getting at us is by preying on our flesh or the flesh of those around us or connected to us. This is why we need Christ to rule and reign in us. He will when we die to the flesh.

Warfare Team Player: Holy Spirit

John 16:13-15: *However, when He, the Spirit of truth, has come, He will guide you into all truth; for He will not speak on His own authority, but whatever He hears He will speak; and He will tell you things to come. He will glorify Me, for He will take of what is Mine and declare it to you. All things that the Father has are Mine. Therefore I said that He will take of Mine and declare it to you.*

Here we find Jesus speaking about the Holy Spirit again. He speaks what He hears, and when He speaks it to us, it becomes revelation to us. He reveals things to us to bring glory to Jesus Christ. Don't take revelation from the Holy Spirit for granted because it truly is an honor and a privilege to hear from heaven. We are only able to do greater works on earth because of the Holy Spirit in us. However, we know that all things God has are also Jesus's and also the Holy Spirit's. Hence, they are also ours as children of God.

Again, the Holy Spirit reveals Jesus to us. You can't get to Jesus without the Holy Spirit, and you can't get the Holy Spirit without Jesus. Revelation is necessary as a child of God. Scripture says that "where there is no revelation, the people cast off restraint…" (Proverbs 29:18). When it talks about revelation, it is referring to prophecy, preaching of God's Word, or divine revelation from God. When this is limited, people run wild and have no self-control. It is needed because if we don't know what God is speaking to us individually and corporately, we will literally be lost. The Holy Spirit not only gives us revelation in spiritual warfare, but He is also the power that works in us to overthrow demons and their works. **If you don't get revelation from God through the Holy Spirit, you are living in what God did, not what God is doing!** This only causes spiritual frustration. God doesn't have to do a rerun because He always produces new episodes in your life.

Scripture is just information if we don't get revelation from it. We need Scripture, but we also need revelation. This is why Satan sends demons to study us. He knows the Scriptures. Although Satan was a cherub angel who once had a lot of wisdom and knowledge of God, he is now stalking us to see what God is up to because he has no revelation. However, he still has a lot of knowledge about God and tries to twist God's Word and use it against us. We can gain more insight into the power of Holy Spirit in the book of Romans.

Romans 8:11: *But if the Spirit of Him who raised Jesus from the dead dwells in you, He who raised Christ from the dead will also give life to your mortal bodies through His Spirit who dwells in you.*

The Holy Spirit came upon Mary and ushered the seed of Jesus Christ on earth into her womb. It was not God the Father who raised Jesus from the dead, it was the Holy Spirit, and that same Holy Spirit now dwells in children of God. So, the Holy Spirit made the conception of Jesus on earth happen and also raised Jesus from the dead. Now God the Father is in heaven, God the Son is in heaven, and God the Holy Spirit dwells in us. Since we are in Christ, we can bring what is in the third heaven (where God's throne is) down here on earth (first heaven).

The Holy Spirit is not a thing, an it, a force, or a feeling. The Holy Spirit is a person, just as God and Jesus are within the Trinity. The Holy Spirit is waiting on you to GO and make disciples of Christ as Jesus commanded. As you go, He will make sure the miracles, signs, and wonders follow you. The Holy Spirit in you is a weapon of mass destruction against all the works of the enemy that cross your path. The Holy Spirit wants to do so much through you, but you must go and do so He can do great things through you.
The Holy Spirit is enough by Himself to also defeat the enemy. Again, we have no excuse with all this power and authority we have been given. This is why angels are perplexed as to why we just don't get it and do it. You have such an advantage on earth as a follower of Christ that it almost seems unfair from a flesh perspective. Thank God we're spirit! It's past time that we all wake up to the greater that truly dwells within us. There are lives that have been bound by the enemy, and they're waiting on you to bring the power of the kingdom of God into their lives!

Warfare Team Player: Heavenly Host

Revelation 12:7-10: *And war broke out in heaven: Michael and his angels fought with the dragon; and the dragon and his angels fought, but they did not prevail, nor was a place found for them in heaven any longer. So the great dragon was cast out, that serpent of old, called the Devil and Satan, who deceives the whole world; he was cast to the earth, and his angels were cast out with him.*

Then I heard a loud voice saying in heaven, "Now salvation, and strength, and the kingdom of our God, and the power of His Christ have come, for the accuser of our brethren, who accused them before our God day and night, has been cast down."

Here we see the vision that John had of a war in heaven. Although Satan had already been cast down before humans were created, he still tries to bring accusations against children of God. Michael, who is the first in rank among the heavenly host (warring angels), and the angels under his command (God being the commander-in-chief) have fought and will fight against Satan. Archangel means "chief angel." Michael is in charge of all of the heavenly host who fight for us in the second heaven, which is why we should pray because we put them to flight. The Greek word for host means an army. Michael is in charge of the army in heaven. They are the soldiers. They have a base set up in heaven just like militaries on earth have bases set up. Granted, all human armies combined are no match for the fire power of heaven's army. Satan's army is also no match for heaven's army. That's good news for us. Heaven's army remains ready to go to fight at any given moment as the need arises.

Satan also has his army of demons who sided with him. When the enemy attacks, you must pray and speak against those spirits in Jesus's name. As you pray, the heavenly host begin to fight for you. Do your part, and they will do their part. Some demons don't leave without a fight, so you must use the authority of Christ and tell them to go. Keep fighting until they go! Satan knows that his time is short on earth, so he tries to cause havoc in the lives of followers of Christ. He tries to retaliate against us. However, we already know we've won.

Notice that Satan and his demons did not prevail against Michael and the rest of the heavenly host. Michael and his team alone are enough for us to win in battle. This again shows how much we have on our side. Again, there is no excuse for us not to go and do what Christ commanded. When you are under demonic attack, you can command the heavenly host to come and fight on your behalf! We know for certain that battles on earth are reflective of battles in heaven. We also know that Satan has already been cast down and kicked out of heaven onto earth. This passage is about the war over the church. Demons try to retaliate against the body of Christ every day, but we retaliate by showing up every day. We're the church, and we always win.

Warfare Team Player: Brothers and Sisters in Christ

It's a great thing that you can come in agreement with God's Word in prayer. Everyone doesn't have to see it, but come in agreement with God's Word, and His Word alone serves as your witness (Matthew 18:19-20). This has much power. Literally, the Word becomes alive and serves as your witness. You and the Word make two. Now just imagine when you and others also pray and use the Word.

Everyone in the army of God must fulfill their responsibilities. We all need each other. This is why when one is weak, the other should be strong. This is why godly covenants are so important. You need to be surrounded by the right people in the proper seasons. Some people will be in your life forever, but others will be for a season. Don't keep people around when their season has expired. It doesn't mean something is wrong with them, but some can be a hindrance to the process. We still need them to fulfill their role in the body of Christ, but they just may not have a full-time role in your life.

One thing that is for certain is that when you come together with other warriors in Christ, you will send the enemy running because we carry too much fire power. I have learned from experience not to try to go at it alone. At the end of the Warriors Prayer Closet (my public morning prayer on social media), I always remind everyone that we are not in this alone. We pray together, go to war together, and celebrate our victories together. I used to try to go at it alone, but I know the power of bringing others together to pray and war for certain things.

I remember a deliverance session for a woman where some leaders from my church were praying behind the scenes. The enemy was really battling in the deliverance session to block her vision. My leaders kept praying for her to see what the enemy was trying to block. She was getting weary, and I was getting tired. The prayers kept her and me going. It was a powerful prophetic deliverance. We refused to leave until we saw the victory that night because it was so close. I know it was the weight of the group prayers that got her deliverance that night and gave me the strength to keep going. That is the power of corporate prayer. It literally sets the captives free.

Part II. On the Offensive: Assassins' Weaponry of Retaliation

Chapter 8: Putting Angels to Work in Warfare

God has assigned angels to protect you in warfare, and it's another reminder that you're never alone. You must be reminded that everyone in God's army plays a significant role. There are angels who help us carry out our roles on earth. They help you execute some of your assignments. There are some things the enemy has thrown at you that you knew nothing about because God sent an angel to block them. There is spiritual activity going on consistently. While our flesh is resting, our spirit never sleeps, and angels and demons don't sleep. You are a warrior for Christ, and angels have been assigned to you to help keep your spiritual weapons sharpened. Even while you sleep, the enemy tries to attack, but you have angels working on your behalf. You should never take prayer lightly because prayer keeps your angels fully employed in your life.

The Holy Spirit teaches you, and angels help you enforce what you've been taught. They push you to keep going. Angels tend to have a difficult time understanding why, as humans, we struggle with prayer and study of God's Word. They have a hard time understanding why we just don't stand on faith and walk in obedience at times. They faithfully serve God and expect that we will, too. The same way we learn from them, they also learn by watching us to know how to better deal with us in the earth. God is not looking for you to recreate the wheel; He's just looking for you to execute the plan He has already set in place.

We know that we absolutely are NOT to worship angels, but we worship God. Angels are on divine assignment from God to assist us. They are working for God on our behalf. When we pray, God often uses angels to deliver the answer to our prayers. Don't let what you see or hear in the physical take you off your prayer game.

Prayer will break down the walls the enemy built to block you. Oftentimes, the heavenly host tear down those walls. As an ambassador of heaven, angels are a part of your team to help you establish God's kingdom on earth. You should utilize them more often. Angels are here on assignment to help us. God revealed to me that there are more angels being sent to earth in this season than God has ever sent on earth in our lifetime to help us carry out His will. They are ready to go to work, but some of their work is based on us doing our part. The full effectiveness of some angels sent to earth is based on our prayers and our obedience to the will of God. So, we must do our part.

You will have encounters with angels knowingly and unknowingly as you continue to seek God and carry out His will in the earth. There are angels who are trained and briefed specifically for various significant seasons in the body of Christ, and it's an honor that God would send them to partner with us. Angels are here for you, and it's time to start getting more acquainted with their work so you can make their jobs a bit easier.

As angels go back and forth from heaven to earth, as you make your requests to God, they're able to go and get what you need. Scripture says that God shall supply all of our need according to His riches in glory, and He often uses angels to bring from heaven what you need. Angels are invested in your success because God is invested in your success. You represent heaven. Just like our emotions don't move heaven, they don't move angels either. They respond to your faith and God's Word. Angels are waiting for us to give them instructions in line with the will of God. For every assignment God gives you, He assigns angels to help you. You just have to give them instructions. Angels are ready for you to put them to work! They are going to help usher in the greatest revival of our time, and that's why we must continue to do our part. Whatever God is telling you to do, do it and do it swiftly because there is a sense of urgency. You don't want someone else doing your assignment because what's attached to that assignment was for you.

God is a loving God. He loves all His children, but His will is very important. What one person does not do, He will raise up another to do. This is your time of divine favor! You will experience unprecedented levels of favor as you obey God. Angels will help thrust you forward.

We often hear references made about angels. Some use the term to describe individuals who were a blessing in their lives. So, they may say that you were an angel. Sometimes we hear individuals talking about guardian angels watching over us. However, in order to begin to talk about angels, we must understand their characteristics. According to Strong's Concordance, the word angel is derived from the Hebrew word "mal'ak," pronounced mal-awk. It means *messenger or ambassador; to dispatch as a deputy*. This Hebrew word for angel is used 213 times in the Old Testament. It is also derived from the Greek word "aggelos," pronounced awng-el-os. This means *to bring tidings; A messenger; Someone sent by God to proclaim His message, which can be human or heavenly being*. This Greek word for angel is used 176 times in the New Testament, usually in reference to heavenly angels, but depending on the context, sometimes it refers to a human messenger (i.e., a spiritual leader). To sum it up, when the word angel is used in Scripture, it is often defined as a messenger. However, a messenger angel, also known as a courier angel, is not the only type of angel. These angels do have higher levels of involvement with matters concerning humans along with the heavenly host.

Angels minister to us. We begin to see one main function of the angels who are involved in human affairs on earth in **Hebrews 1:13-14:**

But to which of the angels has He ever said: "Sit at My right hand, Till I make Your enemies Your footstool"? Are they not all ministering spirits sent forth to minister for those who will inherit salvation?

Angels are heavenly spirit beings. This passage shows that angels are spirits who are sent forth to minister to those who inherit salvation (humans). This is for those who accept Christ. They bring messages, and they also bring assistance to us here on earth. This again shows that we have so much more working in our favor. God assigned angels to work in your life because it takes a team to take over on earth for the kingdom of God. Only Jesus is seated at the right hand of God, but we are seated in Christ. So, we have access to the things of God, including angels. God sent angels to help us, but we should help ourselves by praying to God because it keeps us on track.

Angels are sent to help us, but they already know God's Word. They don't do what we command based on our opinions. They respond to His Word. They are sent to fulfill God's will in our lives. Angels are defenders of God's will, and when we do God's will, they are naturally defenders of us. The job of the heavenly host is to war against Satan and his demons. God's angels have never backed down from a fight, and we shouldn't either in spiritual warfare because we are to rule on earth!

Angels also actually have intellect. We can see this in **1 Peter 1:10-12 (emphasis mine):**

*Of this salvation the prophets have inquired and searched carefully, who prophesied of the grace that would come to you, searching what, or what manner of time, the Spirit of Christ who was in them was indicating when He testified beforehand the sufferings of Christ and the glories that would follow. To them it was revealed that, not to themselves, but to us they were ministering the things which now have been reported to you through those who have preached the gospel to you by the Holy Spirit sent from heaven, **things which angels desire to look into.**

This passage shows that even the angels do not know everything. Only God is all-knowing. Prophets who prophesied of the coming of Christ still only knew in part the fullness of what salvation would entail. It was not fully revealed to them, but we now know what did happen as Jesus died for our sins. God revealed to the prophets of old things that were to come. However, He revealed it to them knowing they would not witness Christ's coming on earth to save us. So, as the story of human salvation had begun to unfold, even the angels stooped down to look into the matter. The idea of human salvation intrigues them, and they desire to know more about it. The angels desire to know more about the mysteries of the gospel. They too cannot fully understand the mysteries until they are revealed to them.

Angels have free will to make a choice just as humans do, but they are fully submitted to the will of God, and we should be, too! Angels are still curious about salvation because they were created sinless. So, what it is like to go from sin to righteousness is very intriguing to them. They don't live on earth as we do, although our guardian angels do for the most part. They want to know more about that mystery that we get to live out and experience ourselves. God made you different not to punish you but because of the love He has for you. Your unique difference is why the world needs you. So, angels are able to quickly respond to your commands as you walk in divine authority.

Angels also have a will. We see this in **Jude 6-7:**

And the angels who did not keep their proper domain, but left their own abode, He has reserved in everlasting chains under darkness for the judgment of the great day; as Sodom and Gomorrah, and the cities around them in a similar manner to these, having given themselves over to sexual immorality and gone after strange flesh, are set forth as an example, suffering the vengeance of eternal fire.

This shows that angels have a will. They can choose. There were angels in heaven who did not keep their rank because they went against God's will. These are those who were evicted with Satan. These angels who were the highest of intelligent creatures left their habitation in the spirit realm and sinned by entering the human realm to marry humans. In other words, they left their office and attempted to go in and invade the offices of others. This is similar to how a demonic spirit can believe they are married to a person and work to prevent them from getting married or make them marry the wrong person. We will get into that in more detail later in the book. These angels were once pure and holy and honorable. These angels who rebelled against God and wanted higher honors are now called principalities. They were some of the fallen angels who rebelled with Satan. Some of these fallen angels are already in chains and imprisoned until they receive their final punishment.

Angels also have emotions. They can be happy or saddened by certain things we do or do not do. They also rejoice for us as we carry out the will of God. We have so much that we can use against the enemy. There are angels who only function in heaven, and there are angels who have been given responsibility on earth.

God has assigned angels to work with you, and the more you get used to utilizing them, the more productive you will be. Your prayers give the angels assigned to work with you the legal right to engage the enemy on your behalf. This is why prayer and angelic activity go hand in hand. Where there is little prayer, there is little angelic activity. When there is much prayer, there is much angelic activity. Angels were created by God for God, and He loved us so much that He made some angels to work with us. When you put angels to work on your behalf, they make your assignment easier. When you understand the order of God's kingdom, it helps you see how important your role is. Every created being in God's kingdom has a role to play, and God has sent angels to help you fulfill your role. Jesus showed us that not only could He deploy the heavenly host to fight on His behalf if He wanted to, but we can do the same and we need to.

Matthew 26:50-54: *But Jesus said to him, "Friend, why have you come?" Then they came and laid hands on Jesus and took Him. And suddenly, one of those who were with Jesus stretched out his hand and drew his sword, struck the servant of the high priest, and cut off his ear. But Jesus said to him, "Put your sword in its place, for all who take the sword will perish by the sword. Or do you think that I cannot now pray to My Father, and He will provide Me* *with more than twelve legions of angels? How then could the Scriptures be fulfilled, that it must happen thus?"*

Jesus had been betrayed and was in the process of being arrested. One of his disciples, who we know was Peter, pulled out a sword and cut off the ear of one of the servants who came to arrest Jesus. Jesus rebuked him because it was not time to fight. It was not time to pull out a sword. When you use the right strategy at the right time in spiritual warfare, you get results in the spirit that manifest in the natural. In this case, if you pull out a sword to fight when it's not a time to fight, you may die by that same sword. Peter was getting in the way of all of our lives being saved. Jesus corrected Peter and reminded him that He could have prayed to God and He could send twelve legions of angels to fight. A legion usually consisted of 6,000 soldiers, so twelve legions would be 72,000 angels coming to fight.

Again, the angels who fight for us are known as the heavenly host. They weren't created to defend heaven, but they defend us. Jesus's role in the battle was to be the sacrifice for us so that we could be back in right relationship with God. However, our role is to be a living sacrifice unto God and submit fully to His will. This again shows the power of prayer. If Jesus, who was our example, could have prayed to God and God would have provided Him with more than 72,000 angels coming to fight one battle, you have that same right. You have that same power and authority because our life is hidden in Christ. You have the ability through prayer to cause thousands of angels to fight on your behalf, which is way more than enough because you're that important in heaven.

Psalm 91:9-12: *Because you have made the LORD, who is my refuge,*
Even the Most High, your dwelling place,
No evil shall befall you,
Nor shall any plague come near your dwelling;
For He shall give His angels charge over you,
To keep you in all your ways.
In their hands they shall bear you up,

Lest you dash your foot against a stone.

There are angels who defend us and look after us. Notice that there is a prerequisite in order for God to command His angels to protect us. We must make God our refuge. In other words, we must trust in Him. You must trust God in all things. Don't just say it, but show it. If you don't put your full trust in God in all things, you limit and delay the work of angels assigned to you. Give God your complete trust, and angels will move on your behalf. You're not in it alone. Angels will defend you with every act of faith and obedience to God.

Demons can't get to you when you're in Christ; they just try to cause issues to try to get you to step out of Christ! The battle is truly not ours. Satan thinks he can mess with God by robbing you, but all it does is add more blessings onto your life. Just watch and see. Evil will not be able to triumph over you. Even if it appears to be so, we know that God always has the final say. No matter how rough it seems, keep the faith. You've been in a serious battle for what seems like a long time, but angels are coming to relieve you. Demons tried to throw a party on your behalf, but they were set up to get a front-row seat on your comeback tour.

Angels either minister to you before battle or after battle. No matter what, we still win because the enemy is already a defeated foe. These angels are even at work when we are asleep. The enemy also attempts to attack us even while we are asleep, especially late at night (third watch), which is when witches and demons set their traps and are the busiest. You may not always be able to see everything in the spirit, but thank God that He told your angels to guard you, and they can see clearly. You can't afford to not pray because your prayers put angels to work on your behalf. They go where you can't go. These angels also nurture us during times of weakness. Once again, we must notice that these are God's angels and they work for God, so we are NEVER to worship an angel. They are on assignment from God; therefore, we worship God for using angels to minister unto us.

No matter how far it feels like you've sunk, God is able to pull you out. God will shame the enemy. You may have fallen into a pit, but not only will you get up, but you will take over the territory the pit is in. There's no time to dwell in misery because God has assignments for you. You have personal angels who serve as your bodyguard when you are carrying out God's will. So, you are covered.

Exodus 23:20-23: *"Behold, I send an Angel before you to keep you in the way and to bring you into the place which I have prepared. Beware of Him and obey His voice; do not provoke Him, for He will not pardon your transgressions; for My name is in Him. But if you indeed obey His voice and do all that I speak, then I will be an enemy to your enemies and an adversary to your adversaries. For My Angel will go before you and bring you in to the Amorites and the Hittites and the Perizzites and the Canaanites and the Hivites and the Jebusites; and I will cut them off."*

Here we see God instructing Moses. He said that He would send an angel before him to keep him and to bring him to the place God prepared. God sends angels to escort you into the place He has prepared for you on earth and in heaven. In this passage, it's believed that God was referencing Christ, who appeared because He can pardon sins. They could not identify Him as being Christ at this time because it was not yet time for Him to come to earth in the flesh. Either way, it is evident that God will still send angels to help us reach a destination.

Some things are sometimes out of our immediate reach in spiritual warfare, but that's why God sends angels to grab them for you. Jesus is not an angel, but if this was in fact Him, He was disguised as being an angel because it was not yet His time. God's timing is important not because He needs time but because you live in time, and you're important to Him!
God told Moses that He would be an enemy to his enemies. God sends angels with specific instructions, and we must be obedient to

those instructions. When we obey God's instructions, He will be an enemy to our enemies. When you're doing the will of the Lord, your enemies are God's enemies. They aren't coming against you, but they're coming against God! You must understand that you're not some little weakling. You're powerful in God. This is why you cannot allow the opinions of others or your current situation to determine who you are.

Matthew 18:10 (emphasis mine): *"Take heed that you do not despise one of these little ones, for I say to you that in heaven **their angels always see the face of My Father who is in heaven.**"*

Here we find Jesus talking about saints of God who may be looked down upon as the least. We should not look down on anyone, especially those who are followers of Christ. This is so because children of God have angels assigned to us in heaven who always see God's face. Jesus was not just talking about little children, but all children of God who humble themselves before Him as innocent little children. So, don't look down on anyone. As a child of God, your status is always the status of royalty, no matter where you are in life at the moment. Situations change, but you're always God's child. You are high profile because your angels who are guardian angels have direct access to the throne of God and can see God at any time on your behalf! They can report to Him when someone attempts to harm us. We must be careful because an angel can also report to God what wrong we may have done to someone else. Thank God for the blood of Jesus. Our angels can always schedule an appointment with God. Again, this is why prayer is vital. Your prayers also put your guardian angel to work. God clears His schedule when you set an appointment through prayer. Guardian angels are the messenger angels who are the closest to humans. They protect and deliver messages. There are also demons who attempt to oppress and attack humans. However, we know that Scripture says no weapon formed against us shall prosper (Isaiah 54:17). Our guardian angel is assigned to us not just when we're born, but at the time we were conceived. Everything God creates, Satan tries to duplicate. So, at the moment of conception,

Satan assigns a demonic familiar spirit to us to watch us and may even attempt to attack in the womb.

Guardian angels escort us to heaven when we go back to be with the Lord. This is another reminder that life begins at conception because that's when our spirit was blown into a body in our mother's womb. Aborted babies still have a guardian angel who just takes them back to heaven. Those babies are taken care of in heaven and won't grow completely up because the parent who aborted, if they repent and live for God and make it to heaven, will still get to take care of them in heaven. Departed loved ones help take care of the baby until the parents come to heaven. This mystery of heaven has also been reported by others who have been caught up to heaven and reported what they have seen.

So, your angels have an all-access pass to the literal throne of God. No matter how low you may feel or if someone sees you as less than, you have angels who represent you and protect you and can literally see God at any time. How can another child of God be better than you when you both came out of the same God? As humans, we cannot physically see God and live. Humans cannot see God face to face, but our spirits can. This is bigger than if you were the best friend of the president. In other words, you are important because your angels who represent you get to see the King of Kings all the time with you in mind. Angels also report to God about you. They give God spiritual updates on you, the good and bad, like a spiritual report card.

With that being said, it will help to understand what functions certain angels have. There are approximately nine types of angels, but I will address the ones that deal more directly with things on earth and the atmosphere.

Ephesians 1:20-21: *Which He worked in Christ when He raised Him from the dead and seated Him at His right hand in the heavenly places, far above all principality and power and might and dominion, and every name that is named, not only in this age but also in that which is to come.*

This passage talks about four types of angels (and demons), which I have learned much about through the years.

Dominions- They govern the activity of angels lower in rank than they are. They serve as the intermediary between higher-ranking and lower-ranking angels. So, they are like a bridge of communication between angels. There are also demonic dominions attempting to duplicate heavenly dominions.

Virtues/Might- They are in charge of the celestial bodies like planets. In other words, they overlook the cosmos/universe to make sure it stays in order. The demonic ones love to try to manipulate the celestial bodies. They try to use the sun, moon, and stars to send curses to people. They can also operate in the atmosphere to cause storms.

Powers- Keepers of our collective history. They are also guardians of peace and order to enforce order in the world. They are the bearers of the conscience and behavior of all of humanity. There are also demonic powers that try to hold us in the past by bringing up our past history to try to use it against us. There are some angels who just record our lives. Some of them look like big eyeballs with wings. Satan also has demons with recorders in them to report on us and to take photos. Those demons are demonic eavesdroppers, scanners, watchers, etc. They keep records on us, too.

Principalities- Rule over kingdoms, cities, states, countries, continents, etc., and any large groups within the earth realm. They govern within the earth realm and may also influence decision-making within government and any collective groups of people. As discussed, these principalities operate in the second heaven. There are good and bad principalities. We are familiar with evil principalities being assigned over regions, but God also has angels that He assigns to regions. That angel will help us in our assigned territory so that we will be able to effectively rule in it.
Although it was not mentioned in this passage of Scripture, we should also address a fifth type of angel known as Thrones. You can find this angel referenced in Colossians 1:16.

Thrones- Symbols of God's justice and authority. They carry out the divine justice of God. They can work with the heavenly host to execute judgments made in the courts of heaven. There are also demonic thrones that are symbols of Satan's injustice and want to invoke injustice in the world.

We must understand that God's justice will be carried out in the world regardless of the injustice that appears to be going on in our communities and cities. Angels are here to work with you, so get in the habit of utilizing their services. They make a huge difference in our lives when we partner with them to carry out the will of God in the earth.

Chapter 9: Engaging the Enemy and Exposing Witchcraft

Once you have an understanding that you have God, the authority of Jesus Christ, the power of the Holy Spirit, and angels all on your side as a child of God, you are ready to effectively engage the enemy in spiritual warfare. There is a dark world around us, but that's why God sent you to be a light. Satan has many agents that work for him, and there are spiritual agents and human agents who serve him. The good news is that we who are on God's team are far more powerful. As a child of God, you have access to all power, but God wants us in a place where all power can flow through us. You have been fitted and clothed to walk in the power of the Holy Spirit, but your vessel must be submitted in a way that you can continually walk in that power.

The Holy Spirit is the power, but there are derivatives of His power. For example, orange juice is a derivative of the orange. Apple juice is a derivative of an apple. So, the anointing we walk in is a derivative of the Holy Spirit. We are able to walk in greater levels of the power as we gain access to it. Gaining access begins with faith and completely surrendering our will to God.
Spiritual warfare is a topic some try to avoid, but you're already in the war, so you need to know how to fight what's fighting you. God has not given us the spirit of fear. Fear is from the enemy. There's nothing to be afraid of concerning the enemy, but there are things God wants you to be aware of so you are prepared for the enemy. Witchcraft is the practices by witches and wizards in which they use black magic, which is the evoking of evil spirits for an evil purpose or to gain some hidden knowledge. This is why there are spying spirits whose job is to spy on us. The good news is that you have the ability to strike them with blindness or scatter them in the spirit. It's something you can add onto your prayer life. You can say that you strike every monitoring spirit with blindness or you send the blood of Jesus to blind every demonic third eye that's monitoring you. These spirits monitor you so they can report back to their boss on how to attack you or even what's going on. Satan is not like God, and he cannot be everywhere at once. So, he needs agents to spy and try to steal intel from us. Remember, Satan

cannot get revelation; only humans can get it from the Holy Spirit. So, demons and human agents of Satan can often get a lot of information from us. They can also see what's surrounding us or what's on us in the spirit. They know what you like, dislike, etc. That's how they know how to tempt us.

No matter what the enemy does, you have all of heaven's defense on your side. However, it's important to know how to use your weapons. God wants us to be aware of the tactics of the enemy. Witchcraft is a major route in which Satan uses human agents to attack God's people. No matter the attack of the enemy, as a child of God, you have the ability to send a far more powerful counterattack. The key is in knowing how to counterattack. Yes, the Lord does fight our battles because we can't fight spiritual wars in the natural. However, God fights those battles through us. He gave us the power and authority to handle business on earth. God doesn't expect you to do it alone. Demons love to cause confusion, and that's in an attempt to go unnoticed. Demons have a way of hiding, but ask God to expose what they're doing in your life. God is not getting off His throne. We are to rule. Those operating in witchcraft are always trying to send curses, but you can block the curse. The enemy wants to rob you of the abundant life Christ promised on earth, but you must exercise your legal right to all Christ came to give. Satan may send agents to work against you, but God sent angels to work for you!

Deuteronomy 18:9-14 (emphasis mine): *"When you come into the land which the LORD your God is giving you, you shall not learn to follow the abominations of those nations. **There shall not be found among you anyone who makes his son or his daughter pass through the fire, or one who practices witchcraft, or a soothsayer, or one who interprets omens, or a sorcerer, or one who conjures spells, or a medium, or a spiritist, or one who calls up the dead.** For all who do these things are an abomination to the LORD, and because of these abominations the LORD your God drives them out from before you. You shall be blameless before the LORD your God. For these nations which you will dispossess*

112

listened to soothsayers and diviners; but as for you, the LORD your God has not appointed such for you."

We see here some who practice the occult, such as a witch, soothsayer, sorcerer, medium, etc. This passage lets us know that all who operate in these are an abomination (disgrace) to the Lord. There were warnings throughout Scripture about it. If someone denies Christ, your light needs to shine so they can see the power of Christ at work in your life. There are some who are blinded by the enemy, but you have the ability to fight in the spirit so their eyes will be opened. There is nothing to be afraid of because you have power over the enemy, and you need to exercise that power. The enemy is trying to curse you, but God's blessing can destroy a curse.

There were some during that time in Israel's history who allowed their children to pass through fire as an act of worship to a false god. There are people in your city and region who still participate in these practices. Witches' covens are all over. There could be one in your neighborhood. A coven is a gathering of witches and warlocks who come together regularly. They gather to cast spells, send curses, strategize, summon demons, etc. If there is demonic activity where God has placed you, you have the power and authority to do something about it in the spirit. Don't sit back and allow darkness to surround where God has placed you. War in the spirit until you see the results you're satisfied with.

Here are some definitions to help you understand these occult practices:

Witchcraft- The practices by witches and wizards (warlocks) in which they use black magic, which is the evoking of evil spirits for an evil purpose or to gain some hidden knowledge. The main difference between a witch and a sorcerer is that witches use demonic powers they were given, but sorcerers use other things like magic, potions, etc. Witches don't need potions, charms, etc. Witches are demon possessed, and demons fight for position

113

within them. Witches have demonic powers and can do many things.

Sorcerer- Consults evil spirits to gain hidden knowledge and uses magic, potions, charms, etc. Any individual who purchases certain charms, potions, etc., and uses them on a person is able to operate in sorcery. They aren't nearly as powerful as witches but still very dangerous.

Soothsayer (Divination)- A fortune teller who claims they can tell the future, reveal secrets, or interpret dreams through magic or reading signs. This is not of God. This is different from prophets to whom God reveals secrets and future events, etc. Soothsayers/psychics get their information from demons, but prophets get revelation through the Holy Spirit.

Medium (Necromancy)- Communicates between the spirit world and humans. They often communicate with the dead, which is a demonic spirit posing as the actual deceased person. They communicate with the dead for information. I have seen previews for reality TV shows that literally follow the life of a medium as though it's perfectly ok.

Spiritist (Wizard/Warlock)- A male witch who uses black magic.

Conscious witchcraft- An individual willingly and knowingly knows what they're doing. They know they're working for Satan.

Unconscious witchcraft (blind witch)- An individual was initiated unknowingly into witchcraft.

Witches are female, and wizards/warlocks are male. Witches typically have higher ranks and are considered more powerful, but there are also high-ranking wizards. Witches/wizards become witches either generationally by inheriting it through another witch in the family (often a parent or grandparent who dedicated them to it from birth), through initiation into it, or through association with another witch/wizard through what's known as witchcraft contamination.

There's also what's known as a blind witch, as I mentioned earlier. This is someone who was initiated in some way unknowingly, and witches use this individual at night to do some of their work and to torment them. They often do this by entering the dreams of the individual. The individual can sometimes find themselves traveling to unknown places in their dreams and waking up extremely exhausted no matter how much sleep they get or with constant pain. The witches use the blind witch's body as a vehicle. They go to their witches' meeting and can ride on the body of the person who has been enslaved, chase them in their dreams, etc. In these dreams, if the person is eating food, cooking food, serving food, drinking blood, being fed, etc., witches can also use that to contaminate an individual. This allows witches to make the individual like a slave to do their bidding. They gained this access to the blind witch through some type of initiation from the individual's bloodline. They can whistle while the individuals are sleeping, and all the unconscious witches come to join them. The blind witch will sometimes wake up with pain in the back, spine, etc., because the witches rode on them as a vehicle. In unconscious witchcraft, a conscious wizard, witch, or sorcerer can also use the blind witch's image to attack people. A blind witch may know nothing about it, but the person who it was done to will recognize your face. If you dreamed about a person you don't know, sometimes it's a blind witch being used to torment you in your dreams. Dreams are very important to watch.

Witches can also work through dreams in another way. If a person dreams that someone is trying to put witchcraft on them and does nothing about it, within six months that person could become a blind witch/wizard. I have countless stories from these type of initiations from many deliverance sessions. Some witches/wizards have such a high rank in the demonic that they can look at a person and cause harm. A wizard or witch cannot destroy a committed Christian. They must find a way to cause the Christian to sin. If a Christian sins and doesn't repent, a witch/wizard will get that person to sin again. The hedge around the Christian will eventually begin to crack, and the witch or wizard will have access to kill the person.

You should be upset at what the enemy thinks they will get away with, but they aren't getting away with it on your watch. I give them two options: repent or die. If they come after us in the spirit, we will fight back. This is all handled in the spirit. We don't fight in the flesh. We are to handle it in the spirit, and it will impact the human agents of Satan in the natural. It's in their best interest to repent and get saved because God doesn't want any to perish, and He wants all to repent (2 Peter 3:9). There are witches and warlocks who have repented and given up their witchcraft. There are some who are now on fire for God. Unfortunately, there are also some who are willing to die for their witchcraft. If they keep attacking us, there will be serious consequences. We have no problem utilizing our spiritual weapons, and I always send a warning in the spirit for them to repent or die. However, if they are on assignment to try to kill us, we will kill them in the realm of the spirit before they kill us. This goes with the rules of engagement on the battlefield. The Word says to not allow a witch/sorceress to live (Exodus 22:18). As a spiritual assassin, we give them the choice to repent or die. It would be great if they truly repented. Warfare is a real fight, and there will be casualties, but we won't be any of them.

Three Realms of Witches

1.) It's all about sexual perversion. They walk naked and have sex in the streets in the realm of the spirit. They use spiritual eyes that are given to them to allow them to see things that are invisible. This is how they can give an accurate word. It's one way they try to deceive the church, by giving accurate words so that they can then slip in false words and curses.

2.) There are a lot of restaurants that they travel to in the spirit realm where they eat, and what they eat changes them. They lose all sympathy toward human life. They then see humans as potential blood sacrifices. There was a former warlock whose wife had initiated him, and before he got involved because of fear, he saw her take out the eyes of a baby girl and cut off the limbs as a sacrifice.

3.) They bring one of three items usually, which is a piece of hair, clothes, or the nail of someone on earth. They call them "utensils." In this realm, humans are bound. Their soul is bound by the witches and warlocks, but they are still alive on earth. They bring those "utensils" of the human they want to control on earth to this realm. They do incantations, then the soul of the person will appear. They call it an **astral double.** It's the soul of the individual that looks exactly like the person on earth. Whatever the witch/warlock does to the astral double, that will happen to the human on earth if there is access to them. They can imprison this person, have sex with them, and even marry them in the spirit realm. There can be demonic spiritual marriages through incubus and succubus demons, also known as spirit husbands and wives, through witches/warlocks who use the astral double. The spirit husband (incubus) and spirit wife (succubus) will have sex with humans in their dreams. They also aim to prevent marriage, cause marital problems, often cause pregnancy and fertility issues, and a number of other things. I will go more in detail about those spirits in a later chapter. Witches/warlocks/sorcerers will even hide their identity by using an astral double on earth. They will dress it in clothes and deceive people.

If a Christian sinned and just repented, witches and warlocks would come after them trying to make them backslide. They will be trying for six months. This shows you their persistence. If it doesn't work, they will then try to go into the person's business/career to impact finances. They try to get your boss/manager/supervisor to oppress you and get you upset and even try to get you fired. If none of that works, they stop trying until a new plan is developed. However, if the Christian backslides, they know it's an opportunity they have not gotten in a while to gain access, so they try to kill the person to make sure they don't have a chance to repent. They cannot gain access when the Christian's light is shining bright and the wall of fire is around them. They also notice that we're not walking alone. They can see angels walking with us. They know they can't get to us then. So, the only way is through sin or the Christian being connected to someone who they can use to get through that wall.

They have a couple of other methods. They can also turn into different animals, and that demonic ability is known as **"shape shifting."** They can turn into birds, alligators, goats, ants, spiders, snakes, etc. Turning to cats allows witches and wizards to get to humans. When they turn to a rat, it allows them to get into the house and turn to a shadow at night and then back into a human to suck the blood of someone. Remember that they're possessed, and demons feed off of blood. It gives them more strength. We have discussed how a spirit husband or wife can have sex with humans in their dreams to hinder progress, but witches and warlocks also attend courses in the satanic world to learn how to turn into a spirit husband or wife as well.

You must use your weapons. Send the fire of God. Send the blood of Jesus to destroy the curses and works of the enemy. You must use your authority. The blood of Jesus frightens demons, but it doesn't bind demons. We must use our authority and tell the demons what to do.

Organization of Sorcerers

The sorcery world is very organized and has its own government. Women hold the highest positions in the sorcery system. Satan keeps a document of records about everything people do on earth. It's called the Book of the Dead. It contains every evil deed done by people on earth. They're kept so that demons can legally control and impact lives of people all around the world. He also will use this book to bring accusations against the people before God.

118

First position- Presidents and Queens- They give instructions in witchcraft. They sit on chairs made out of human bones.

Second position- Supreme Sorcerers (Neighborhood Chief of Sorcerers)- In any neighborhood, there is a neighborhood chief of sorcerers. They are in charge of all the sorcerers in a neighborhood, and he is the one who goes to the main department to pass on the report of the neighborhood. The chief does not work alone. He works with the avenue chief and the street chief. Every neighborhood has an avenue or street chief assigned to it. They establish demonic laws to govern the area, for example, poverty, few marriages, crime.

White magic deals with problems of physical and mental disease, accidents, natural disasters, etc. These curses are often done in the daytime and often involve a public ceremony. Some people may think they are using white magic for good such as trying to get rid of evil, sending a curse to get someone to like them, getting a specific job or position, more money, etc. There are some marriages that were formed out of witchcraft. But Satan does not have a good side. There is no such thing as good witchcraft, and there is no such thing as a good witch. They are simply being deceived by demons. Seeking help from a witch for any type of help is the same thing as praying to a false god. It's all demonic.

Black magic is black because those who practice it work in the dark. Its goal is to bring evil and harm.

Both white and black magic are bad. Former witches will tell you that they felt they had so much power and thought they actually controlled some of the demons, but in all actuality, they were the ones being controlled by Satan.

Any time a wizard wants to visit Satan, he has to perform two sacrifices. The Sacrifice of Condemnation and the Sacrifice of the Red Carpet. The wizard must provide two family member names to the secretary of Satan. The secretary calls the family member's name three times, and they appear on the table or in a mirror. With his hands, the head sorcerer kills that family member. Once the skin is dried, it is divided into two. With the first part of the skin, the black book is made, called the Book of Condemnation. Whatever is written about that family begins to happen because of what the wizard in their family did.

With second part of skin, the red book is created called the Book of Execution. All members of the family were written. The wizard has to name someone. Once their name is scratched out, the person dies. A demon is also often sent to the cemetery to extract blood. When it is collected in a vase or some vial, it is slipped into the castle of Lucifer. When Satan sees it, he drinks it and that pleases him. After that, the wizard can enter. Satan already has a death date planned for those whose blood he drinks, and when the allotted time expires, that's when physical death occurs. If anyone in the occult has a meeting with Satan and is even one minute late, Satan will destroy them. So often, witches, wizards, and sorcerers arrive an hour early.

Some sorcerers have what's called mystic eyes used to see everything. They can see if a woman is pregnant before she knows it. They can see true Christians, lukewarm Christians, and unbelievers. They can see a pastor who is preaching but not living up to what they're preaching, and they will appear naked. For every person they kill, they get two mystic eyes.

We must pray for discernment because there are individuals who practice these today. Some are open about it, but the discernment is needed for those who try to hide behind the name of God to carry out these demonic functions. Not every person who says "God" is referring to Jesus, so make sure they serve Christ and not some other god. We aren't to hate people, but we have every right to hate Satan and his demons with righteous indignation!

Use your weapons against witchcraft. One weapon is the Word of God. Jeremiah 23:29 says, "'Is not My word like a fire?' says the LORD,/'And like a hammer that breaks the rock in pieces?'" God was speaking to Jeremiah about the judgment He was going to bring against Israel. There were false prophets who were lying about God. They were saying what God never said. They also made a lot of people think Jeremiah was crazy for telling the actual truth. There will be some who will oppose you, but when you're on assignment from God, they're opposing God. If they were smart, they'd move aside. Jeremiah was speaking an unpopular message. What God gave you to do may not seem popular today, but you can bank on it that it will be powerful.

The people wanted to continue to go forth and sin and only call on God when they were in trouble. Jeremiah was warning the people. God gave them multiple chances, but they still disobeyed. Don't prostitute God's love for you! Give Him the honor and obedience He deserves. These false prophets were claiming they had a word from God, but their words had no true power. God's Word comes with fire and power that breaks demonic foundations like a hammer. While we're talking about breaking foundations, we also need to discuss demonic umbilical cords that too many are still attached to.

Breaking Demonic Umbilical Cords

Your physical umbilical cord may have been cut, but if there was a generational curse that was passed down or even a word curse spoken while you were in the womb, that demonic umbilical cord might still be there. That's one way demons can keep a curse going or draw human blood because of that cord that must be broken. A physical umbilical cord is the lifeline of the fetus because it's made up of blood vessels and it carries oxygen and the necessary nutrients to the baby. Demonic umbilical cords allow demons to feed off humans like leeches if undetected. If it is still attached in any way, demons use this to feed you fear, rejection, and anything else to take you out. It's often rooted in something from childhood, in connection with your parents, or any generational curse. You must open your mouth and sever any demonic umbilical cord. Send the fire of God to destroy it. You can also open your mouth and say, "I cut any demonic umbilical cords in my life with the sword of the Lord." Witches and warlocks will try to use these demonic umbilical cords to gain access to you and to keep the demons they use fed.

Demonic/Evil Altars

Witches and warlocks set up evil altars when they meet in their covens. They make sacrifices unto demons, send out curses, etc., at these altars. They erect altars to try to stop your destiny, block finances, block marriages, cause sickness, etc. Send the fire of God to destroy these evil altars or drown them in the blood of Jesus.

Numbers 23:1-2: *Then Balaam said to Balak, "Build seven altars for me here, and prepare for me here seven bulls and seven rams." And Balak did just as Balaam had spoken, and Balak and Balaam offered a bull and a ram on each altar.*

Balaam was a perfect example of a prophet of God going bad for the sake of money and greed. You must be comfortable with who you are in God. Your gifts are not for sale because the anointing on your life can't be bought! Balak was the king of Moab, and he was afraid that the Israelites might destroy him and his city, so he called Balaam because he wanted him to curse the people so that he could defeat them. Balaam had a reputation as a prophet, that whatever he spoke came to pass because, prior to this, Balaam only spoke what God said.

The men came to Balaam with money as though he was some type of soothsayer. However, Balaam consulted God, and God told him that he could not curse the people because they were blessed. Balak sent more men more honorable than the first and begged Balaam to come and said he would give him anything he asked for. Balaam prayed to God, and God said he could go, but he must only speak what God told him to speak. God kept telling him that the people were blessed. God has blessed you; therefore, any curses sent against you are illegal and must be broken in Jesus's name.

Balaam instructed Balak to build seven altars. Balak worshipped Baal, the false god, so to have Balak built an altar was already a bad idea. Even if Balaam planned to offer sacrifices to God, he had Balak build the altar to attempt to curse God's people. Many altars were raised up and sacrifices made to idols. Witches and warlocks and worshippers of Satan also raise up altars and offer sacrifices and make vows at these demonic altars and send curses from these evil altars just as Balak attempted to do. Those demonic altars are an abomination to God. You must send the fire of God to destroy every demonic altar erected against you and every curse that has been spoken against you.

Pray this prayer target: I send Holy Ghost fire to locate every evil altar erected against me and my family! Be destroyed by fire, by fire, by fire in Jesus's name!

Demonic Calendars

Satan also has a calendar, and witches and warlocks and worshippers of Satan go by this calendar. They have holidays where certain rituals are done. Any Friday the 13th is a high satanic holiday, so blood is required, and they do a human sacrifice. The full moon in any month is also a human sacrifice. One of the highest satanic holidays for the individual is their birthday. The calendar may change some from year to year depending on the cult and what day certain celebrations occur for Christians.

Some cults keep women they kidnap or who are initiated, and they impregnate the women and use the baby as a blood sacrifice. They call it breeding. Most of these demonic cults have at least one, if not more, doctors or medical professionals and funeral directors as members. To be clear, I'm not saying all doctors, medical professionals, or funeral directors are a part of covens. I'm saying that some covens have professionals who operate in witchcraft. There are many strong children of God who are doctors, medical professionals and funeral directors.
Now those professionals who are witches and warlocks help with the young girls who are pregnant to make sure they have what's needed during the pregnancy, and the funeral worker can cremate or dispose of any bodies used as sacrifices. Some sacrifices are

blood sacrifices, and some are sexual. In some covens, on Christmas Eve, the sacrifice is an infant male, and they often give infant body parts as gifts. The date or holiday determines the type of sacrifice required, whether it be blood sacrifice and whether it be the blood of animals, humans, or both. Also, it determines if they perform some type of sexual act on the victim, whether it be oral, vaginal, anal, etc. They also outline the age and gender of the victim.

It's a dark world that is very real, but thank God we have power over it all. It's our job to let our light shine in the world for Christ, and there are a lot of places that need your light!

Witchcraft in the Church

Satan has several assignments in reference to the church:

1.) Make Christians ignorant of the Word of God.

2.) Create dullness during tithes and offerings because he knows if he can keep Christians in poverty, it can draw them closer to him. Tell Christians not to give tithes and offerings and that it's their pastors stealing the money.

3.) Block the projects of the church by sending witches to become leaders in the church.

4.) Get involved in praise and worship by manipulating musicians and singers. People who don't have a life of prayer and sanctification can cause contamination.

Demonic Fasting

Yes, we must fast and pray as followers of Christ. It is very critical that we live a fasted life to effectively walk in the power and authority of Christ. However, we are not the only ones who fast. Please understand this: witches and warlocks go on fasts, too.

While we fast for our power from God to be in full operation, witches and warlocks fast for power from Satan. If they're trying to come against a church, they go on a dry fast, meaning no food or water. They eat and drink nothing and utter satanic declarations. You must ask yourself this question: *Do workers of Satan live more of a fasted life to do evil than you do for Christ?*

Many witches slip into the church. Some will sit in the church and send curses to cause division in an attempt to move up in rank in Satan's kingdom. They send seducing spirits to try to break your faith.

Demonic Strategies to Cause Deception in the Church

If a committed follower of Christ fasts for three days, for example, a witch typically has to fast for fifteen days to tempt a follower of Christ to sin. In other words, more is required for them to get to a committed follower of Christ. Most witches assigned to the church can prophecy. They will give accurate prophecies for a time that will come to pass so that they gain the trust of the people. After that, it's all deception. Remember, they gain information from demons. They will try to cause divisions in the church and give false prophecies to try to cause more division in the church.

There are also false healing pastors who are out there who put sickness on people without the people knowing. Then they take the curse of sickness off as though they are healing them only to add more curses. It's an attempt to deceive children of God. We had many who have come to us for deliverance who had consulted with witchdoctors and psychics for healing or solutions to problems. Remember, there is no such thing as a good witch. They come to us because they realize curses have been put on them and they want them broken off. They didn't know any better when they originally consulted with the kingdom of darkness.

There was someone who came to my wife and me for deliverance and told us how their family would always be divided until they went to the root doctor. They would all come together for that.

This individual recalled how they all had to drink this weird-looking green liquid. It was supposedly to help them and to ward off evil, but it was witchcraft initiation. Say it with me as I reiterate again, "There is no such thing as good witchcraft, and there is no such thing as a good witch."

I have so many stories from our deliverance sessions. I remember a young woman—for the sake of this book, we will use a random name of Suzie. Suzie came to us for deliverance. Her grandmother had initiated her as a child. She was a blind witch and did not know it. First, Suzie remembered her mother taking her to a country in West Africa called Benin. This is the birthplace of Voodoo. Some from Haiti and those who are at very high ranks in witchcraft all over the world have trained in Benin. Her mom took her there to try to find answers to her problems. Say it with me again: there is no such thing as good witchcraft, and there is no such thing as a good witch.

What's unfortunate is that those curses continued on the bloodline. All the men who married her mom's siblings died before age sixty. All of the women on her mom's side had failed second marriages. It was a bloodline curse, and bloodline demons waged war against marriages on the bloodline. Suzie remembered her grandmother putting on all white and offering sacrifices. Suzie's grandmother was a priestess in witchcraft. Her grandmother took her and her cousins to the Atlantic Ocean and sacrificed them. She found out that her grandmother had to make a choice to please the demons. She either had to make a vow that her grandchild would die at a young age or not be able to get married. So, since her grandmother loved her, she chose to make the vow that her grandchild would never get married.

Her grandmother would pour blood on the water. She would take chicken blood and put it on her forehead and ask her to take the water from the sea and give her a bath. This is known as "spiritual bathing." These ritual baths or spiritual baths seem harmless to some. They are even led to believe that it wards off evil. However, it's an initiation process. It simply ties the individual to demons. In many cases, it invites a demonic spirit husband or wife to be married to that person in the spirit, which of course blocks them from getting married in the natural.

Suzie's grandmother would be dressed in a white outfit. People would go to the sea and make a vow and throw money into the sea. Sometimes that money washed on the shore. Suzie was initiated unknowingly. She would find that money and go and buy stuff with it. It was money sacrificed to idols, and it was not meant to be spent. So, naturally there was a curse on her finances and a curse that she would never get married. Suzie's grandmother had weekly sacrifices on Thursdays, and Suzie was also born on a Thursday. Suzie was the first in her family to accept Christ, so you know the enemy really had a target on her back. Thank God she went through deliverance and the curses were lifted.

Just like Suzie's mother went to a witch doctor, there are many who still do that today thinking they are doing a good thing. We had another young lady—let's call her Sarah—who came to us with an all-too-familiar story. She was in a church under the leadership of someone who was a witch. Sarah didn't know it until after she had left. There was extreme control and even threats of death if she disconnected from that leadership. That was obvious witchcraft, but it is much more subtle at some other witchcraft churches posing as authentic churches. You must pray for discernment. Sarah came to us, and Christ set her free during our deliverance sessions with her. When we walked her through deliverance, the demonic spirit who was in charge of all the other spirits (we know it as the strongman or ancestral demon) manifested in her body, and we commanded it to tell us how it entered. The strongman told us that it entered through impartation from the pastor she was under. Now if that doesn't open your eyes, I don't know what will. I'm not telling you about these stories to instill fear, but it's to instill awareness. Everyone shouting Jesus isn't even talking about Jesus.

Contrary to popular belief and probably what you've heard, not all demons are afraid to say the name of Jesus. It all depends on the situation. I heard a story once of a demon that told someone they were a false Jesus. Remember, there is an antichrist spirit. That antichrist spirit can say Jesus boldly because they're not talking about Jesus who died on the cross for our sins, but they're talking about the false Jesus who is tied to the spirit of the antichrist. Hence, the name anti-christ. Test the spirits. Try the spirits. Pray for discernment. Trust your discernment. If you sense something is off in your spirit, pay attention. Don't dismiss it just because they are a pastor, minister, evangelist, prophet, apostle, or whatever title they might have. Test the spirits. Pray for discernment.

Satan also gives strategy to his human agents. One strategy is to look at three key needs of most Christians: marriage, finances, and their aspirations. If they can't seem to penetrate the Christian because of their righteousness, they will focus on their marriage or their desire to get married. They will try to create doubt and disappointment and cause them to make the wrong choice and marry who Satan assigned rather than who God assigned. Satan has many businesses run by his human agents. So, they will try to arrange for the Christian to become employed by a company Satan has control over that is surrounded by many of his human agents working there. The Christian will then be paid a salary with the cursed money and will sign a contract with Satan without knowing it.

Another strategy is hours before Christians plan to attend a worship service, Satan can instruct a demon to visit the homes of Christians. The demon can get through to blow over them and make them heavy and not go to church.

When a Christian is about to sin, a thought comes in their mind, and the witch monitoring them will be able to see them appear in her mirror. They are persistent, but there are certain things they won't try if they think it won't work against that Christian. They study to see what popped up in the demonic mirror to see the weakness. This demonic mirror allows them to see the bad thoughts of Christians, or anyone in general, and the weakness. They won't make the attack until the thought is where they want it. Please understand this significant difference: Demons cannot read our minds, but they can pick up on negative thoughts because they send demonic waves. It's something that's in common with them.

Revelation 3:14-16: *"And to the angel of the church of the Laodiceans write, 'These things says the Amen, the Faithful and True Witness, the Beginning of the creation of God: "I know your works, that you are neither cold nor hot. I could wish you were cold or hot. So then, because you are lukewarm, and neither cold nor hot, I will vomit you out of My mouth."'"*

The seven churches in Asia were each given an overview of their current condition. Of the seven churches, four demonstrated a spirit of compromise—Ephesus, Pergamum, Thyatira, and Laodicea. The Laodiceans were lukewarm followers of Christ. Far too many churches have become lukewarm and have a form of godliness, but God has left the building. They have mastered the formalities of church, but they are walking in no power. Witches, warlocks, sorcerers, and demons can see if a Christian is truly sold out for God or if they are lukewarm. They can easily target lukewarm Christians. They have a field day attacking lukewarm Christians.

Just because someone is doing what appears to be work for God doesn't mean they're being used by God. They will come in the church and pretend to be Christians. It's part of their assignment, and Satan holds them accountable if they don't fulfill the assignment. This is how contamination gets in the church. There are witches assigned to every church, and some get in and some don't. How effective they are will depend on the particular church.

Sexual perversion is one of their favorite tactics. If a witch or warlock sleeps with a leader in the church, the anointing is weakened and the fire around that leader is removed. The witch can then replace that anointing with demonic power without the leader knowing it. That leader can then pray for people to heal them, but the healing is a transfer of demonic spirits. Of course, those individuals will eventually have more problems in the long run because of the transferring of spirits because that leader was no longer releasing the anointing but was releasing demons.

I am all about healing the sick because it's what God mandated us to do as children of God. We have seen so many healed and delivered through the power of God. Yet, we see how the enemy tries to sneak in and do counterfeit miracles through false prophets. They also aim to cause affairs in the church and destroy marriages. It's not an easy assignment for these witches, but they do whatever they can to try to get through. They can also see in the houses of new converts and try to cause them to sin so that the flame of fire surrounding them can be quenched. Sin gives demons access. It takes off protection from around the Christian, and the flame of fire is turned off or reduced significantly. Lukewarm Christians are already being used in Satan's kingdom to make weak Christians sin.

If a Christian is surrounded by fire, the enemy studies who is around them. If they have a friend who is not Christian or a lukewarm Christian, they will use that friend or person they're connected to as a stumbling block. Demons, witches, warlocks, sorcerers, etc., cannot get to a Christian who is surrounded by the fire of God. They need an opening. They need some type of legal right.

Witchcraft Operating Against Your Blessings

I'll go into more details later in the book pertaining to your wealth, but there are some key things to understand. One major goal of the enemy is to steal from you, but thank God that you've been given weapons to defend what's yours. The bottom line is the enemy doesn't want you to prosper. The enemy knows they can't stop you when you walk in obedience, so they do what they can to get you to walk in disobedience. There are blessings that have been released in your territory, and you need to war against the enemy who think it's their territory! Blessings are your divine right as a child of God. Everyone wants blessings, but not everyone knows how to fight the enemy who came to take them. You know how, and demons picked the wrong one. Witches and warlocks are targeting your blessings by targeting you, but every curse they send, you send it back to the sender. They have the wrong address. You're not operating in witchcraft in doing that because you're not sending a curse to a person; you're simply rejecting what was sent to you.

You're in a fight. It's not for the faint of heart. It doesn't matter how many people try to preach you happy. A feel-good message that isn't backed by power is just a motivational speech. Satan can give those to his agents. Not only that, he can even give power to them. So, the church must wake up to our power. Witches, warlocks, and sorcerers have Bibles. Yes, they have the same Bibles we have. The Word is powerful, but its power lies in the source activating the Word. When God is the source, you will see power.

We are not glorifying the enemy, but we're exposing the enemy. Any army knows they must study their enemy. The enemy studies us. Don't let the enemy know more about you than you know about you. You must study. The place to learn about you is the Word of God. In the Word is where you'll know about yourself, not in your personality and preferences. Demons have been known to sit on personalities before deliverance. Anyone who downplays demonic activity is someone who's being used by demons. You must expose the problem in order to cast out the problem. Satan wants to rule the world, but God gave you power and authority and the jurisdiction to rule the world around you!

The enemy is very crafty, but ask God for wisdom because no demon can outthink the wisdom of God. We don't bow down to demons, but we fight and make them bow down to the power of God in us. We see this in the book of Daniel.

Daniel 3:15-18: *"Now if you are ready at the time you hear the sound of the horn, flute, harp, lyre, and psaltery, in symphony with all kinds of music, and you fall down and worship the image which I have made, good! But if you do not worship, you shall be cast immediately into the midst of a burning fiery furnace. And who is the god who will deliver you from my hands?"*

Shadrach, Meshach, and Abed-Nego answered and said to the king, "O Nebuchadnezzar, we have no need to answer you in this matter. If that is the case, our God whom we serve is able to deliver us from the burning fiery furnace, and He will deliver us from your hand, O king. But if not, let it be known to you, O king, that we do not serve your gods, nor will we worship the gold image which you have set up."

King Nebuchadnezzar had set up a golden image of an idol and commanded everyone to bow down and worship it at the sound of the music. However, Shadrach, Meshach, and Abed-Nego only served the true and living God and refused to bow down to a false god. Some of the people told the king about it, and he became angry and ordered them to be brought to him. These men openly defied the command of the enemy. They had bold faith. It was not in themselves but in God. Your faith should be so tied up in God that it will literally bring God's presence in any situation. Some people talk a good game, but when evil is staring them straight in the face, they run! Don't run from what God sent you to conquer. These three men made it clear that they would not bow down to a false idol and that the God they served was able to deliver them from the fiery furnace.

Even if God chose not to, they would still not serve an idol because they knew God was still able to deliver them. God is a deliverer, and they knew it. Your faith puts problems on God, but your feelings put them on you. Go with faith! Your faith may be tried and tested in a number of different areas, but you should always stand on the fact that God is able to deliver you. God's not concerned with what the enemy says as much as He is concerned with your response. Respond in faith. An attack of the enemy shouldn't impact your response. Demons and witches are looking for a reaction, but your response should always be faith in God. Even if God gave you instructions and no one else understands, go with God. You must be bold. You can't defeat the enemy with fear because fear is a demonic spirit on assignment. You defeat them with the power of the Holy Spirit.

These three men came out of the fiery furnace in one night because they trusted God. The children of Israel came out of bondage in Egypt in one night because of Moses's obedience to God and their obedience to God. Your response can literally change your life overnight. Faith is a prerequisite for spiritual warfare because we know we can't please God without it. In order to engage the enemy, we must be trained. We must be disciplined. Apostle Paul shined some light on this for us in Scripture.

2 Timothy 2:3-6: *You therefore must endure hardship as a good soldier of Jesus Christ. No one engaged in warfare entangles himself with the affairs of this life, that he may please him who enlisted him as a soldier. And also if anyone competes in athletics, he is not crowned unless he competes according to the rules. The hardworking farmer must be first to partake of the crops.*

Apostle Paul was speaking to his spiritual son Timothy. He was giving him instructions on church order and discipline. Here we see that as a soldier in God's army, you don't get caught up in what you think you want. You should get caught up in pleasing God. Trying to please people will leave you frustrated because people's minds change. Pleasing God is much easier because He doesn't change. When we please God, we get what we need and want because His will becomes our wants. When we focus on what God wants us to do, we become better soldiers and avoid some pitfalls in this life. However, when we allow the cares of this world to suck us in, we lose focus. There's nothing the world has to offer you that is worth running from God.

Do God's will, and you will get God's will for your life. If we don't go by the rules, we cannot get our eternal crown. When we work hard at doing God's will, we will partake in the benefits of it just as a hard-working farmer is able to be the first to enjoy the fruit of their labor when the crops have grown. There is no question that it is not always easy being a soldier of Christ. There are some hardships that we will face. However, every hardship has made you stronger and wiser, and you are able to help other soldiers because of it. God never said the fight would be easy, but He promised that no weapon of the enemy will be able to prosper against us. This is why it is a team effort because we never go through anything in life in which the lessons benefit only us. Don't throw yourself a pity party. When you have endured some of the challenges and training as a soldier, you receive the rewards. God's army is not for the weak of heart. His training can be tough,

133

but it is done in love because He knows what we will need to survive and to defeat the enemy. God is pushing you. He doesn't give you problems or place problems on you. He pushes you to seek Him, to study, fight in prayer, etc. That is work, but it doesn't have to be hard work. The enemy doesn't get tired, so it's important that we continuously seek God so our strength is renewed so we can keep beating on the enemy. He also knows that we must be strong to carry out His will. When your faith is tested, it produces patience/endurance over time. Demons attack with the hope that you will be too tired to fight back, but you can always phone home to heaven for backup.

As you become more patient and stronger, you will mature. You will become complete for the task at hand, and you will lack nothing. You will have everything you need. The more the enemy steals from you, the more you'll get. Not only will you get an upgrade from what was taken, but it'll come with interest. So, you can have joy in the midst of your trials, because your trial has nothing to do with your joy. Your joy is not tied to your situation, but it's tied to God and His promises for you. So, don't be shocked or frustrated at the trials. Just respond with faith. Just because you faced it before doesn't mean you should jump ahead of God. You must still get instructions. There's not a challenge that will ever be bigger than Christ who is in you. We must also detest the works of the enemy. Proverbs 8:13 says, *"The fear of the LORD is to hate evil; Pride and arrogance and the evil way and the perverse mouth I hate."*

As a child of God, you must detest evil because God detests evil. Just because it seems nice doesn't mean it's from God. Satan is crafty. A person can say and even do nice things, but if they reject Christ, they are lost. God doesn't like pride and arrogance. So, we shouldn't like pride and arrogance. When you fight the enemy in spiritual warfare, don't boast in who you are, but boast in who God is through you. You must fully recognize that you are literally in war. Spiritual warfare is going on, and you're the center of attention. Let God remind the enemy how big God truly is through you.

Chapter 10: Demonic Plots and Patterns

Everything in the spiritual realm is strategic. Nothing just happens by coincidence, so you need to stay sharp through prayer. The enemy doesn't accidentally attack you, but it is planned out. There's no such thing as an accident in the spirit. It may look like an accident on earth, but the enemy planned it in the spirit. You must pray. There is always a war going on around us. There was literally a war going on before you were conceived in your mother's womb, while you were in her womb, and after you were born. Don't take it lightly.

Demons hate you, and they don't hate you because you're so good, but they hate you because you matter to God. That's not your problem. It's not your problem, but they plot to try to cause you problems. Everything the enemy throws at you was methodically planned out, and you can go in the spirit realm in prayer and cast down those plans. It's their goal that you never find that out. They want you to think you just have to put up with whatever comes your way. You don't have to put up with anything that is blatantly against the will of God. You have the power and authority to do something about it! Just because something has been going on in your life for a while doesn't mean you have to accept it. Don't accept attacks of the enemy. You are equipped to fight back. However, if the enemy plans, we too should have a plan. If demons study us, we too should study the things of God so we know how to effectively counterattack. Angels who do work on earth study God's blueprint. Demons who operate on earth study Satan's blueprint. So, we too must study God's blueprint. This starts with prayer and study of God's Word. If demons study you, you should be studying, too. If they put in the work, there's no excuse for us not to put in the work to do God's will. Demons want to sell you a lie so you never buy into the truth. The more you seek Christ, the more truth you will have to expose the lies! You have more power than you may realize. Some things we can't control, but some things that the enemy plots in the spirit we can expose and prevent when we get serious about prayer. Prayer and God's Word open your eyes to levels you could never obtain without them. It's one

thing to know the enemy is plotting, but it's another thing to be able to see the plot being formed. God can reveal it to you through revelation from the Holy Spirit, dreams, visions, etc.
No attack of the enemy nor any enemy is more powerful than the Holy Spirit living in you. You have a great advantage in spiritual warfare, but you must know how to work it to your advantage. It's not enough to just have power, but you have to know how to work the power God gave you against the enemy. The Holy Spirit is not broken; He is waiting for you to get up and go so He can get up and work in and through you.

Demons try to gauge where you are in your thinking and how you will respond. This is also why they try to sow seeds of certain thoughts in your mind. They do this based on tests they have thrown at you in the past. Demons create patterns in your life based on the pattern that worked before, and they only change it when it doesn't work. However, they will often try it multiple times before changing the pattern in hopes of catching you with your guard down. If you're experiencing the same vicious cycle in life, there's a seed the enemy sowed that you must command to be uprooted in Jesus's name!

Some won't just leave immediately the first time you say it, so you must be relentless in prayer and warfare until it happens. Don't quit fighting in the spirit because demons hope you get tired during warfare and lose the strength or courage to fight. Keep fighting. Again, it goes back to strategy. Familiar spirits are demons who study you and your likes, dislikes, strengths, weaknesses, etc. They're looking for an opening to attack. Demonic familiar spirits create a report on you and take it back to their headquarters so they can form a plan to attack you. Fight back!

This is again why you must understand that your life is to be taken seriously. You're important enough for angels and demons to fight over you. God doesn't waste time nor space, and everything God does, Satan tries to duplicate. God can use one thing to accomplish multiple things, and one thing can change your entire life forever. Satan tries to accomplish a similar thing. He sends his demons to do a job that is meant to create a long-term effect. For example, they will try to contaminate someone's life and try to get that person to pass it down to their child, and their child to pass it to their child. That's how generational curses are formed. It's a curse that was planted many generations ago that is passed down until it is finally destroyed. Demons hope you never even recognize it. This goes back to patterns. Every demonic plot has an end goal to create a long-term effect with the hope of killing us. They use sickness, manipulation, people, etc. This is why you should never accept anything that has happened generationally in your family that is not of God. It doesn't matter if there is a history of diabetes, cancer, alcoholism, sexual sins, infidelity, etc., in your family. Don't accept that—reject it. None of those are God's will, so you can attack them. An important thing to also remember is that just because you avoid it doesn't mean the curse has been uprooted in your family. One generation can even be skipped over because of what was accomplished in warfare. However, the enemy will try to get around you and get to another generation. So, now that you know, you can be the one to break the curse once and for all by engaging the enemy in warfare and uprooting the curse so no other generation will have to face that again. God chose you to disrupt the plans the enemy tried to use to take out your family. It may isolate you for a season, but you will win! This is where persistence comes into play. You must be persistent in prayer and studying of God's Word. No Christian has an excuse not to study the weapon that Scripture is. You can begin by learning one verse per week to build your Word base. You can only truly sustain your effectiveness in warfare when the Word of God is in you, and what's in you will be used against the enemy. Some demons have gotten comfortable, and it's time for you to make them uncomfortable by walking in the power of the Holy Spirit in you. They have been warring against you in your own territory, and it's time to war back. A child of God never runs and hides from the works of the enemy. We respond with power! Every structure can only remain standing when it has a firm foundation. Every demonic foundation that has been set up in and around your life must be destroyed. You have the power to destroy it! You can destroy the structure, but if the ground or foundation on which it was built still exists, something new can be built on it. You don't ask a demon to leave, but you must command them to leave in Jesus's name or they will suffer the consequences. Satan and the demons under his evil leadership look to build a foundation first in the lives of all people. His ultimate goal is to corrupt all of God's creation. Satan understands that he cannot build without a foundation. So, he tries to sow negative seeds in the minds of God's children. You need to get out of your mind and get the mind of Christ. Demons try to get you to believe a complete lie so that lie can take root in your life. Don't believe what demons are trying to get you to see, but believe what God has already said. God said you're a conqueror, so believe it!

Once a foundation is set, demons then use that to attract things to it. It's like a magnet. Oftentimes, when you are attracting or falling for the same tricks, it's not you. It's a foundation that demons or witches/warlocks laid that then attracts things to itself. You must destroy the foundation. If you feel like you're going around in circles, it's not by coincidence! Demons are trying to confuse you. Confuse them with your praise. They're trying to wear you down to where you have little strength to put up a fight. You don't always need strength to fight in the spirit. Send a heavenly host to fight on your behalf. Someone can be a good person at heart but have a bad foundation that has been laid somewhere along the way. It could have come from a bad or traumatic experience or anything Satan can use to try to gain access. The enemy has tried to use past experiences to gain access to your life, but you need to send the blood of Jesus to uproot negative seeds of the past. It's something you can do daily until you see change. Spiritual warfare is not something you do one time, but you engage in it as long as the enemy is engaging you and until the problem is gone.

So, we must learn how to locate and destroy the foundation Satan has attempted to form in our lives. The mistake that is often made is that what was built on the foundation was cast down, but the foundation was not uprooted. If the foundation is not destroyed, it makes building on it again easy. Don't only cast out a demon, but also send the fire of God to destroy the entire camp so setting back up will be that much harder for them. The enemy will attempt to trap you, but you either participate in your deliverance or participate in your bondage. Set yourself free and obey God! Don't give in to your feelings, but give in to your faith. Your flesh is an easy target for the enemy. This is why we must daily put our life down and pick up Christ. Some days are harder than others, but when you're committed to Christ, hard days will never be able to remain comfortable around you.

Once you're convinced that you've already won every battle you'll face, you won't be the one always frustrated, but you will frustrate demons. You are not a pushover. You are not some weak Christian, but you are an enforcer of your God-given territory. It may seem like sometimes you are moving forward and then are being pushed backward. It may sometimes feel like you're a part of some big joke, but your life is important. Your life is under attack because you cause major problems to Satan's kingdom. The good news is you're more powerful than the attack. It doesn't always feel that way, but that's why we aren't to live in our feelings. What has been attacking you has attacked you so strongly because they thought you were too weak to fight back. God is renewing your strength! The demonic foundations that have been set up in your life will be destroyed. It's not your job to go and pick a fight with demons just because, but it's certainly within your spiritual rights to finish the fight they started. However, you can definitely pick a fight and declare war when they are in your way. You uproot and plant. So, if they are in your territory, that's a reason to pick a fight. You are entitled to peace. Your mind belongs to God, so if the enemy has been messing with it, you must persistently fight back in the spirit. Your life is not a game, and when the enemy tries to play with it, you can show them how serious your power is by throwing them out. Some of you are still dealing with residue from past attacks. Deliverance is a right. God will not partially deliver you, but He will completely deliver you! Let's explore some ways that Satan tries to plot against the children of God.

Spirit of Error

1 Timothy 4:1: *Now the Spirit expressly says that in latter times some will depart from the faith, giving heed to deceiving spirits and doctrines of demons.*

This was a part of a letter the apostle Paul wrote to his spiritual son Timothy whom he mentored in the gospel. At this time, Timothy is believed to have been overseeing the church at Ephesus, and Paul was encouraging him and giving him instruction on how to deal with certain things going on in Ephesus. One thing that had to be addressed was the false teachers who were popping up and leading people astray. Apostle Paul addressed the issue of people being deceived, which caused them to depart from the faith. They were susceptible to deceiving spirits.

Deceiving spirits are demons who deceive. All demons deceive, but they go about it in different ways. They have different assignments. This particular demonic spirit that was being exposed was the "spirit of error." Essentially, this spirit opposes the spirit of the truth of God and His Word. Its assignment is to push false doctrine. It makes doctrine sound enough like truth, but it puts a little twist in there to completely contaminate the truth. This spirit causes people to walk in error and believe it to be truth. This spirit is still in operation today. This spirit will have someone boldly declare what is false. They will walk in error with arrogance and confidence, and some will claim Christ. It sways people away from the truth. Satan sends the spirit of error to blind people from the truth of Christ. Pray to God to not fall into the trap of the spirit of error!

This spirit also influences people to be offended by the truth and become overly sensitive and critical of people who speak the truth by calling them judgmental. The truth should convict. People who are easily offended by truth are influenced by the spirit of error. Jesus offended darkness because He brought light. Don't feel bad if people are offended when you speak truth. The truth of Christ should convict as you offend darkness and bring light! The demonic spirit of error makes room to push the agenda of Satan, and this spirit does that through the distribution of the doctrine of demons. According to Strong's Concordance, the Greek word for doctrine means teaching or instruction. So, the doctrines of demons are the teachings influenced by and taught by demons. They influence others to believe it and to teach it to others. Some people are well aware of it, and others are deceived and teach it without really knowing it per se. There are some entire non-Christian and even Christian groups that are influenced by the spirit of error. Of course, deliverance is needed, and it begins with the basics by coming in contact with the truth of God's Word. This is why it's important to know God's Word. Many have been led astray because something sounded good or made sense to their intellect, but in all actuality, it opposes God's Word. They claim to be enlightening the people. There are some groups that try to push that the story of Jesus was copied from another story. All lies. They pull people in to the lies by giving them some truth, like where some of their true roots originated. It's intriguing, and you see the truth in some of it. They make others feel like they've been lied to. It has some truth, but then it's enough to draw people in and then sprinkle in the lies. A good word is not a good word if it contradicts God's Word! Those who didn't know the truth of God's Word were easily deceived. Intellect alone is a demon's playground. It is never a replacement for intellect covered by the blood of Jesus. We must have a renewed mind. The Bible is not just a cool book to read when you feel like it. It's what we need to live and fight the enemy who is trying to destroy us!

There are three doctrines outlined in Scripture:

1. Sound doctrine- Sound doctrine is healthy teaching. According to Strong's Concordance, the Greek word for "sound" means true, healthy, and uncorrupt. Sound doctrine is true, healthy, and uncorrupt teaching, which is the truth of God's Word.

141

2. The apostles' doctrine- This was the teachings of the apostles in Scripture, and they taught what Christ taught and what was revealed to them by the Holy Spirit. They first just delivered the message orally, but it was later written down, which gave us the entire New Testament. The apostles' doctrine is sound doctrine because it upholds the truth of God's Word. It is true and uncorrupt. Acts 2:42 talks about the apostles' doctrine.

3. Doctrines of demons- It's mentioned in 1 Timothy 4:1. It is teaching influenced by demons. It is taught by demons, and demons also influence others to teach it. It is deceptive because it will use some of the truth of God's Word but twist it. Satan did this exact thing when he tried to tempt Jesus after Jesus came off a fast. Satan twisted the Word of God, but Jesus knew the Word and was able to rebuke Satan (Matthew 4). It opposes sound doctrine because this is unhealthy teaching and it is false and corrupt.

John 8:44-47: *"You are of your father the devil, and the desires of your father you want to do. He was a murderer from the beginning, and does not stand in the truth, because there is no truth in him. When he speaks a lie, he speaks from his own resources, for he is a liar and the father of it. But because I tell the truth, you do not believe Me. Which of you convicts Me of sin? And if I tell the truth, why do you not believe Me? He who is of God hears God's words; therefore you do not hear, because you are not of God."*

Here we find Jesus having a conversation with the Pharisees and Sadducees. They were supposed to be well versed in the law, but many of them didn't acknowledge Jesus and His authority. They claimed to be the descendants of Abraham and thus children of God, but Christ rebuked them and told them that their father was the devil because not only were they rejecting Jesus's teaching, but they were also plotting to kill him. Satan had influenced them that much, and Jesus recognized it. They weren't opposing Him but God, because God sent Him. Don't be concerned with who might oppose you or talk about you; be concerned with fulfilling what

God told you to do. These men were influenced by the spirit of error, as they rejected the truth of God.

These men were not bringing glory to God, but they were bringing glory to Satan. They weren't doing God's will, but they were fulfilling Satan's will, and Jesus labeled them children of the devil. If someone defends what opposes the truth of God, they're working either temporarily or permanently for Satan, unknowingly or knowingly. Defend the truth! Jesus gave them a list of reasons why, from their actions, their father was Satan. He speaks a lie, and a lie never comes from God, but it comes from Satan and out of Satan's own nature. He is a liar and the father of lies. The spirit of error not only got these men to believe a lie, but they were so adamant about the lie they were influenced to plot to kill Jesus to defend the lie. Not only did they have the spirit of error, but they also were influenced by a lying spirit and the spirit of murder. We see how one spirit, if not rebuked and cast out, can make room to invite other spirits. Ultimately, it was all influenced by Satan. Everything God creates, Satan tries to duplicate. God is the Father of Lights, and we are those lights. That's why we are supposed to be the light of the world and to let our light shine (Matthew 5:14-16). Satan is the father of lies, and those spirits lie, and they influence people to lie and live a life of lies. God is king and has sons and daughters. Satan is a king in his kingdom and has sons and daughters. In the natural sense, he can use people in such a way that they become his children. He also initiates people into his kingdom of darkness, and some of those people initiate their children into his kingdom. In the spiritual realm, Satan doesn't see the angels who were kicked out with him as coworkers or his peers, but he sees some of them as sons. He definitely sees demons as such. As God's children, we are God's sons and daughters. God gives us territory to rule in on earth, and we go from the status of just a son or daughter to a place of rulership/kingship and dominion on earth as kings and priests.

Hence, God is our king and is king over all His children. Jesus is over us and is called King of Kings. Jesus showed us how to be kings. When I say king or sons, I'm being gender inclusive because it is referring to men and women. In God's government, He gave us power and authority on earth to rule on earth. He gives His angels various functions/roles. Satan again tries to duplicate what God does. So, Satan calls his fallen angels, demons, and witches and warlocks sons or daughters, and he gives them territory to try to gain influence in. He has an order, and he takes his sons and daughters who are fallen angels and makes them princes/principalities. They rule over kingdoms, cities, states, countries, continents, etc., and any large groups within the earth realm, as I discussed earlier.

Demons aren't fallen angels, but they are disembodied spirits who roam the earth trying to live in humans. Demons are the spirits of the Nephilim giants who were wiped out in the great flood. The Nephilim came about when fallen angels mated with humans, creating half-human, half-fallen angel creatures. So demons are of lower rank than principalities. Yet, that's who we fight against most. The principalities send out the orders, and demons and human agents attempt to carry them out. Satan may try to copy what God does, but he will never be able to do what God does! When you engage the enemy in spiritual warfare, you aren't engaging them as just a child of God, but it's king vs. king. We are kings in God's government, and we war against kings in Satan's government of various ranks. Hundreds or thousands of demons can be working against us at one time because they operate in networks. Witches and warlocks also operate in networks or teams. We must go from just the place of being sons and daughters and realize we have duty as kings and queens. Sons and daughters have an inheritance, and we inherit the things of God. We inherit His promises for us. Ultimately, God is our inheritance. Sons and daughters inherit, but it's only when we walk in the anointing as kings that we have jurisdiction to rule on earth on behalf of God. Even in earthly government, a child of a king cannot legally begin ruling, declaring war, etc., until they are anointed and appointed as king or queen. As I stated early in this book, spiritual warfare is a war between two governments, and one is evil and the other is good. Fight on the good side, which is the side of Christ.

We find another example in Scripture with the famous story of David and Goliath.

1 Samuel 17:16, 45-47: *And the Philistine drew near and presented himself forty days, morning and evening...*

Then David said to the Philistine, "You come to me with a sword, with a spear, and with a javelin. But I come to you in the name of the LORD of hosts, the God of the armies of Israel, whom you have defied. This day the LORD will deliver you into my hand, and I will strike you and take your head from you. And this day I will give the carcasses of the camp of the Philistines to the birds of the air and the wild beasts of the earth, that all the earth may know that there is a God in Israel. Then all this assembly shall know that the LORD does not save with sword and spear; for the battle is the LORD's, and He will give you into our hands."

We know the story of David and Goliath. David was the least likely person to have defeated this giant who had been trained in war from his youth. The army of Israel had many great soldiers including Saul, but everyone was afraid of Goliath. We can identify a demonic pattern here. The spirit of fear worked against the Israelite army, so Satan kept using it. He influenced the Philistine army to keep showing up every day for forty days, morning and evening, because it worked. He didn't have to do anything except keep showing up. The fear was working on them and wearing them down before the physical fight. The enemy tries to weaken you in your mind so they can have an easier fight. Pray for the mind of Christ!

It didn't change until David showed up. God gave David courage and strength to overcome Goliath. The enemy will keep trying to bully you so you leave the territory God assigned you. Don't run; defend your territory in the spirit. God may use you to do the very thing everyone else is afraid to do or they may think you are crazy for doing it. David's older brother had previously told David to stop asking questions about Goliath because he felt David only came down to them because he was trying to find an excuse to come and see the battle. David spoke words only God could have given him to speak. There will be situations that you are in when the Holy Spirit will rise up in you and speak words you know couldn't come from you.

David told Goliath at the very beginning that the battle belonged to God. He also prophesied to Goliath exactly what would happen. So, David knew that God was using him. Saul tried to give David his armor and sword, but David had not tested it. David had to use what God gave him. Sometimes what you need is right within your reach and you cannot go by what someone else thinks is right for you. If you want to break a demonic pattern that was formed in your life, don't respond in your feelings. Attack it with God's Word and prayer.

We can also find in Scripture a demonic plot that was set up to destroy an entire race of people.

Esther 4:13-17: *And Mordecai told them to answer Esther: "Do not think in your heart that you will escape in the king's palace any more than all the other Jews. For if you remain completely silent at this time, relief and deliverance will arise for the Jews from another place, but you and your father's house will perish. Yet who knows whether you have come to the kingdom for such a time as this?"*

Then Esther told them to reply to Mordecai: "Go, gather all the Jews who are present in Shushan, and fast for me; neither eat nor drink for three days, night or day. My maids and I will fast likewise. And so I will go to the king, which is against the law; and if I perish, I perish!" So Mordecai went his way and did according to all that Esther commanded him.

Here we find Queen Esther and Mordecai. Mordecai was a man who sat at the king's gate and played some minor role on the king's staff. Mordecai helped raise Esther, but this was kept a secret from the king. Haman, who became the king's right-hand man, did not like Mordecai because Mordecai would not bow down to him like the others. Mordecai stated that he was a Jew. So, of course he was not going to bow down to a man, but only to God. Haman did not like this and fooled the king into making a decree that all the Jews would be killed. Esther was also a Jew. So, Mordecai was seeking Esther's help to save him and the other Jews.

How Esther became queen was a divine connection. Now she had an opportunity to save an entire population. One divine connection can not only change your life forever, but it can change the lives of others forever! Esther knew it was against the law to approach the king without being summoned, even though she was the queen. Mordecai insisted that if Esther remained silent, God would raise someone else up to replace her to deliver the Jews. He also suggested that it could be that her purpose in becoming queen was for a time like this. Esther was under a lot of pressure to complete her assignment. It was dangerous because of all that was at stake, but she was willing to take the risk to save her people. She asked Mordecai to gather the Jews in the area and fast and pray for three days, and she would do the same along with her maids. Not every assignment God gives will seem easy, but if He gave it to you, there's a guarantee He will complete it through you if you let Him. She took the risk, the people were saved, and Haman's evil plan backfired on him.

This is not a time to be silent in the things God is urging you to do. God is giving you more responsibility, and you must stand in the confidence in knowing that He already qualified you. Esther rose to the position she was in as queen for many reasons, but she was given the great assignment of helping to save an entire nation. Sometimes what God has purposed us to do will take a lot of courage. It's an honor because God trusted you with it. If you live for God today, your life will speak for you even when you're gone. Purpose comes with pressure, but it takes a big person to accomplish a big job. There is joy in knowing that your work for the Lord is not in vain. There are generations depending on you. Your decision to follow God's will for your life will benefit current and future generations. When you say yes to God, things beyond your wildest dreams will say yes to you!

Demonic Cycles and the Demon who Oversees Witchcraft

When someone gives their life to Christ, demons count fifty-two days and try to find an opening again. They continue this fifty-two-day cycle. This is not an exact science because the enemy is always trying to find a way to attack, but this is just one strategy of the enemy. During this time, they send 200-300 evil spirits to track you. They will try to send many distractions in an attempt to get you to lose focus. This is why you may notice certain cycles popping back up or when you notice old exes pop up at the same time or certain bad or suspicious things start happening in or around your life that you've already overcome. It's a demonic attack. No matter what cycle the enemy tries to continue in your life, you have the power of the Holy Spirit to break it.

We find in Scripture how the enemy can send an entire army to try to capture one person. The bigger of a threat you become to Satan's kingdom, the bigger of a target you become. That's actually an honor. Your name should be a topic of conversation in the camps of the enemy because it means you're a real threat, and you are causing real problems. It's not something to be afraid of. They targeted Jesus, and they will target us, but we win! At one time, you may have had one witch assigned to you, but as you become a bigger threat, it could turn into several witches and even an entire witches' coven that has been assigned to target you. Then you graduate from just local witches trying to target you to an entire witchcraft network internationally meeting together to talk strategy and exchange notes on how they can somehow try to stop you. We know we're victorious, but we must understand who is fighting against us. We see a great example in Scripture.

2 Kings 1:9-14: *Then the king sent to him a captain of fifty with his fifty men. So he went up to him; and there he was, sitting on the* *top of a hill. And he spoke to him: "Man of God, the king has said, 'Come down!'"*

So Elijah answered and said to the captain of fifty, "If I am a man of God, then let fire come down from heaven and consume you and your fifty men." And fire came down from heaven and consumed him and his fifty. Then he sent to him another captain of fifty with his fifty men.

And he answered and said to him: "Man of God, thus has the king said, 'Come down quickly!'"

So Elijah answered and said to them, "If I am a man of God, let fire come down from heaven and consume you and your fifty men." And the fire of God came down from heaven and consumed him and his fifty.

Again, he sent a third captain of fifty with his fifty men. And the third captain of fifty went up, and came and fell on his knees before Elijah, and pleaded with him, and said to him: "Man of God, please let my life and the life of these fifty servants of yours be precious in your sight. Look, fire has come down from heaven and burned up the first two captains of fifties with their fifties. But let my life now be precious in your sight."

Here we find the prophet Elijah sending fire from heaven. King Ahaziah of Israel, who was the son of the deceased Ahab as well as Jezebel (who was still alive at the time), had fallen through the lattice/window of his upper room, and he was injured. King Ahaziah had done evil in the sight of God just as his mom and dad did, and he also worshipped the false god Baal, provoking God's anger.

King Ahaziah sent messengers to go to Ekron to inquire of the false god Baal-Zebub to see if he would recover from his injury. So, we see demonic activity being summoned. Baal-Zebub was known to them as the "god of the flies" or "lord of the flies." In the Greek, it's Beelzebub (Matthew 12:25-28). This false god was supposedly able to deliver them from the plague of flies that often infested the area. Of course, this idol worship angered God. The temple where they worshipped this demon was in Ekron. Ekron was a city near the sea where many flies would swarm around because of the atmosphere.

Beelzebub is called the prince of demons. He is a fallen angel who controls all types of witchcraft. The demonic king of Babylon falls somewhere in this category as well. Beelzebub doesn't report to other powers or principalities. He reports directly to Satan. Beelzebub, the lord of the flies, is in charge of many witches and warlocks. Really, any principality has demons, witches, and warlocks under their command. Witches can send demonic flies, gnats, wasps, etc., to monitor you. They can also use spiders, dogs, and many other animals. Oftentimes, if you are attacked by any such creatures in your dreams, it's witchcraft being sent to you, but you have power over it.

God sent an angel to inform the prophet Elijah of what the king was doing, and God sent Elijah to stop the messengers and tell them that King Ahaziah would die. God will often show His people what the enemy is planning so you can stop it in the spirit. When Ahaziah found out who told them that, he was angry and sent a captain of fifty to capture Elijah. The armies of Israel were divided into thousands, hundreds, and fifties and led by one captain. We see this demonic influence trying to seize and destroy the child of God. The king sent all these men to capture one man. It shows how threatened he was by Elijah. Demons are fearful of your power in Christ, so they do everything they can to try to get you to live outside of faith. When a person or place is delivered from demons, it can be hundreds or thousands of demons at once. The enemy is desperate in their attempts to destroy you; they will send many demons at once, but God gave you the power to defeat them. Satan may send many demons to attack you, but God will send angels to rescue you. You are never alone in spiritual warfare! When you war, angels are also warring on your behalf.

So, we see the first group of fifty reach Elijah and command him to come down at the king's request. These men were under demonic influence and probably demonic possession. So, notice that they recognized who he was and acknowledged him as a man of God, although they were mocking him. Demons are fully aware of who you are in God. They aren't afraid of who you are in the flesh, but they're terrified of who you are in God!

So, Elijah said that if he was a man of God, let fire come down from heaven and consume the captain and his fifty men, and it happened. Elijah was able to call fire down from heaven. This fire was God's anger that came with it, as we know God was angry with the people for worshipping a false god. Elijah served notice on the demonic principality in his territory. When demons try to mess things up in your life, you need to call down the fire of God to wipe them out. You have the authority of Christ to call down the fire of God to destroy demonic walls that have been set up in your life that you can't see.

Here we see a demonic pattern. The enemy won't always learn their lesson the first time. They try to keep attacking in the same area and in the same way until they realize it won't work. If demons are persistent at attacking, Christians must be persistent at counterattacking in spiritual warfare. So, King Ahaziah sent another group of fifty soldiers along with their captain with the same request and the same mockery. Elijah responded in the same way and called down the fire of God from heaven. Elijah knew the enemy was not only blatantly insulting him, but they were insulting God, who sent Elijah. Elijah knew it was demonic, and he knew God was not pleased. When you know God is not pleased with a thing, you can easily send down the fire of God to destroy its works.

When you call down the fire of God from heaven, you're literally manifesting the anger of God on earth against the enemy! Now King Ahaziah sent a third group of fifty and their captain. By this time, Elijah had already caused so much damage to the demonic foundation in the region that the demons were now retreating and begging him to stop. The third group came, and the captain begged Elijah not to send fire down. Keep in mind that this physical battle was a direct correlation to a spiritual battle, so demons were literally wounded and their camp destroyed. This third captain was really showing how the demons were now begging for Elijah to stop causing damage to their camp.

This is similar to how when Jesus cast Legion out of a man that the demons begged Jesus not to cast them out of the country and to allow them to go into the herd of swine (Mark 5:12). After you are done in warfare, demons will be begging in the spirit for you to stop causing so much damage to their camp. When you constantly wound demons in battle, although they may be commanded by their boss to try again, they'll beg you not to torment them. Elijah had already sent God's fire of anger from heaven twice, and that was too many times for the demons in that area. They didn't want any more because there was no trace of what came before them.

The fire of God destroyed 102 evil men leaving no trace behind. So, the demons influencing those 102 men had no place to go and were forced to try to find another home. When demons attack in your territory, your warfare will force them to find another home. The same ability Elijah had to call down the fire of God from heaven is the same ability you have. James 5:17 reminds us that Elijah was a human being just like us and was able to pray that it wouldn't rain, and it didn't rain for three and a half years because of his prayers. This is the same Elijah who called this fire to come down from heaven. So, you need to start using the fire of God and use it in the right way. I will discuss it in more detail in chapter 13. The fire of God is a destroyer of demonic works. Thank God for giving you a weapon of destruction to destroy what's trying to destroy you.

Chapter 11: How to War through Praise and Worship

Praising and worshipping God are not just showing honor to God, but they are also an act of spiritual warfare against the enemy. You should make a conscious decision to do this often. Our praise and worship aren't what God needs, but they're what He delights in. Also, it's what we need to be renewed and to fight the enemy. It's amazing how much is working in your favor. No demonic attack can withstand the pressure and force that comes with the power and authority and all the other weapons God entrusted to you. You shake up demonic foundations when you praise and worship God. The two are separate, but they often go hand in hand. When you praise God, you are driven by His power. When you worship God, you are driven by His presence. This is why praise can be loud, emotional, passionate, full of energy, etc. Worshipping God can bring tears to your eyes, and sometimes you have few words to say because of His presence being magnified in your life. When you praise God, it hurts the ears of demons and it annoys them. So, while you're praising God, also know that it is an act of spiritual warfare. When you worship God, demons tend to run away until you're done because you create waves in the spirit and angels also show up with you. Praising God is a weapon against the enemy, and worship brings shame to demons because it reminds them of their defeat and what they lost. It is truly an honor and a privilege to be in a position to be able to serve the true and living God! Satan was demoted and excommunicated from heaven, and he's jealous that what he once had access to we now have. You can't afford not to give God the praise and to worship Him. It should be a part of your daily diet.

Not every demon will respond the same way to the use of each spiritual weapon, so use as many as you know. There was a time in my life, years ago, when I was experiencing heavy demonic attacks as soon as I drifted off to sleep. My prayer life was increasing during this time, so quite naturally, it caused Satan to send higher-ranking demons to try to slow me down. Normally when I would be attacked during those times and tried to come out of spiritual consciousness (as dreams are), back into natural consciousness, I would plead the blood of Jesus or just say, "Jesus." Normally, that would quickly give me enough strength to overcome. However, during that season, the demons weren't responding to it as quickly, so I added in worship, and it instantly caused them to lift the attack and flee. It wasn't anything I thought of, but it was just revelation of the Holy Spirit at that time. It was a greater level of attack, and it required a combination of spiritual weapons to weaken the enemy. This is why we need to remember about all our weapons. Sometimes, you might have to plead the blood, call on Jesus, worship, and call the heavenly host to fight. Demons tremble at your worship of Christ because your worship gets the attention of heaven and the reinforcement you need in warfare.

You should not stop persistently seeking God. Everything and everyone on earth has the ability and choice to praise God, but as God's chosen on earth, we ought to lead the praise party! You confuse the enemy when you praise God in a situation that you normally would have had a breakdown in. There is power in your praise. Worship has a smell. When you glorify God through praise and worship, you send an aroma to heaven that is pleasing to the Lord. It's opposite for the enemy. Your worship to God creates an offensive smell to the enemy. Stink up the enemy's camp. If you want to spoil the enemy's appetite, make sure that praise and worship unto God is on your menu. The only thing is that some demons will enter a church if they know they are able to influence others or to set traps. Some demons are on assignment to enter churches to deceive, and your praise has the ability to make them change plans for that day.

Your hands and feet are not only instruments to give praise unto God, but they're also mighty weapons against the enemy as you praise. Not only are your hands and feet important, but your mouth is another very powerful tool in spiritual warfare. When you sing unto God, you distract the enemy because they love music, but only music they can control. This is why demons try to control the airwaves. This is why they love to influence the lyrics of music artists. Words are seeds. That's why you should be careful what type of music you listen to because your ears are gates into your

154

life and seeds can be planted, good or bad. Satan has an elaborate plan, and as stated before, he and his demons are patient. They can sow seeds that are scheduled to be released at a later date. So, if you're a parent, you should also monitor what your children listen to because there are some demonic seeds you can prevent from being sown.

Eyes are also gates, and demons use certain things to try to sow seeds to get you to do things contrary to God. This is why you must also guard what you watch. Entertainment can quickly turn into much more. Always watching or entertaining drama or negativity can invite drama and negativity into your life unknowingly because that's how the enemy works. What you must realize is that when you feed into those things, it's actually a form of praise. Are you praising drama more than God? No Christian would naturally say yes, but it's something to think about and watch closely. When you send praise and worship up to God, the life power of the Holy Spirit is renewing you. Every time you praise God, you literally start a praise party in heaven.

Let's discuss three specific types of warfare weapons pertaining to praise and worship:

1.) Warfare Weapon of Hands

2.) Warfare Weapon of Feet

3.) Warfare Weapon of Voice

Warfare Weapon of Hands

Ezekiel 21:14, 17: *"You therefore, son of man, prophesy,*
And strike your hands together.
The third time let the sword do double damage.
It is the sword that slays,
The sword that slays the great men,

That enters their private chambers…
"I also will beat My fists together,
And I will cause My fury to rest;
I, the LORD, have spoken."

In these two verses, we find God talking to the prophet Ezekiel. God was going to bring judgment on Jerusalem because of their continual sin and ignoring the warnings God sent through prophets like Ezekiel. Demons are also warned by God. We have the authority of Christ to warn demons to back off before the fight gets ugly. What we lost temporarily won't compare to their loss! In verse 14, God told Ezekiel to strike his hands together or to clap his hands. "Let the sword do double damage" was referencing the damage God was going to allow the enemy army to do to the Israelites because of their constant worshipping of idols. So, the judgment was not just on the people, but it was also on the demons the people were worshipping. Ezekiel clapping his hands was to be an expression of righteous anger. Clapping of the hands here encouraged the sword to be drawn. When you clap your hands when you engage the enemy in spiritual warfare, you're encouraging angels to make use of the sword. Clapping your hands during warfare prayers is symbolic of God bringing judgment upon the enemy. If you watch any of my videos or are in worship services with me, when I'm engaging the enemy in warfare, you will often see me clapping my hands. I'm striking the enemy with the sword of the Lord in doing that.

Not only did God tell Ezekiel to clap his hands, but God also clapped His hands in verse 17. It showed His righteous anger over the continual sin and evil practices of the people. It represents God's fury because God also said He will clap His hands and will cause His fury to rest. So, once the judgment was done, He would stop it. He wouldn't allow it to continue beyond accomplishing its task. When you clap your hands in spiritual warfare, you are able to release God's righteous fury upon the enemy. At this point, the children of Israel became an enemy of God because they were worshipping idols, which of course are demons. Notice how God told Ezekiel to clap his hands, and it was in unison with the sword.

156

When the enemy attacks you and you clap your hands, you're literally counterattacking them in the spirit, and each clap strikes the enemy.

Ezekiel's claps represented something prophetically as well. God said the sword would do double damage the third time. This was prophetic because Jerusalem had three events happen when the Babylonians captured them. King Zedekiah was captured; the city was taken; and Gedaliah, who King Nebuchadnezzar II of Babylon put in charge of the remnant of Jews, was killed. Others believe the three symbolizes the three different kings of Judah who were captured: Jehoiakim, Jeconiah, and Zedekiah.

We can explore another example in Scripture.

Psalm 144:1: *Blessed be the LORD my Rock,*

Who trains my hands for war,

And my fingers for battle.

Here we see the words of King David, who was praising God for preparing him to fight. Thank God for preparing you in advance to fight in a spiritual war you didn't even know you would be in. David was a great man of war and a leader of armies. We know that he slayed Goliath. His fingers were skilled as he was able to use the bow in physical warfare.

However, this also has a spiritual meaning. David's hands were used in physical battle and in spiritual battles. Your hands serve more than a physical purpose; they also serve a spiritual purpose to war against the enemy in the spirit. This same David also had very skilled hands and fingers as he played the harp. King Saul was troubled by an evil spirit because the spirit of the Lord left him. So, it had left room for an evil spirit to legally torment Saul. David came in and played the harp, and the tormenting spirit went away and Saul was refreshed (1 Samuel 16:23). The power of the Holy Spirit can flow through your hands to set someone free from a demonic attack. Sometimes all you have to do is wave your hands toward heaven, and it's a sign for angels to go to work on your behalf!

Warfare Weapon of Feet

Ezekiel 6:11: *Thus says the Lord GOD: "Pound your fists and stamp your feet, and say, 'Alas, for all the evil abominations of the house of Israel! For they shall fall by the sword, by famine, and by pestilence.'"*

We see God giving the prophet Ezekiel instructions to clap his hands and stomp his foot, which is a sign of grief and righteous anger. All the evil the Israelites had done caused them to fall by the sword and famine and a plague. If one didn't take some people out, the other two would. Clapping hands and stomping feet in this case was also a sign of the destruction that was to come. When you literally stomp your feet in spiritual warfare, you're actually bruising the head of any enemy that tries to enter your life. When you clap your hands and stomp your feet in prayer, you're warning the enemy to back off or get dealt with!

You can see how this plays out in spiritual warfare. The sword pierces the enemy and wounds them, causing them to flee. Famine is a dry place for them. They need to feed off of people. They need blood sacrifices, and you can starve them when they have nothing to latch onto in your life. The plague sent against the enemy is when masses of people come together on one accord to take back territory from the enemy. Your feet are a dangerous weapon against the enemy because where the soles of your feet touch there's an opportunity to take territory back from them. Stomping your feet in prayer with anger against the enemy shakes and can crush demonic foundations around you. God will make your enemies ashes under your feet (Malachi 4:3).

Luke 10:19: *Behold, I give you the authority to trample on serpents and scorpions, and over all the power of the enemy, and nothing shall by any means hurt you.*

Jesus gave you authority to walk over any enemy that tries to harm you. He let us know that not only do we have authority over all power of the enemy, but you can trample them. That means they are truly beneath you. When you walk in your Christ-given authority, you can use your feet to help keep any demon that attacks under your feet in the spirit. Even in Ephesians 6, about the armor of God, it talks about your feet being shod with the preparation of the gospel of peace. It's a metaphor that was comparing the physical boot in warfare to the spiritual boot in warfare. The Good News keeps us standing firm and can bruise the enemy's head. Many Roman army boots were studded with sharp nails on the bottom. When you stomp your feet in praising God, it's like driving nails into the enemy. If the enemy kicks, make sure you kick back in the spirit!

Warfare Weapon of Voice

Joshua 6:20-21: *So the people shouted when the priests blew the trumpets. And it happened when the people heard the sound of the trumpet, and the people shouted with a great shout, that the wall fell down flat. Then the people went up into the city, every man straight before him, and they took the city. And they utterly destroyed all that was in the city, both man and woman, young and old, ox and sheep and donkey, with the edge of the sword.*

Here, we find Joshua and the Israelites following God's instructions, which led to the destruction of the wall of Jericho. Jericho was a major city of the Canaanites, who were an enemy of God. This city was well-fortified with a massive wall of defense. The Canaanites occupied the Promised Land that God promised to the children of Israel. The wall stood in the way of God's promise to His children. No matter how big the wall, if it stands in the way of where God is leading you, it will come down!

The wall was a physical stronghold, but it also has a spiritual meaning. We've discussed before that a demonic stronghold is based on arguments and reasoning philosophers and teachers use to attempt to discredit the Word of God. It is also an incorrect thought pattern. So, this physical stronghold was a wall of defense opposing God. The wall was in the way. The enemy will erect walls in your life to try to make you feel you can't get around them, but God gave you power to knock them down. God told Joshua that He had already given Jericho into their hands. God told this to him before it literally happened. God will often tell you that you have something before you physically have it because it's already done in the spirit. You've already defeated the enemy. God gave Joshua specific instructions. It's key that you follow the right strategy for each battle that will come through the Holy Spirit. The army could not physically penetrate the wall that was built. The only way through at that time was an act of God. For six days, they were to march around the city once per day, and the seventh day, they were to march around the city seven times. After the seventh time, the priests were instructed to blow the trumpet, and when the people heard it, they were to make a great shout and the wall would come down. They did just that. Their voice was warfare.

When you shout with a loud voice unto God against the enemy, you weaken and break down demonic walls set up against your life. There is power in your voice as a warrior for God, and God gave it to you as a weapon against the enemy. Not only did the shout break down the wall, but God then gave them the grace to go into the city and destroy it. Not only can you overcome demonic attacks, but God can use you in such a way that demons leave embarrassed after the attack. The enemy will try to make noise in your life, but your noise can send confusion to their camp and cause their plans to come crashing down.

We also can revisit 2 Chronicles and find another powerful example of what your voice can do.

2 Chronicles 20:17-22: *"' You will not need to fight in this battle. Position yourselves, stand still and see the salvation of the LORD, who is with you, O Judah and Jerusalem!' Do not fear or be dismayed; tomorrow go out against them, for the LORD is with you."*

And Jehoshaphat bowed his head with his face to the ground, and all Judah and the inhabitants of Jerusalem bowed before the LORD, worshiping the LORD. Then the Levites of the children of the Kohathites and of the children of the Korahites stood up to praise the LORD God of Israel with voices loud and high.

So they rose early in the morning and went out into the Wilderness of Tekoa; and as they went out, Jehoshaphat stood and said, "Hear me, O Judah and you inhabitants of Jerusalem: Believe in the LORD your God, and you shall be established; believe His prophets, and you shall prosper." And when he had consulted with the people, he appointed those who should sing to the LORD, and who should praise the beauty of holiness, as they went out before the army and were saying:

"Praise the LORD,

For His mercy endures forever."

Now when they began to sing and to praise, the LORD set ambushes against the people of Ammon, Moab, and Mount Seir, who had come against Judah; and they were defeated.

Notice that they lifted up their voices loud and high. Spiritual warfare is not quiet. As stated before, you must open up your mouth because your sound causes damage to the enemy's camp. It's not by accident that every individual has a unique voice pattern that is unlike another. No two voice patterns are exactly alike. Imagine what happens when multiple voices come together for God. When we raise our voices together in praise unto God, demons pause because every voice is different, and it confuses them at the point of attack.

Demonic Glory and Demonic Tongues

Satan knows what it's like to be in God's glory. He was a custodian of God's glory. He knows how to display a form of godliness. He knows how to create false glory. There are some atmospheres that some believe have God's glory, but it's demonic glory. It's Satan's knockoff of the glory of God. If God's glory leaves a church or any place, Satan quickly tries to slip in. Some have mastered "doing church," and they can dance and shout when the music plays and go through the motions of the service without God's glory being present. Also, if a church has become contaminated because leaders and others are greatly contaminated, it welcomes Satan in legally. It gives demons full access to contaminate worship, and that's how some can also speak in demonic tongues as opposed to tongues from the Holy Spirit. Ezekiel 28 shines some light on this.

Ezekiel 28:12-17 (emphasis mine): *"Son of man, take up a lamentation for the king of Tyre, and say to him, 'Thus says the Lord GOD:*

"You were the seal of perfection,
Full of wisdom and perfect in beauty.
You were in Eden, the garden of God;
Every precious stone was your covering:
The sardius, topaz, and diamond,
Beryl, onyx, and jasper,
Sapphire, turquoise, and emerald with gold.
The workmanship of your timbrels and pipes
Was prepared for you on the day you were created.

"You were the anointed cherub who covers;
I established you;
You were on the holy mountain of God;
You walked back and forth in the midst of fiery stones.
You were perfect in your ways from the day you were created,
Till iniquity was found in you.

"By the abundance of your trading
You became filled with violence within,
And you sinned;
Therefore I cast you as a profane thing
Out of the mountain of God;
And I destroyed you, O covering cherub,
From the midst of the fiery stones.

"Your heart was lifted up because of your beauty;
You corrupted your wisdom for the sake of your splendor;
I cast you to the ground,
I laid you before kings,
That they might gaze at you. "

This chapter was a prophecy with double meaning. God told Ezekiel about the judgment of the earthly king of Tyre, and in verses 11-19, God told Ezekiel about the judgment of the spiritual king of Tyre, which was Lucifer. Lucifer was a cherub and was placed in charge of the cherubim. He was the highest model of perfection until he sinned against God. He became prideful because of his beauty and wisdom. He also became filled with violence. Lucifer's name means "light bearer," "shining one," or "star of morning." He was indeed an angel of light, thus a cherub. Because of his brightness, beauty, and wisdom, Satan attempts to deceive followers of Christ. He corrupted his wisdom for the sake of his beauty. Because he was cast down, we now have power and authority over Satan and his demons through the power of God in us.

Verse 13 talks about all the gemstones that covered Lucifer. Satan was over the worship angels. Satan could create music. He still can today. One third of the angels were under him and were created to worship. Those angels were never replaced in heaven, but we replaced them. Satan was the only angel with the gemstones because it had to do with worship. Verse 14 talks about how Lucifer walked back and forth in the midst of fiery stones. The stones being referenced are gemstones that are in God because in God's heart are huge gemstones of fire. Lucifer would stand inside of God and open his wings and make music, and when the angels worshipped, the fire of God's love would hit the gemstones in God along with those on Satan, and a huge rainbow would form in the throne room of God. Apostle John had a glimpse in Revelation 4:3; he also talks about the rainbow around the throne and how God appeared like a jasper or sardius stone. He clearly saw gemstones.

163

So, we see even more revelation as to why Satan really thought he could be God. He was also the only angel who could create music within himself. Verse 16 tells us that God kicked him out of His heart from among the fiery stones. This reminds us that angels also had and have a will. When Christ rose from the dead, He not only got the keys of hell and death, but He also stripped Satan of the gemstones that were once on him so he could no longer say he was like God or looked like God.

Now when we worship, not only do angels ride on the waves of our worship, but God's burning fire of love consumes the gemstones in Him when we worship, and it lights up the throne room. Satan hates that he lost that. We can even see in Scripture that God calls us precious living stones. First Peter 2:5 says, "You also, as living stones, are being built up a spiritual house, a holy priesthood, to offer up spiritual sacrifices acceptable to God through Jesus Christ." The reference to holy priesthood and offering up spiritual sacrifices has to do with prayer and worship.

Of course, everything God creates, Satan tries to duplicate. In some occult practices, as a part of their ritual, they walk on burning coals of fire, and some in new age occult practices also summon demons through crystals and various types of gemstones. We see how Satan can contaminate things, but thanks be to God that we can combat his tactics with authentic worship. We can combat it by fully surrendering to God and truly chasing after Him to come out of darkness and into His marvelous light. You have weapons of praise that you need to use more often.

Chapter 12: The Blood Power Activated

The blood of Jesus is so powerful because it covers us in warfare, cleanses us of sin, and presents us spotless before God. It serves so many functions. Shedding of blood has always played a role since the beginning of mankind. We talk about the blood, proclaim the blood, sing about the blood, but we need to really understand the power of the blood. Godly covenant requires blood. The old covenant God made was a covenant with Abraham, and it required the blood of animals when the covenant was made. All of the descendants of Abraham in the Old Testament had the opportunity to enter into this blood covenant through circumcision, which of course produced blood. According to Strong's Concordance, the Hebrew word for covenant in the Old Testament is "karath," which means to cut. So, one would cut or make a covenant by cutting flesh. God made a blood covenant with Abraham, and that was the old covenant.

The covenant God made with us through the sacrifice of Jesus is the new covenant. It also required blood. Jesus's sacrifice would have been illegal in God's government without the shedding of His blood. Thank God for the power of the blood! When you hear Scripture say how "He was wounded for our transgressions, He was bruised for our iniquities...by His stripes we are healed" (Isaiah 53:5), all of that points to blood. Wounded, bruised, beaten: all drew blood. There's no stronger contract than that sealed with blood. The blood of Jesus is the signature we need to access all the things of God.

Even in marriage, there was a blood covenant because the woman was to be a virgin, and the blood from her having sex for the first time consummated the marriage. Not only that, but with a healthy cervix, a woman can still bleed a little internally after intercourse if there is enough friction. Hence, when two people have intercourse, they make a blood covenant. In warfare, not only do soul ties need to be broken, but blood covenants need to be broken as well. Jesus's blood did it once and for all for us. The Bible is the blood covenant God made with us, and when we accept His Word, it activates the promises in the covenant. It changes one's perspective because the Bible is not just a book. The Bible is not just a book to help us get by, but it is a legally binding contract sealed in blood that presents to us life and death. It gives spiritual life to those who obey it and spiritual death to those who disobey. You were blood-bought by Christ, and it's far greater than anything money could ever hope to buy because you are priceless. A godly covenant also comes with a name change. God changed Abram's name to Abraham. And Sarai became Sarah (Genesis 17). God changed Jacob's name to Israel. When you're in Christ, your name holds weight in the spirit because it's covered in the blood. People will begin to hear your name differently.

If godly covenant requires blood, then demonic covenant requires blood because Satan tries to duplicate what God does in his own way. The demonic world wants human sacrifice of blood. They want death. They want to literally cause us pain and harm. They're seeking blood. Witchcraft and other demonic occult practices always have some sacrifice of blood. This is also one reason why you see suicide bombers claiming to die for God, but they're making a blood covenant with Satan just as those who worshipped idols sacrificed their children as an act of worship to demons. Not only that, but they're operating in a spirit of error because they haven't accepted Christ and they incorrectly believe they're dying for a just cause. The true and living God does not require that. Yes, people have died for Christ because of attacks of the enemy, but their blood was not required because only Jesus's blood could do what it did for us. We are to be living sacrifices, and that's presenting ourselves to God for duty and putting our wills aside. Many great men and women of God died on the spiritual battlefield for the Lord. Their labor was not in vain, but their blood could not save, forgive sins, or defeat demons.

The blood of Jesus goes beyond just covering our sins. The blood of Jesus is a weapon of warfare. We must understand that God is a God of order. There are legalities in the spirit realm. Adam gave up dominion to Satan. Satan cannot take our dominion on earth—that can only be given away. So, we must fight in the spirit to keep our

God-given territory! Adam gave dominion to Satan in certain territories because of his sin. Those who came after Adam and lived in sin also gave territory and gave up dominion to Satan and his demons. This is why there are demons who have been controlling certain regions for centuries. It's a battle over territory. God has raised you up as a defender of His territory on earth, and He gave you power and authority to drive demons off of your land. If you walk in sin and disobedience, you come up from under the blood of Jesus and are giving demons a key to your house! This is why they feel they own you in certain areas. This could be based on the patterns of the past or something in your bloodline.

Jesus's blood is alive! You must open your mouth and put the blood to work by applying the blood of Jesus in your life and your territory. Jesus didn't take His blood with Him to heaven because there is no flesh in heaven. He left His blood on earth for us to put it to work. You have to look at the blood in a different way. He left it as a tool and a weapon for us. Jesus's blood didn't stop working. It's your responsibility on earth to open up your mouth and tell it where to flow. You can't physically see the blood of Jesus because it's spiritually discerned. You can't see it, but you can speak it because it's voice activated.

The blood cleanses us from unrighteousness. It's a cleaning agent as well. The blood of Jesus cleanses us, but when you plead the blood of Jesus, you're throwing dirt on plans of the enemy. When you declare the blood of Jesus against the enemy, it shames them because it's a clear indicator that they lost. The blood of Jesus ought to be a part of your warfare. When you proclaim the blood of Jesus, you're literally proclaiming victory in battle as you're in the battle because it's a symbol of victory. The blood of Jesus gets out the residue demons left behind. Sometimes you need to ask God to wash you in the blood. It doesn't just clean you from sin and bring about healing. It also flushes out any seeds the enemy sowed in your life. Just as you wash daily, you should ask God to wash you in the blood of Jesus daily, just in case a demonic seed was left behind overnight. Let's explore some Scriptures as the Holy Spirit gives us more revelation on the blood of Jesus.

John 19:33-34: *But when they came to Jesus and saw that He was already dead, they did not break His legs. But one of the soldiers pierced His side with a spear, and immediately blood and water came out.*

Here, we find Jesus on the cross. The new covenant began when Jesus died and His blood poured out. The enemy made a mistake because killing one man gave the entire world an opportunity to take part in the new covenant. The enemy had better be careful because what they sent to kill you will make your name and influence greater than before when God's finished.

From a medical perspective, it's believed that Jesus was pierced in His heart. The pericardium is a thin, double-layered sac that covers the heart. It contains some watery fluid called pericardial fluid that reduces friction within the pericardium as the heart beats. When Jesus died, and we can gather that it was when his blood hit the ground, the earth shook and the veil of the temple was also torn according to Matthew 27. Not only that, but some who were dead were raised from the dead. Prior to this no one who had died had gone to heaven yet; now anyone who dies immediately goes to heaven or hell. Everything changed because of Jesus's sacrifice. The blood of Jesus is so powerful it can raise the dead like the Holy Spirit. It can also raise you out of a tough situation! If the blood of Jesus can raise the dead, it can certainly defend you against the enemy, but you must give the blood a target. The blood also caused the earth to quake. The blood of Jesus causes demonic foundations to be shaken in your life.
When we talk about the blood, we must also realize that there is literally life in the blood.

Leviticus 17:10-11: *" 'And whatever man of the house of Israel, or of the strangers who dwell among you, who eats any blood, I will set My face against that person who eats blood, and will cut him off from among his people. For the life of the flesh is in the blood, and I have given it to you upon the altar to make atonement for your souls; for it is the blood that makes atonement for the soul.' "*

This passage dealt with the old law that one was not to eat anything with blood, such as a piece of meat with blood. Under Christ, this law is no longer in effect. The reason they weren't allowed to eat any part of an animal with blood in it was because during that time, the blood of animals was used as a sacrifice unto God to atone for sins. So, during that time, eating something with blood in it (similar to a rare steak) was forbidden because they were eating something that could literally atone for sins. The life or soul of the flesh was in the blood. It was only reserved at that time to make atonement for sins, which is to make amends for and reconcile us back to God.

This, of course, was a foreshadowing of Christ's coming. It's a price paid for our sins. Even if you give blood, a needle must still penetrate your skin and stick into your vein. Blood being shed always has a cost. Jesus paid the greatest cost for His blood to be shed. Now we're the beneficiary of His blood transfer.

We see how important blood was from the beginning. If there is no blood in the physical body, the body will die. That's why someone or an animal can physically die from too much blood loss. When the enemy sends toxins in your life, you need to call forth the blood of Jesus so that it can clean you inside and out! It's not enough to say you have Jesus and not utilize all that comes with having Jesus. You can't truly say you have Jesus without operating in the power that comes with Jesus. When you accept Christ, you now have access to all things that are of God. You get the Holy Spirit, the authority of Christ, and the blood of Jesus. However, none of them will be able to effectively work in your life without you doing something. There are laws in the heavens. The blood of Jesus is what God sees when we repent of our sins. It keeps Him from having to cover His eyes or take us out because He now sees the blood of Jesus.

However, the blood of Jesus doesn't go to war for you and to work for you without your permission. Demons are afraid of Jesus's blood when it's on you because it's not just serving as a sin cleanser, but now it becomes a weapon. The blood truly does transform. Just like Scripture talks about the Word of God being alive, the blood of Jesus is alive. It responds to us and for us in warfare. When we accept Christ, we enter the blood covenant, and instead of physical circumcision, our hearts are circumcised and renewed unto God. We must also be reminded that the blood of Jesus is how we came under the new covenant.

The blood of Jesus gave you a blood-bought right to receive everything that comes with being in covenant with God. Demons may come in to try to take what came with your covenant with God, but they technically are illegal when faced with the blood of Jesus. The blood of Jesus is tied to your inheritance, so if a demon tries to steal what God said is yours, use the blood of Jesus to fight back. God made a guarantee to us. It was not a negotiated contract. Don't neglect the blood of Jesus in your life. Not only do you need to use the authority of Jesus against demons, but also use His blood! His blood is also very important in spiritual warfare. There are some demons who may try to hide in your life behind things, but release the blood of Jesus to drown them out. We need the authority of Christ because it's a backstage pass to legally war in the spirit realm and arrest demons. The blood blocks demons. It's a defensive weapon.

The Blood of Jesus Has a Voice

Hebrews 12:24 (emphasis mine): *To Jesus the Mediator of the new covenant, and to **the blood of sprinkling that speaks** better things than that of Abel.*

Here the writer is talking about the new covenant in Christ that is even better than the old covenant. Jesus is the mediator of this new covenant. Jesus stands between us and God, urges us to keep coming to God, and is our advocate to God our Father against the accusations of the enemy. In the old covenant, blood of animal sacrifices was sprinkled on the altar and on the person, but now the blood of Jesus is sprinkled on us. This passage shows us that the blood of Jesus speaks. Our blood even speaks. Our blood and our pain cries unto God when we don't say a word because there is life in the blood.

Cain and Abel made a sacrifice unto God in the Old Testament. Cain tilled the ground and brought an offering to God from some of what he produced. Abel tended sheep and offered unto God the firstborn of the flock. God respected Abel's offering but not Cain's. There was something Cain didn't do so that God didn't accept it. He had sin in his heart. He had the wrong heart motive. Abel also offered a blood sacrifice of the animal. Cain was angry because God respected Abel's offering over his, so Cain killed Abel. Cain tried to act like he didn't know where Abel was after God questioned him. God said that Abel's blood cried out to Him from the ground (Genesis 4:10). That is an indicator that bloodshed is not overlooked. God sees it.

Christ's blood reconciles us to God and cries out for peace, and it lashes out in vengeance against the enemy when we send it. In spiritual warfare, when we release the blood of Jesus, it speaks against darkness. It speaks and brings vengeance upon demons! That's why it's important to plead the blood of Jesus against the enemy. When we release the blood of Jesus against the enemy, the blood speaks more than we do because it has a job to do in warfare when we allow it.

Revelation 1:5-6: *And from Jesus Christ, the faithful witness, the firstborn from the dead, and the ruler over the kings of the earth.*

To Him who loved us and washed us from our sins in His own blood, and has made us kings and priests to His God and Father, to Him be glory and dominion forever and ever. Amen.
Here we find an account of apostle John's revelation. He talks about Jesus being the firstborn from the dead, and the ruler over the kings of the earth. We know that we're kings and queens in God's government. We are also priests unto God. Christ is the ruler over all the kings of the earth, and that's referring to us because it's referring to those in God's government. Christ loves

us and washed us from our sins. We were once in bondage to sin, but Christ's blood set us free. Celebrate the blood!

Notice that after John spoke of Christ loving us and washing us from our sins in His own blood that it goes on to say He made us kings and priests to God. If you want to rule on earth for God as a ruler in His earthly kingdom, you must continually be washed in the blood of Jesus. You must have the blood. You must use the blood. As a king in God's government, in order to effectively engage a king in Satan's government, you must cover yourself in the blood of Jesus. Demons want us to shed blood because they draw power from it, but our blood has no power. We draw from Jesus's blood, which has all power! You do great damage to demons when you use the power of the Holy Spirit, authority of Jesus Christ, and the power of the blood all at once. You're hitting them from so many different angles they won't know what hit them.

Revelation 12:10-12: *Then I heard a loud voice saying in heaven, "Now salvation, and strength, and the kingdom of our God, and the power of His Christ have come, for the accuser of our brethren, who accused them before our God day and night, has been cast down. And they overcame him by the blood of the Lamb and by the word of their testimony, and they did not love their lives to the death. Therefore rejoice, O heavens, and you who dwell in them! Woe to the inhabitants of the earth and the sea! For the devil has come down to you, having great wrath, because he knows that he has a short time."*

We already know that Scripture tells us that death and life is in the power of the tongue (Proverbs 18:21). This passage speaks of a war in the spiritual realm between heavenly angels and Satan and his demonic angels. We can also overcome the enemy through the words of our testimony. Telling our testimony of what God has done for us and how God delivered us is a major shot at Satan. The word of your testimony is a powerful weapon against the enemy because it's a reminder to them that you overcame the attack.

172

We also overcome by the blood of the lamb, which is the blood of Jesus. You must put the blood of Jesus to work in your life daily because the enemy doesn't stop planning to find a way to attack daily. There may be places where because of the setting, you can't engage in warfare like you would in your private time with God or in a different setting, but you can send the blood. Send the blood of Jesus against the enemy because it can go places you can't get to. Satan also has some understanding of times and seasons. He doesn't know everything God will do and how God will do it, but Satan is aggressive because he knows he has a short time to try to kill, steal, and destroy. Satan always tries to get us to go against God's will. He knows when angels are dispatched, and he sends his demons to try to stop them from carrying out their assignments in our lives. They run reports on you. They know what's going on in your life that's good and what they caused. When you utilize your spiritual weapons, the next time demons run a report on you, they will see that your wall of defense grew overnight. The battle is over territory. It all belongs to God, but Satan tries to keep us from our inheritance. When you want to send confusion to demonic camps, say it and send the blood of Jesus. The blood will go to shake things and so will angels.

Chapter 13: Releasing the Destructive Power of the Fire of God

This is one of my favorite weapons to use. There are times in warfare where I just send fire nonstop. There are times when I just send God's fire for thirty minutes, burning up everything in its path that's not of God. The enemy hates the fire of God. You have extreme fire power to use against the enemy, and that fire power comes with the fire of God. You can destroy the works of the enemy by fire and by force. The fire of God is something that you must learn how to use and when to use. Demons don't like when you send the fire of God against them because it is very destructive to them! They understand how dangerous it is, so they hope you never know how effective it is to use. When you send the fire of God in warfare, you literally send a weapon of mass destruction against the enemy. This weapon is powerful, and we can access it even more as we build our relationship with God. The fire of God doesn't simply spoil the plans of the enemy; the fire of God literally destroys the plans of the enemy. It is destructive in nature, and you must see it as such. As warriors for Christ, the fire of God is used for one reason and one reason only: to destroy the works of darkness.

It is fire for a reason. The fire of God destroys the works of the enemy, but the same fire purifies our lives! If something the enemy has done or is doing in your life needs to be destroyed, you need to call down the fire of God. The fire of God is also a changing agent in the lives of His people. Once the fire of God ignites on the inside of you or gets on you, the only thing you can do is change. If someone has some bad habits that need to change, you can send the fire of God to burn away what doesn't belong in their life. The fire of God brings about change. God's love is a burning fire, and His love changes hearts. God's love changes minds. The fire of God is nothing to play with because it can actually take people out. God used His fire to entirely destroy Sodom and Gomorrah because of all of their sinful practices. God destroyed the entire earth with water the first time, and He said He would never destroy earth with water again (Genesis 9:11). However, He did say fire would be used in His judgment the next time (2 Peter 3:10). The enemy is hoping that you never learn about how God's fire works because it will be another weapon you can use in warfare. To effectively use a spiritual weapon on a consistent basis, you must truly know its function and how to use it. This is why God is equipping us so we will have no excuses. When you send the fire of God, it blows up demonic camps set up in and around your life. It forces them to move elsewhere or try to rebuild! You want to make them uncomfortable. You want demons to wish they had left you alone by the time you finish fighting them in spiritual warfare. You should want to be so good in spiritual warfare that when demons plan a new attack, they'll remember what you did the last time.

You have a responsibility in spiritual warfare to also help your brothers and sisters in Christ. If you see demons are attacking someone in your territory, it's your responsibility as a ruler in God's government to reestablish order. Every person may not be your assignment, but your territory is. We need all our other warriors in God's army to stay in position, too. God is training you to effectively fight in spiritual warfare so you can also train others. We must keep our weapons sharp as well. Many of our spiritual weapons serve defensive and offensive purposes, but we must put the weapons to work for ourselves. Spiritual weapons will definitely work for you against the enemy in spiritual warfare, but you must put them to work. This is a key takeaway in understanding spiritual warfare. You must employ the weapons in your life. The spiritual weapons God gave you to use in warfare are only as effective as your willingness to work them. The weapons are flawless!

Of course, Satan tries to duplicate everything God creates. So, demons can use their fire as well to try to consume us, destroy us, or to burn up things in our life. That's why we must use our weapons against them because our weapons are far more powerful. The fire of God will destroy your obstacles, and God will send an angel to rescue you out of the damage it will leave behind. God sent an angel to rescue Lot and his family before the destruction of Sodom and Gomorrah. The fire of God leaves debris behind, and it's a reminder to demons that God is working in your life on your behalf. When you think of the fire of God in warfare, your first thought should be destruction because that's exactly what it will bring.

Hebrews 12:28-29: *Therefore, since we are receiving a kingdom which cannot be shaken, let us have grace, by which we may serve God acceptably with reverence and godly fear. For our God is a consuming fire.*

When we receive Jesus Christ in our lives, we also receive the kingdom of God. We become a part of God's kingdom. When you receive Christ, you get responsibility in God's kingdom and power and authority to function in God's kingdom. Not only that, but God's kingdom is unshakeable. If you are royalty in God's kingdom and God's kingdom is unshakeable, that makes you unshakeable because you're in Christ. We also have grace from God, and we should serve Him and honor Him. You should serve God because He is on the winning side! God is a consuming fire, and there is no power that has ever or will ever be greater. Verse 29 is taken from Deuteronomy 4:24. God is a consuming fire. Yes, He is love and He is forgiving, but He is the same consuming fire that He was under the old covenant, even under the new covenant. He still despises sin and evil. He is still a jealous God in that He doesn't want us to worship anyone or anything but Him. God's fire destroys the works of sin, and you ought to use it when the enemy won't get off your back. This passage is a reminder that God does not play in the face of evil. He is to be taken very seriously. It's your job to remind the enemy that God is a consuming fire, and you remind them by sending His fire their way!

Deuteronomy 32:22-23: *"'For a fire is kindled in My anger,*
And shall burn to the lowest hell;
It shall consume the earth with her increase,
And set on fire the foundations of the mountains.

'I will heap disasters on them;
I will spend My arrows on them.'"

This passage speaks of the destruction God would send to Israel because of their faithlessness, continual sin and disobedience to God, and worshipping idols. Because of this, God was going to send destruction to Judea. This passage is very clear. God's fire is kindled in His anger. When you send the fire of God, you send God's anger against the enemy because God detests evil. Not only is it God's anger, but it is also God's judgment. God's fire is often connected with judgment. When you release God's fire from heaven against the enemy, it sends God's judgment against them for what they've done to you.

You see how destructive God's fire is from this passage. He said that His fire would burn to the lowest hell, consume the earth's increase (crops), and burn the foundations of the mountains. God's fire would not only destroy the vegetation in the land, but it would also go beyond that and destroy the root and the foundations, leaving no place for it to grow back. God's fire destroys a demonic operation set up in your life to the point they have to start all over from scratch. When you send the fire of God, it doesn't just destroy the surface of a thing, but it destroys the root of what the enemy sent in your life! The fire of God does not deal with the symptoms, but it goes straight for the root and destroys it.
You must understand the magnitude of sending the fire of God. It is no joke. When you call down the fire of God to earth, it brings an end to a thing, period! The enemy is afraid of the fire of God because it not only destroys their works, but it also brings judgment with it. So, that's a double problem. It burns going in and coming out. When you ask God to send the fire of God from heaven, that fire will not stop until it destroys the target. You see in this passage that after God sent the fire, He would also send arrows. The fire of God is truly a lethal missile. Calling for the fire of God to be sent from heaven is a loud and clear response to the enemy of "I'm going to tell my daddy on you!" Not only that, but

we get to use God's fire for ourselves. We can see an example in Luke.

Luke 9:53-56: *But they did not receive Him, because His face was set for the journey to Jerusalem. And when His disciples James and John saw this, they said, "Lord, do You want us to command fire to come down from heaven and consume them, just as Elijah did?" But He turned and rebuked them, and said, "You do not know what manner of spirit you are of. For the Son of Man did not come to destroy men's lives but to save them." And they went to another village.*

This is more proof that we have the ability to call down fire from heaven to consume the enemy and all works of darkness. James and John were upset that the people in a particular Samaritan village did not receive Jesus. So, they asked Jesus if He wanted them to command fire to come down from heaven and consume the people. For starters, they didn't pause for one moment to ask Jesus if they had the ability to do that. They knew they had the ability, but they asked Jesus if He wanted them to make the call and send the fire. You must know that you have the ability to do all God said you can do. It's just a matter of actually accepting it and doing it.

This was a teaching moment. While they were ready to send the anger and judgment of God against a people similar to how Elijah did, they were actually going about it the wrong way and would not have gotten the results anyway. Jesus let them know that He didn't come to destroy people but to save them. In other words, He was saying that a seed was sown in the lives of these people, and it was still possible that they might become saved later. Not only that, but in Elijah's case, those people were trying to destroy him and the works of God. These particular Samaritans were not hospitable at this time because it appeared Jesus was going to Jerusalem. The Jews and Samaritans debated over where the best place was to worship. The Jews felt it was Jerusalem, and Samaritans felt it should be at Mount Gerizim. So, since it appeared Jesus was going to Jerusalem instead, they didn't receive him. Perhaps they would have received Him if He chose to worship there. The problem was not the rejection, but the Samaritans had not come into the truth. They still had a chance to come to the knowledge of the truth of God through Christ. They could still be evangelized. So, taking them out by fire was not the right call.

James's and John's spirits were not right in them in wanting to do this because it was not based on a true zeal for God and righteous indignation against the enemy, but it was more on their own self-righteous mind-set. It was like saying, "Who do those Samaritans think they are to not receive us?" God rebuked them because they were being susceptible to a religious spirit. That was clearly not from God. Thus, Jesus rebuked them. We must be careful to not want to send God's judgment just because we're angry about something that offended our flesh. The fire of God is not to be used for selfish reasons, but it must be used for godly reasons and that's to oppose evil works of the enemy. That's the only way it will be authorized for our use anyway.

At this point, the Samaritans were not really guilty of anything except ignorance and poor hospitality. Though it was definitely wrong, they didn't need God's wrath just yet; they needed the love of God that could have been demonstrated through James and John had they not had a flesh moment. So, as Jesus had already told the disciples earlier in Luke 9:5, if people didn't receive them in a home, they were to wipe the dust off their feet as a testimony against that house and go to another home that would receive them. That's just what He did here. The love of God is always sent first to give people a chance before the judgment of God comes. Show God's love. We're not in a flesh war, but it's spiritual. It's your job to show God's love to people and send His wrath to demons. God said that vengeance belongs to Him. He will handle those who mistreat you, but it's your job to use the weapons He gave you to handle Satan's workers.

2 Chronicles 7:1-3: *When Solomon had finished praying, fire came down from heaven and consumed the burnt offering and the*

sacrifices; and the glory of the LORD filled the temple. And the priests could not enter the house of the LORD, because the glory of the LORD had filled the LORD's house. When all the children of Israel saw how the fire came down, and the glory of the LORD on the temple, they bowed their faces to the ground on the pavement, and worshiped and praised the LORD, saying:
"For He is good,
For His mercy endures forever."

Solomon ruled as king after his father David died, and Solomon built a temple for God. He dedicated the temple unto God. He made sacrifices unto God as an offering. During this time, they had to use animals as a sacrifice or offerings to God for sin, sacrifices of thanksgiving, sacrifices of devotion to God, etc. We know that Jesus came in the New Testament, and He was the ultimate sacrifice for us. So, when we accept Christ, we no longer belong to ourselves. It's a blessing that you belong to God and not yourself because God takes care of you far better than you could ever take care of yourself. Our body belongs to God because He created it from the dust of the earth so that our spirit could have a vehicle to live in on earth legally.

So, the fire no longer consumes burnt offerings of animals, but it can consume you and me. How so? Romans 12:1 tells us to present our bodies as a living sacrifice. Notice that the fire came after prayer. This again shows that prayer can literally send fire down from heaven to wipe out the enemy or to ignite us. Prayer is vital because the glory of God showing up can always be linked back to a prayer of faith. As a living sacrifice, we are crucifying our flesh. We are putting down our will and picking up God's will! You cannot get the fullness of God's glory in your life without literally giving up your life and picking up Christ, who is your life. Christ is literally our life. He wants to continue His work through us. We are a continuation of Christ in the earth.

So, we see that the glory of the Lord entered the temple, and it was so powerful, everyone stopped what they were doing. The priests could not even enter back into the temple because God's glory had filled it. God Himself showed up. It was the manifested presence of God. All the people could do was bow down and worship God. God's glory is going to increase in your life, and the more it increases, the more you will see things drastically change everywhere you go. We see how powerful the glory of God is. Flesh can do nothing in God's presence except get out of the way, and the Holy Spirit completely takes over and we can worship God fully. It's not a flesh experience or a soul experience; it is a spirit experience. There are no words that can describe the glory of God showing up in any place. It is not always in a physical church, but it can show up in our lives. The glory of God that is coming upon your life will be a loud statement to the world that God still reigns and that He reigns in you. Not only does He reign in you, but His glory can rest upon you! As His glory rests on you, you will be that much more dangerous to the enemy in warfare.

2 Thessalonians 1:4-9 (emphasis mine): *So that we ourselves boast of you among the churches of God for your patience and faith in all your persecutions and tribulations that you endure, which is manifest evidence of the righteous judgment of God, that you may be counted worthy of the kingdom of God, for which you also suffer; since it is a righteous thing with God to repay with tribulation those who trouble you, and to give you who are troubled rest with us when the Lord Jesus is revealed from heaven with His mighty angels, **in flaming fire taking vengeance on those who do not know God, and on those who do not obey the gospel of our Lord Jesus Christ.** These shall be punished with everlasting destruction from the presence of the Lord and from the glory of His power.*

Apostle Paul was commending those who walked in faith in the midst of persecution and tribulation. They were suffering because of their stand for the kingdom of God. The enemy was attacking them for it, but Paul assured them that God would repay those who persecuted them. He also said that God would give the faithful rest. He was talking about after death. However, it also applies while on earth. They saw many victories on earth through the many lives that were saved under their ministry.

God will vindicate you. Sometimes God sends His fire without anyone calling for it, and if that happens, it's so much worse because He sends it only after many warnings! This passage outlines when God will take it upon Himself to bring the vengeance without us calling for the fire. We see the reference to the flaming fire in verse 8. It is a flaming fire of vengeance. The fire of God brings God's vengeance to disobedience and all those working for Satan's kingdom. They are not only in trouble now, but they will be in trouble eternally. The fire of God brings destruction to the enemy now, and it's the same fire that will entirely destroy Satan and all his kingdom in the end. Evil will be punished forever in the final judgment. There's no greater punishment than being banished from the presence of the Lord forever! Demons have already earned it. Their final judgment will come, but in the meantime, you must continue on with the fight and use your spiritual weapons. You are an agent of fire because you have access to call down the fire of God from heaven at any time to defeat the enemy.

Chapter 14: Calling Forth the Four Winds

When certain things are going on in your life, you need the winds of God from heaven to blow upon you. It is an effective warfare weapon and an effective tool for your daily life. You will be much more effective in fighting against the enemy when you understand that you have a limitless supply of weapons you can use. The four winds of heaven are a necessity in the lives of warriors for Christ. The four winds represent the four corners of the earth. There is a North Wind, South Wind, East Wind, and West Wind. Each wind has a specific function. You need the four winds of heaven to blow in your life so you can shut the works of the enemy down in your life. The four winds of heaven do work you can't do yourself. So, it's your job as royalty in God's kingdom to tell the winds to blow! One common denominator in spiritual warfare is your role to speak to your weapons. You were sent on earth to rule, and it's your job to tell the weapons God gave you for battle what you need them to do. When you gain an understanding of how to call forth the four winds of heaven, you will be able to deploy yet another weapon against the enemy. The enemy attacks from all directions, but you can call forth the wind of heaven that brings destruction to blow against the enemy. You must remember that you have access to all of heaven's resources, and you can ask for what you need on earth to be sent from heaven!

Attacks will come, but you are equipped. God doesn't always need to send help because sometimes you already have help, and you need to use what He gave you. God takes it personally when the enemy attacks you because you're doing God's business. So, He gave you more ammo than you need to ensure victory. The four winds are more ammo that you can use in spiritual warfare. Some are offensive, and others are defensive. So, don't grow weary. Don't faint now because you were not born to lose. God will restore you in battle when you need strength because you're fighting the battle in His name, and His name only knows victory. You must employ the four winds of heaven in your life. They will blow and accomplish what they were sent to do. The four winds impact various aspects of life. Sometimes the enemy will try to use winds or storms to blow against you, but you can counterattack by knowing how the four winds of heaven operate. The enemy can send storms in our lives, but you can also send storms in the lives of the enemy. Open your mouth and tell the winds to blow! We have sat back for far too long allowing the enemy to play in our lives or on our territory. It's time to make demons pay for causing havoc in certain areas of your life for so long. Send a destructive wind from heaven against them. The enemy sent some winds in your life to blow away what God said you can have. It's time to blow back and command it to be returned!

Each of the four winds of heaven serve a function that you can deploy in your life. We will discuss the role of each.

1.) East Wind   2.) West Wind   3.) North Wind

4.) South Wind

Daniel 7:1-2 (emphasis mine): *In the first year of Belshazzar king of Babylon, Daniel had a dream and visions of his head while on his bed. Then he wrote down the dream, telling the main facts. Daniel spoke, saying, "I saw in my vision by night, and behold, **the four winds of heaven were stirring up the Great Sea."***

Daniel had a prophetic vision of something that was going to happen among some of the nations during that time. However, we see the four winds of heaven mentioned. Wind is also one symbol of the Holy Spirit.

East Wind

The East Wind of heaven brings destruction. It destroys the works of the enemy and sin. Pray to God to send an East Wind against the enemy. The East Wind wrecks things. It causes things to dry up and brings famine. If you need something to dry up in your life, you can send for the East Wind of heaven to blow to dry it up. The East Wind of heaven brings judgment against the enemy. To send God's judgment against demons, call forth the East Wind to blow.

184

The East Wind also brings forth the demonstration of the power of God. You will often see miracles, signs, and wonders as the East Wind of heaven blows. If you need a miracle in your life or the life of another, you can call forth the East Wind of heaven to blow!

Exodus 10:12-14: *Then the LORD said to Moses, "Stretch out your hand over the land of Egypt for the locusts, that they may come upon the land of Egypt, and eat every herb of the land—all that the hail has left." So Moses stretched out his rod over the land of Egypt, and the LORD brought an east wind on the land all that day and all that night. When it was morning, the east wind brought the locusts. And the locusts went up over all the land of Egypt and rested on all the territory of Egypt. They were very severe; previously there had been no such locusts as they, nor shall there be such after them.*

Moses was obeying the instructions of the Lord. God was bringing judgment against Pharaoh and all of Egypt for not letting the children of Israel go free from bondage. This was the eighth plague God sent against Egypt. Your obedience to God will always give you favor with the hand of God. We see that it not only brought destruction, but it also brought forth judgment. The enemy may try to hold you in bondage, but you can send the East Wind of heaven to blow to bring God's judgment against them. The locusts destroyed the crops. In other words, they brought a famine. You can have the East Wind of heaven blow to bring a famine to the enemy's camp. What came with the East Wind was so severe that no locust of that type had ever been on the land, nor will there ever be again. You are so special to God that there are some things that God will do in your life that He has never done before in your life! We see how destructive the East Wind was. When you call forth the East Wind from heaven, it will send a plague upon the enemy's camp.

Exodus 14:21-22 (emphasis mine): *Then Moses stretched out his hand over the sea; **and the LORD caused the sea to go back by a strong east wind all that night, and made the sea into dry land,***

and the waters were divided. So the children of Israel went into the midst of the sea on the dry ground, and the waters were a wall to them on their right hand and on their left.

In this passage, God was rescuing the children of Israel from the hands of the enemy, Pharaoh and Egypt. We see that this was a miracle. Moses stretched forth his hand and God sent the east wind to divide the sea so that the children of Israel could walk on dry ground. When you call forth the East Wind of heaven to blow in your life, it will cause what's blocking you from moving forward to be removed. We see that they were able to walk on dry ground. If the enemy sends a flood in your life, you can call for the East Wind of heaven to clear a path for you to walk on solid ground. Moses demonstrated the power of God as he stretched forth his hand over the sea. It was truly a miracle. There is truly miracle-working power living in you, and all you need to do is tap into it and use it for the glory of God. Just as Moses demonstrated the power of God, we are expected to demonstrate the power of God. There may be things in your life that you seem to be drowning in, but you can call forth the East Wind of heaven to blow the waters back. Notice that the wind continued to blow until the task was completed. When you call for the winds of heaven to blow in your life, they will blow until you get to the place you need to get to. They are persistent, so we should be persistent.

West Wind

The West Wind of heaven brings deliverance! If you or someone you know needs deliverance out of a tough situation, you can call forth the West Wind of heaven to blow.

Exodus 10:16-19: *Then Pharaoh called for Moses and Aaron in haste, and said, "I have sinned against the LORD your God and against you. Now therefore, please forgive my sin only this once, and entreat the LORD your God, that He may take away from me this death only." So he went out from Pharaoh and entreated the LORD. And the LORD turned a very strong west wind, which took* *the locusts away and blew them into the Red Sea. There remained not one locust in all the territory of Egypt.*

The East Wind had done so much destruction (Exodus 10:13-14) that Pharaoh was repentant. He was afraid and begged for Moses and Aaron to pray to God that the plague would be lifted. It was so bad, Pharaoh called it a death! Pharaoh wanted deliverance from the destruction of the East Wind of heaven. If the enemy caused destruction in your life, you can call forth the West Wind of heaven to blow it away. We see how Moses, under the influence of God, used one wind to bring the locusts that caused destruction (East Wind) and used another wind to take the destruction away (West Wind).

Notice that Pharaoh called for Moses and Aaron in haste. That means it was an urgent matter. You can cause so much destruction in the enemy's camp that they will beg you to take it away. We also see here that the West Wind was very strong. It had to be strong enough to blow the locusts that covered the entire land away and blow them into the Red Sea. The West Wind of heaven is powerful enough to blow any obstacle—no matter how big it may seem—out of your life. Parts of your life may seem to be in shambles, but there is nothing that can be so shattered that God cannot fix it.

North Wind

The North Wind of heaven brings with it the presence of God. If you need the manifested presence of God in your life, send for the North Wind of heaven to blow. It truly changes things. The North Wind brings forth rain in your life if you're in a dry place or if things just seem dried up. The North Wind of heaven also brings shaking, conviction, stirring, and rebuking. It can push us when we want to quit. It puts things in order. If your life seems to be in disorder, send forth the North Wind of heaven to blow to restore order. Your job, community, family, etc., may need a shaking or stirring to get things moving again or to wake them up. If things are at a standstill and nothing seems to be moving in your life, call forth the North Wind of heaven to blow to stir things up.

Ezekiel 1:4: *Then I looked, and behold, a whirlwind was coming out of the north, a great cloud with raging fire engulfing itself; and brightness was all around it and radiating out of its midst like the color of amber, out of the midst of the fire.*

This chapter gives an account of Ezekiel's vision of God and His throne. We see that he saw a whirlwind coming out of the north. The North Wind represents God's presence. We also see the cloud that often represented God's presence. He used the cloud to guide the Israelites out of Egypt. This same cloud with fire can consume you and can also turn to judgment against the enemy. It's an honor and a privilege for God to manifest His presence in our lives. This was a great opportunity for Ezekiel. God will give you greater visions of what's to come in your life if you consistently make time for Him.

Song of Solomon 4:16: *Awake, O north wind,*
And come, O south!
Blow upon my garden,
That its spices may flow out.
Let my beloved come to his garden
And eat its pleasant fruits.

This book, also called Song of Songs, is a love story of the love a husband and wife have for one another. Some of it can also be seen as symbolic of the love between Christ and the Church. However, it's definitely a love story. We see that this verse speaks of the North Wind to be awakened or to arise. The North Wind was being told to come to bring the cool air and to purge things. The South Wind came to bring warmth and comfort. The garden is also symbolic of us. We need the North and South Winds to blow upon us that we may grow in God. These winds were called forth to bring the wonderful aroma and perfumes of the garden.

We need the chilly wind of the North Wind of heaven to blow in our lives to prune us so we can produce good fruit. This was the longing and desire of the woman for her husband to enjoy all that came with her and for her to enjoy all that came with him. We need the North Wind of heaven to blow in our lives to stir up the love of God in us that it may be shown in the world through our lives. If you need love to be kindled in your life, send forth the North and South Winds of heaven to blow in your life. They produce a sweet aroma in the spirit realm as they blow upon your life. You want these winds to blow upon you and your future or current spouse. It is a signal in the spirit for God-ordained lovers. Love is attached to the North Wind of heaven because it comes with God's presence. God is love, and in any type of God-ordained relationship, whether intimate or familial, it takes God's love in us to love them and vice versa. In order for God's love to shine forth through you, you must remain in position for God to use you.

Proverbs 25:23: *The north wind brings forth rain,*
And a backbiting tongue an angry countenance.

We see here that the North Wind of heaven brings forth rain. Some versions may say "drives away," but the more accurate translation is "brings forth rain." It's showing that just as the North Wind brings forth rain, a backbiting or slandering tongue brings forth anger. If something is not growing in your life, you can send forth the North Wind to water the seed. Sometimes we have been fighting for so long until we get weary along the way. If you're tired from the battle, send forth the North Wind of heaven to blow to refresh you. Sometimes we need that extra boost to keep going. It may feel like you're losing, but keep sending forth the winds to blow in your life and they will do their job. You will win!
This passage also shows the power of your words. Words are seeds, and you don't want your words to produce anger in your life or anger in another's life if it is not based in truth or love. A slandering tongue is not rooted in love or truth. Send forth the North Wind of heaven to blow to water the good seeds in your life and shake up and uproot the bad seeds sown.

South Wind

The South Wind of heaven brings provision and prosperity. If you're in need of provision in your life, send forth the South Wind to blow in your life. The South Wind also brings joy, peace, and comfort. If you need joy, you can call forth the South Wind of heaven to blow in your life to bring joy and peace.

Psalm 78:26-29: *He caused an east wind to blow in the heavens;*
And by His power He brought in the south wind.
He also rained meat on them like the dust,
Feathered fowl like the sand of the seas;
And He let them fall in the midst of their camp,
All around their dwellings.
So they ate and were well filled,
For He gave them their own desire.

Here we see how the South Wind of heaven brought down food or provision. This account is talking about how God fed the children of Israel in the wilderness with quail after their constant complaining and rebellion. The South Wind brought the provision, but the East Wind brought the destruction and judgment upon them for their disobedience. God didn't take away the provision, but they weren't really able to enjoy it to the fullest because of the judgment against them. You've come too far and gone through too much to get the blessing you prayed for; it would be a shame to not be able to enjoy it.

God wants you to have peace and prosperity. Don't abort what God is birthing out of you. Keep pushing! The provision brought some peace in their lives because it was what they needed since they were in the wilderness. You may be in a wilderness experience, but call forth the South Wind of heaven to blow so that it will bring God's peace. God sent so much meat down to the people that it rained down like dust. God is the God of more than enough. If you're lacking in finances, send forth the South Wind to blow in your life to bring prosperity. The Israelites had no reason to panic or to rebel against God because God always made a way for them. You have no reason to get impatient with God because God has always and will always make a way for you. Things may be uncomfortable right now, but the South Wind of heaven blowing in your life will bring comfort with it!

Calling forth the four winds in your life and during spiritual warfare is an effective tool, and the more you get used to using it, the more weapons you will have at your fingertips at any given moment.

Chapter 15: Fight for Your Family: Warfare Over Your Bloodline

My wife Donna and I can speak from experience: when dealing with deliverance and spiritual warfare, the most common point for demons to enter and or attack is through the bloodline. That's usually the first way they gain legal access to an individual. We understand how powerful blood covenants are because there is life in the blood. When the enemy knows they don't have legal access to you, they will try to gain legal entry through sin in your family bloodline. This is why you can't afford not to pray for your bloodline. There are some battles you will face that have nothing to do with you, but they have to do with what's attached to your bloodline. You are a defender of your bloodline, and if any demon is causing hell in your family, you are qualified to send it back to hell! The problem could have been in your bloodline for centuries, but it can stop with you.

The family unit is so important. Your family is what you were born into, but there are some things that have haunted your bloodline that you were born to change. For some, family is what you were adopted into. However, it does not change what is in your bloodline or what's on the bloodline you were adopted into. Your bloodline was here before you were born. You may have been born into a curse on your bloodline, but you can reverse the curse. You could very well be the interruption in your bloodline. You are not in your family by accident. God looked at your family before you were born and saw the turmoil. He saw what the enemy was doing. So, He sent you from heaven to be born into your family or adopted into your family because He had to send a generational curse breaker to break the curses off your family line. It's called a generational curse for a reason. A generational curse is a systematic attack of the enemy on families by creating vicious cycles in an attempt to keep an entire family in bondage and strip them of purpose and identity, with the end goal of eventually making the family extinct! You can ensure that the family legacy will go on and that the curse is broken. You've heard about this epidemic and attack on the family unit. That was planned by the enemy.

The church has spent so much time dealing with attacks on the church and issues in the church that sometimes the family unit goes unnoticed. It's not necessarily intentional, but it's something that needs to be discussed. There are many moving forward in ministry in the church, but ministry at home is not moving forward. There must be balance. You must fight for and cover family. If there's disorder in your bloodline, the enemy knows they can legally attack. You must fight and pray to restore order to your bloodline. The more it is ignored, the greater the issue can become in the long haul. If issues are not addressed in your generation, you will pass them on to the next generation in your bloodline to have to deal with. There are some things in your bloodline that were supposed to be dealt with, but they were not, so now you must face them and conquer them. If you notice a demonic pattern that has impacted numerous members in your family, it's your responsibility to war and pray to break it. It's not a time to retreat because even if you personally avoid it, it will continue to flow through your bloodline and reach another generation if you don't put a stop to it. The enemy wants you to fight with your family because they know that it also keeps you away from generational blessings. God is a generational God. He blesses individually, but He also blesses generationally. Some blessings are tied directly to your bloodline. We are a part of the body of Christ. We are many members but part of one body. That is generational. That is family. Scripture talks about us being brothers and sisters in Christ, and that is family. God loves families, and that's why He created them! Satan hates family because he cannot have family. He has workers but not true family. The enemy also wants war in your family because they know how powerful a unified bloodline is. Some things can happen quickly when you and family pray for them together. This goes back to generational blessings. That's one reason Satan hates family. Demons try to divide family because they know how much damage a unified family will do to their camp. You may think your family is messed up, but God sent you on earth through that bloodline because you're the one to put a stop to the mess. A change in you will impact future and current generations.

Your bloodline is so important because it was here before you were born and can go on after you leave earth. Your legacy is in your bloodline. What you do matters because it is a reflection of your bloodline. The enemy wants to kill your entire bloodline to stop the family name from moving forward, but you can stop the enemy. Your family is too important to God for you to say you don't care anymore. If He cares, you must care. Don't let the devil have your family. The enemy knows how important your family is, and that's why they are relentless in trying to attack. Don't be discouraged by what's going on in your family; be encouraged that you're doing something about it every time you pray. The enemy hates that you're a part of your bloodline because you're the reason the seeds they sowed don't take root like they used to. You must know that you matter, and your family is depending on you. If you do your part, what has attacked generations before in your bloodline will no longer be able to attack another generation. At minimum, you will have definitely weakened the assault of the enemy on your family. They will know they can't come for your family the way they did before without strong opposition from you.

God truly does supply all of our needs, and He gave us family because family was something we needed. Just because one may feel like they don't need family for physical things or for things they need in day-to-day life, family will still be needed in one way or another, or God would have had no need to create family. God gave you family because it was never His intent for you to be born into the world alone. Even Jesus had to be born into a family. God could have chosen to send Jesus to earth in many ways, but God chose to have Him to be born into a family because family matters to God. I understand that certain things may have happened along the way because the enemy tried to ruin the family. The enemy tries to cause problems in your family because there are generational blessings every family is entitled to that they want to stop. This is why you cannot afford to have division in the family.

The family you were born into, adopted into, or who helped raise you is still family. Whenever one accepts Jesus Christ, we're adopted into the family of God. This again shows how important family is to God. The family unit on one accord is the most powerful institution, along with the church, on the planet. That's why the enemy tries to target both! The enemy knows how powerful family is. Every member in your family plays a pivotal role, and you must carry out your role to ensure that the family unit stays intact. A family divided allows demons to legally steal what rightfully belongs to you. Do your part to bring peace to your family! You have need for your family because God has need for your family to do their part on earth. I do understand that wisdom is needed. Obviously, you can't allow family members to take advantage of you or abuse you. There are some family members that you have to deal with from a distance, but that doesn't stop you from praying for your family.

Let's go a bit deeper as we examine some examples in Scripture.

Judges 2:7-12: *So the people served the LORD all the days of Joshua, and all the days of the elders who outlived Joshua, who had seen all the great works of the LORD which He had done for Israel. Now Joshua the son of Nun, the servant of the LORD, died when he was one hundred and ten years old. And they buried him within the border of his inheritance at Timnath Heres, in the mountains of Ephraim, on the north side of Mount Gaash. When all that generation had been gathered to their fathers, another generation arose after them who did not know the LORD nor the work which He had done for Israel.*

Then the children of Israel did evil in the sight of the LORD, and served the Baals; and they forsook the LORD God of their fathers, who had brought them out of the land of Egypt; and they followed other gods from among the gods of the people who were all around them, and they bowed down to them; and they provoked the LORD to anger.

We see here that after Joshua died and his entire generation had died, there was another generation that followed false gods and abandoned God. We know that Joshua and many in his generation passed the baton, but somewhere along the way, it was dropped by someone for an entire generation to miss it. One generation was so blessed, and then we see another generation that was cursed. You can't afford to play around with the responsibility God gave you. What you do will hold a lot of weight for the generations after you! We have a responsibility to keep moving forward in God and pass our knowledge and information on to others who will eventually take our place and continue the family legacy. It's our duty to give them a head start. Whatever curse the enemy had on your family won't get past you. It ends with you as you face it head on and destroy it in Jesus's name. You will be prosperous and successful and whoever replaces you one day will keep the legacy going. You may have many decades left, but every day counts. The decisions you make today are generational decisions because they will impact generations to come in your family. Do it God's way! Perhaps you were busy making it about you, when in all actuality it's much larger than just you. God trusted you with the assignment. If you abort it, it will mean someone else will have to start over rather than starting where you left off. If you ignore what the enemy has tried to do to your family, you are missing it. God showed you so you can kick those demons out.

God expects every family to establish His kingdom on earth and to leave a legacy on the earth. What is your family legacy? How will your family impact this earth? These are questions you must start thinking about, and then do your part. Every family has had challenges along the way, but every family has the necessary tools to overcome every challenge. Your family should have a blueprint that those born into your family generations from now will be able to follow to keep the legacy alive. No one should have to start over. Again, the baton should be passed on from each generation in your family, not dropped for the next generation to have to try to figure out. Prayer should be a part of that legacy. Your family generation should conquer the mountains of the enemy in such a way that no generation will have to face that mountain again. That can only be accomplished when everyone does their part. Yes, sometimes, you may be the one carrying more of the load. You may feel like you're carrying more of the weight of the family on your shoulders, but that's because God trusts you to preserve the family. However, you are never in it by yourself. The direction of the legacy of your family may be held together now because of your prayers and efforts. Don't give up because family needs you! There may be some who seem like they're too far gone, but don't stop praying for them. There may be some who treat you a certain way, but don't stop showing the love of Christ. The role God gave you in your family is too important for you to fall into the enemy's trap and step outside of your godly character. You're never in a fight against your family, but you're in a fight for your family. You must let demons know they can't have your family! The enemy tries to bring confusion, disorder, sickness, etc., to attack family. God will restore order to your family, and it begins with you getting and staying in order with God. You may not talk to all of your family every day, and there may be some you have not talked to in a very long time. However, you should pray for them every day because there's nothing like family praying for family. The enemy will try to sow seeds to cause miscommunication and have one family member being upset over something that another knows nothing about. There are some who carry around anger, resentment, etc., for reasons they never shared. You can't afford to be silent in your family because God gave you something to say. If you don't talk to family, it's difficult to know what family really needs. You need family, and family needs you. The needs may be different, but they are needs nonetheless.

Your family matters, and that's why God gave you one. Every family has a collective purpose. Do your part to help ensure your family fulfills their God-given purpose in the earth. Your family is a threat to Satan's kingdom! That's why he tries to send curses to put your family in bondage, but you can break them. There are some things that have been plaguing your family for centuries, and nothing has been done about them. Everyone has just been coping and dealing with them personally when they were meant to be dealt with corporately as a family. Demonic curses are meant to be hidden, but God gave you the power and authority and all of heaven's defense team to expose them and destroy them! The enemy may have gained legal access in the spirit to curse your family, but every curse is illegal and you are the curse breaker. It must matter to you what is going on in your family outside of your own home because it impacts you. It impacts the legacy of your family. Your family is precious to God! You could be the very person God raised up to change the path the enemy tried to put your entire family on.

Ungodly patterns that you see impacting multiple members in your family are byproducts of a generational curse. It was an assault on your bloodline by the enemy, and you must see it as such. The enemy is always trying to attack your family, and it's your duty to cover your family in prayer and to fight back.
The easiest counterattack when the enemy attacks your family is for family to be united. It confuses the enemy on where and who to attack. The enemy is always looking for an opening or a weakness to attack. When your family is united, the enemy doesn't have a clear path to attack because on every side they see a big problem. It doesn't mean they won't still attempt to attack, but we know it won't prosper. There are some attacks of sickness that you have seen in your family. Some attacks were on marriages, just about everyone in the family being single mothers, majority of men being noncommittal in relationships, addictions, generational poverty, poverty mind-set, etc. The list goes on and on. It's all a byproduct of a generational curse.

You must fight back. Don't allow demons to bully you. Don't allow demons to bully your family any longer. You are the generational curse breaker, and it's your time to take your place. Don't shy away. Don't shrink back and run from the curse. Don't just say you're just going to live your life because what certain family members are going through is not your problem. Every time the enemy attacks you, it's a problem to God. So, every time the enemy attacks your family, it should be a problem to you. A generational curse on your family is not in God's will! Therefore, He's looking for some curse breakers, and your name came up.

Don't be afraid. You are coming into the greatest season of your life, and God can trust you with responsibility. You are the DNA of God, and God doesn't raise up cowards. He raises warriors to defend His territory and to push His holy agenda.

In order to break a generational curse, you must first know that one exists. Outside of praying for the Holy Spirit to reveal it to you, you can just look at patterns that are ungodly cycles. If you see it impacting multiple family members, it's a curse. For every curse the enemy tries to put on your family, it's a guarantee that God always births curse breakers in the family. The Holy Spirit has opened your eyes to see more because you have been given more responsibility. When God gives you more responsibility, it doesn't make you better than another; it makes you more responsible for what happens. It doesn't mean it's your fault when certain things happen in your family. It means that you have greater responsibility to do something about it, and it begins and ends in the spirit. Just give God a yes to let Him work through you!
The family unit has been under a major attack for some time. It has created a gradual decline of the family unit. Many home dynamics have changed. However, there is a mass renewal of the family that is coming in this great revival, and you get to be a part of it. Don't be sad about the attacks the enemy has waged against your family. Get mad and declare war in the spirit! Fight for your family.
This is another reminder about increasing your prayer life. It is not an option. It is a mandate! If you really understood the difference persistent prayer makes, you would realize that you can't afford not to pray. Prayer to God is a language Satan hates. Your prayers add to your heavenly bank account, giving you more to withdraw. Prayer can bring anything from heaven to earth. Your family is depending on your prayers. There are some prayers that you prayed that are still holding some family members up right now. This is not a time to be silent. This is a time to speak up. This is not a time to be laid back. This is a time for war. Your family is in a war against the enemy, and you must stay on your post and fight.

Genesis 37:1-4: *Now Jacob dwelt in the land where his father was a stranger, in the land of Canaan. This is the history of Jacob.*

Joseph, being seventeen years old, was feeding the flock with his brothers. And the lad was with the sons of Bilhah and the sons of Zilpah, his father's wives; and Joseph brought a bad report of them to his father. Now Israel loved Joseph more than all his children, because he was the son of his old age. Also he made him a tunic of many colors. But when his brothers saw that their father loved him more than all his brothers, they hated him and could not speak peaceably to him.

We know that Joseph was later sold into slavery because of his brothers' jealousy toward him. However, his brothers' jealousy came about because of their father Jacob. It makes no sense for a family member to be jealous of another when they're part of the same bloodline and can share in the same blessings. Jacob showed favoritism, and it was obvious he loved Joseph more than his other sons because he had Joseph when he was older. However, this was generational because Jacob went through a similar thing with his brother, Esau. Jacob knew what it felt like to not be the favorite, but instead of breaking the cycle, he fell into the same cycle and showed favoritism toward Joseph. He was now guilty of the same thing he had gone through. That's similar to someone who was neglected as a child and in turn neglects their own children. Generational curses can only continue when they're allowed to operate in your family. You have the power to shut down that demonic operation.

A generation before Joseph was Jacob and Esau. Esau was the oldest, and their father, Isaac, favored Esau. Esau lost his birthright to Jacob, who was the youngest. There was a family feud with Jacob and Esau. Esau hated Jacob when he found out Jacob got their father's blessing that belonged to him. A family feud that is not properly dealt with will leave a door wide open for the enemy to walk in. Don't let disagreements with a family member continue. Step up and make peace because you represent God and the family name. With help of their mother, Jacob tricked his father, who had become blind in his old age. Jacob made Isaac believe that he was Esau. This spirit of deceit passed generationally to Joseph and his brothers. Joseph's brothers tricked him and got him sold into slavery. They tricked their father, Jacob, to have him believe Joseph was dead. Some family may have hurt you because the enemy tried to stop what God wanted to do. You can change that by making peace with those who hurt you.

Now, a generation later, Jacob's son Reuben was the oldest, but he lost his birthright because he committed adultery with one of his father's concubines. His uncle had lost his birthright to Jacob. So, we see a history of the same problems within this family. It was a demonic pattern. Demonic patterns of the enemy are only patterns because they have been working. You begin breaking the pattern by ensuring it doesn't work with you. Have you conquered what has tried to conquer your family?

Two generations before Joseph, there was conflict between Abraham's sons, Isaac and Ishmael. Abraham had Ishmael through his wife's maid Hagar. She served as a surrogate mother because Sarah had not been able to have children. It was Sarah's idea for Abraham to do this. However, Sarah later had a child, who was named Isaac, with Abraham. So, there was a family feud then. When Isaac was born, Sarah saw Ishmael scoffing or mocking because of Isaac's birth. Ishmael was around fifteen years old. Ishmael was jealous. When Sarah saw this, she told Abraham that Hagar and Ishmael had to go. You may have felt rejected by family, but all it did was push you to a position to be able to turn your bloodline around. It became so bad, Hagar had to leave the country with her son, Ishmael. Now we see a history of the spirit of rejection, deception, and jealousy that was circulating through this bloodline. Rejection is a spirit who wants you to feel like you don't matter because it knows that it doesn't matter. Don't give it the attention it craves. So, we see how these issues continued in the family bloodline from generation to generation until Joseph became the interruption in his bloodline. He became the curse breaker, even though the curse tried to take him out. The enemy is trying to stop you because you are the curse breaker in your family, but you will win! Joseph went through slavery and rose to power to actually save his entire family. You may have felt like the different one in the family, but God can use you to rescue your family. God has placed in you the power to be able to change anything you come in contact with that is not aligned with His will.

Deuteronomy 30:11-16: *"For this commandment which I command you today is not too mysterious for you, nor is it far off. It is not in heaven, that you should say, 'Who will ascend into heaven for us and bring it to us, that we may hear it and do it?' Nor is it beyond the sea, that you should say, 'Who will go over the sea for us and bring it to us, that we may hear it and do it?' But the word is very near you, in your mouth and in your heart, that you may do it.*

"See, I have set before you today life and good, death and evil, in that I command you today to love the LORD your God, to walk in His ways, and to keep His commandments, His statutes, and His judgments, that you may live and multiply; and the LORD your God will bless you in the land which you go to possess."

God was speaking to the children of Israel in this passage, and it applies today. We don't have to look far and wide for God's commands because they have been given to us. His Word is near us and in us once we accept Christ in our lives. The Holy Spirit will guide us, but we must continue to feed our spirit with God's Word so we can know what He said. If we obey God, He will bless us in the territories He has given us. This blessing God spoke of was generational. The blessing here was tied to obedience. Obedience to God opens the door for generational deliverance to occur in your family. There are rewards for obedience and consequences for disobedience. Your obedience matters to God regardless of what someone else does or does not do! Obedience holds a lot of weight in God's kingdom. God has and will place His Word in your mouth and in your heart as you seek Him. As He commanded the children of Israel here, He also commands us to love Him, walk in His ways, and keep His commandments. Through this obedience, we will be blessed everywhere He sends us. Stop simply reacting to the attacks of the enemy and start responding to them with the Word of God. This passage also talks about how we will live and multiply when we love God and walk in His ways. God is big on multiplication. When you are obedient to God, He will multiply what He put in you so that you will produce even more on the earth. God wants to multiply your faithfulness in your family so that your family legacy grows and brings more glory to God on earth. When more is multiplied, the curse can't survive. Generational curses cannot survive in a godly kingdom atmosphere. Your life can set the atmosphere for your family! We can go deeper in this chapter and gain more insight.

Deuteronomy 30:19-20: *"I call heaven and earth as witnesses today against you, that I have set before you life and death, blessing and cursing; therefore choose life, that both you and your descendants may live; that you may love the LORD your God, that you may obey His voice, and that you may cling to Him, for He is your life and the length of your days; and that you may dwell in the land which the LORD swore to your fathers, to Abraham, Isaac, and Jacob, to give them."*

Here we find Moses explaining to the Israelites that they had two choices. He even told them which choice to go with. God gives us simple choices; it's only when our flesh is loud that the choice seems difficult! Who wouldn't choose life? Well, it's easy to say you choose something, but do your actions line up with it? Moses even helped them see what they needed to do. If we choose life, we need to cling to God. The choices you make today will greatly impact the next generation in your bloodline for the good or the bad, so make the God choice! This passage shows us generational blessings and generational curses. Heaven and earth are witnesses to the decisions we make. Some family members made the wrong choice, but you can make the right one. You can activate unclaimed blessings that were forfeited by your ancestors because of their disobedience by simply being obedient.

Deuteronomy 28:1-2: *"Now it shall come to pass, if you diligently obey the voice of the LORD your God, to observe carefully all His commandments which I command you today, that the LORD your God will set you high above all nations of the* *earth. And all these blessings shall come upon you and overtake you, because you obey the voice of the LORD your God."*

When you obey God, you don't have to ask for blessings or look for blessings because the blessings will be looking for you. They will literally overtake you. Obedience automatically promotes you to what God has next for you. Notice that it says **diligently** obey the voice of God. Obedience to God is not a one-time thing, but it must be a lifestyle. Your obedience to God opens doors because obedience gives you a key to the storehouse of heaven.

Once again, we see generational blessings. If you continued to read the passage, verse 4 talks about children being blessed just by parents being obedient to God. Breaking generational curses automatically opens the doors so your family can receive generational blessings. Demons have been stalking your family because your family is able to multiply, and the more you multiply God's love, the greater the impact. Don't you dare give up on your family. Don't you dare write them off. Your family may have been overlooked in the past because of where you came from, but you all will be on display because of where you're going.
Every family has a God-given identity! The enemy has tried to change it, but you can help restore it. Your family identity has been under attack because family is so important. A unified family not only threatens Satan's kingdom, but it brings God's kingdom to earth quicker than you could ever do alone. Your family identity begins with the identity of Christ. You must fight and pray for whatever is not of Christ to go away and stay away. The enemy has been trying to blind members of your family and even you from seeing the Christ nature in your loved ones. Your family was wired to serve Christ, but if there is a shortage in the wire, God has given you the power and authority to fix it. Yes, you can fix it. God didn't send you on earth to just take up space. There are many problems on earth that you can fix because God sent you on earth so He could fix things through you.

Don't take the role God gave you in your family for granted. There's greater responsibility in you than you've allowed yourself to accept. This is a call for you to wake up to your role. This is a call for you to step into place. You staying in position will give other family members who are living below the will of God more opportunities to get in position. You matter. Your prayers matter. The biggest lie the enemy ever got you to believe is that your prayers aren't working in your family! It's the enemy's goal to shut you up because they know death and life are in the power of your tongue. You must declare God's Word over your family because it's God's Word that will change them. Let the Word do the work. You must make it a habit to persistently cover your family in prayer because when you show up in prayer, you send demons running. The persistence is necessary because although they may run, they will do everything they can to try to come back. Don't let a demon outwork you by doing more evil than you are doing good! Chase after God's will like your life depends on it because it does.

The identity of your family matters because your family is to leave an imprint on this earth. Regardless of the history or social status of your family, your family is to find their identity in Christ, which will change everything. Don't shy away from leading in the areas God is calling you to lead. The tragedy isn't just a family that dies without leaving a legacy, but it's those who die with pieces of the legacy that weren't passed on. God placed seeds in you, and it's your job to plant what He put in you daily. You hold a great piece to the lasting legacy of your family on the earth. Be sure that you plant those seeds early and often! Family is too important. God chose to create family because He didn't believe man should be alone. You will never be left alone because loneliness is something God took issue with and handled when He created family in the beginning. You are chosen, and the Word of God tells you this.

1 Peter 2:9-10: *But you are a chosen generation, a royal priesthood, a holy nation, His own special people, that you may proclaim the praises of Him who called you out of darkness into His marvelous light; who once were not a people but are now the people of God, who had not obtained mercy but now have obtained mercy.*

You must first realize that God chose you for something specific. He called you to do something specific. God chose your family to accomplish something specific in the earth, and He will reveal it to you. He has given all of us assignments to accomplish for the kingdom of God. We are royalty because we are members of the body of Christ. We come from a royal lineage, and as priests, we are to offer up praises unto God. It doesn't matter what's said about your family because it doesn't change the facts. God calls your family royalty. Live up to the status! As priests, we can go to God directly for ourselves or on the behalf of another. We are a peculiar people, which means we are God's special people. We belong to Him and are unique in that way. Before we came to accept Christ, we were not a people at all, but now we are children of God who have received His mercy. In other words, we were fatherless without God. We had no identity outside of God. However, when we are connected, we now have all the rights and privileges that come with being a child of God.

God woke you up today because you still have some unfinished business to handle on earth. Your family is here because your family has some unfinished business that God wants to finish on earth through your family. God is bringing your family from out of the darkness and into the light, and it begins with you letting your light shine. The restoration of your family identity will happen. No one is coming to do it in the future because God is ready to start it through you now. War for your family!

Chapter 16: Your Divine Right to Healing: Confronting the Spirit of Infirmity

There are some things you don't need to think about whether they are in God's will because they are already in His Word. It is in the will of God that you are healed in every area in your body and in your life. Healing can be physical, emotional, psychological, etc. Mental illness and any other diseases are not from God, but they are from Satan. As God's children, we can bring healing. One of Satan's tactics is to try to get us to believe that just because someone was born with a certain illness that it was God's will. We were in a spiritual fight in the womb and entered the fight outside the womb. Don't quit because you have a divine right to God's promises!

Not only do you have a divine right to healing, but you also have the power to bring healing to others you come in contact with. God didn't place you where He placed you by accident. Not only do you have power and authority, but God expects you to use the power and authority to evict demons and change lives. We must understand our responsibility as children of God. God gave you power and authority to use on earth so you can bring His kingdom on earth. That's responsibility. I discussed some of that responsibility in chapter 3, but we're going to go deeper when it comes to dealing with sickness and disease. There is always work for you to do. There is always work to do in God's kingdom, so if you feel you aren't doing anything, that's not on God. It's on you to seek His will. Going around healing people in Jesus's name who are sick in body, mind, or soul is enough to keep you busy for a lifetime. There are many sick around you who have been praying for healing, but you may be the answer to that prayer to bring God's kingdom to them. You must walk in godly boldness. The enemy tries to send fear so you don't pray for someone in person who is sick because they know you have the power of the Holy Spirit to bring healing. The more you do it, the more you will conquer fear. It's not you doing the work, but it's the Holy Spirit doing the healing through you. That takes pressure off you. You have the power to bring divine healing to others. You just need to put the Holy Spirit in position to do His job because He won't force it!

Some are still sick near you, not because they didn't pray, but because you passed by them with the power of the Holy Spirit in you to bring healing. That again comes with responsibility. This is one reason we get filled with the Holy Spirit. What's in you should come out so you can go back and get filled again. Too often, we think that when we see someone who is sick in any way that we have an option to declare healing over their lives. Praying for the sick you cross paths with is not an option—it is a mandate from God! He didn't give you power to sit on. Any type of sickness is an attack from the enemy in an attempt to slow you down, but God placed His healing power in you. Just use it.

Everywhere Jesus went, miracles, signs, and wonders followed Him. You now have the authority of Jesus Christ and the power of the Holy Spirit, so everywhere you go, miracles, signs, and wonders should follow you. It's not so much about how special we are, but it's about how powerful God is. It makes us special that we are used by Him! We must activate it, and that comes through prayer, God's Word, and worship. You must pray to the level of your assignment and to the level of your promotion. The power of the Holy Spirit needs full access to flow completely through you. You must see sickness and disease of any kind as your enemy, and it's your job to destroy the enemy in Jesus's name. What Jesus did on earth, we are to do as well.

The spirit of infirmity is an enemy whose job is to inflict people with sickness and disease, but it's our job to overthrow it. You may be thinking that you have declared healing over people who still died of sickness or disease. That's not your issue. Your job is to keep showing up. Keep praying for the sick. When you do it enough, you won't have all that time to focus on what appears to not have worked because there will be so many that have been healed because you showed up. There are some who are losing their minds, but because they come in contact with you, you can usher God's peace into their lives. There are some who are emotionally in turmoil, but you can set them free by the power of the Holy Spirit at work in you. As God's child, you must take the healing power of the Holy Spirit everywhere you go. You bring God's glory on earth. God's glory also brings healing. God desires healing for His people, and He intends to use you to bring forth that healing. You are able to do it because God gave you the ability to do it. The enemy has cursed many bloodlines with generational sickness, but you can break the curse and pray and war for generational healing. There are families who have been keeping the curse going by saying things outside of God's will pertaining to healing. Don't accept a family curse that others seem to be comfortable with; it's your job to reject and break the curse. Again, God is not leaving His throne, and it's our duty to bring His Kingdom on earth. The kingdom of God is a kingdom of power, and as a child of God, you should demonstrate that power to the world. As a child of God, you are a miracle worker because God desires to perform miracles through you. Too many people are trying to fit in with the crowd, but as God's child you're supposed to be different from the crowd. You stand out because God stands out in you. God's kingdom shall come in your life, and the world will have a front-row seat to see it. Your flesh is attached to things of the world, and your spirit is attached to things of God. It's time to raise your level to fully operate in things of the spirit! Don't be frustrated because things aren't going according to your plan, but let it motivate you to chase after God for His plan. You are a living miracle, and many more miracles will be birthed out of you.

This is your season to shine very bright, not because man said it but because God said it. You're not behind schedule, but you're on time on God's schedule, which places you ahead of the world's schedule. The world had plans to change you, but God sent you because He has a plan for you to change the world. God's plan wins. You have needed a miracle, and God is going to release greater than what you need. We have all been in a place in life where we were in dire need of something or some type of change. It could be something physical or even emotional. There are times we are reminded that we can do nothing without Christ and that we are nothing without Christ! We live because He lives. There are those times in life when we know that if God doesn't do it, it just won't be done. That's what a miracle is. It is the supernatural invading the natural, causing something to happen immediately. A miracle defies natural law. It supersedes the natural because a miracle must first happen in the spirit. Because we are spirit beings, we already have the ability to defy natural law.

However, we live in a physical body. So, we must balance living in the world with not being from the world, yet still be able to impact the world by bringing God's kingdom on earth. As an ambassador of Christ, you are expected to bring the supernatural to earth. Heaven begins to invade earth through you because you came from heaven. God wants the supernatural to be a part of your life on a continual basis, and persistent prayer can get you there! You are spirit with a flesh. God created you to walk in the spirit because you are spirit. So, don't allow your flesh to convince you to believe anything outside of God. Many of you are experiencing extreme levels of warfare because the enemy doesn't want you to birth in the spirit what God has placed in you. In understanding this, it helps to put things in perspective. Don't get upset and quit here. The abundant life Christ promised is under attack, but keep fighting because you will enter the Promised Land. You were made for the supernatural because you are supernatural. Our spirits came out of God, so flesh must move aside. The real you is your spirit, not your flesh.

The enemy is trying to break you, but you will break through and God will get the glory out of this. You were created to be walking, living, breathing power. It's time for you to walk in the levels of power God ordained for you to walk in. The attack may have seemed unbearable at times. It seemed like one area after another was under attack, but you must remember that the attack is based off of where you're going, not where you are. The enemy is always planning ahead, but the power of the Holy Spirit that you will walk in will spoil their plans. What God is birthing out of you requires you to walk in greater levels of power of the Holy Spirit because He is trusting you with much. The pressure is intense, but your power is more intense! What you are birthing is unlike anything you've personally experienced before. Miracles will be attracted to you because, by nature, God created you to be a miracle producer. Let the Holy Spirit have full residence in your life.

You must bring healing. Healing is not an option, but you have a divine right to healing because Jesus already died so you could be healed. He didn't die just for our salvation, but He died so we would be healed. Sickness entered the world because of Satan, but healing entered the world because of Jesus! We know the foundational Scripture for healing.

Isaiah 53:5: *But He was wounded for our transgressions,*
He was bruised for our iniquities;
The chastisement for our peace was upon Him,
And by His stripes we are healed.

It's safe to say that it's already done! Jesus Christ was wounded, crushed, beaten, and tormented not just so we could be saved, but so we would be healed. So, when it comes to healing, we must look through the lens of a completed work. We're not just healed from a sin-sick soul, but we also have physical, emotional, psychological healing, etc. Your soul is very critical. We will get to that later in the book. You are not going to **get** healed because you **are** already healed because Jesus already paid for it. Jesus paid for our healing, so if you know someone who's sick in any way, whether physical or emotional, you can grab their healing for them. It was paid for, but sometimes we have to fight the enemy to secure it. If the enemy took your healing, you need to fight and snatch it back because it rightfully belongs to you. Sickness will never be greater than healing. Get your healing and shame the enemy.

Mark 16:15-18: *And He said to them, "Go into all the world and preach the gospel to every creature. He who believes and is baptized will be saved; but he who does not believe will be condemned. And these signs will follow those who believe: In My name they will cast out demons; they will speak with new tongues;*

they will take up serpents; and if they drink anything deadly, it will by no means hurt them; they will lay hands on the sick, and they will recover."

The first thing that was said was "go into all the world." We are to lay hands on the sick. You have the power to lay hands on the sick and they will recover, and you need to go to them. People in need are not hard to find. The instructions Jesus gave to His disciples are the same instructions we have. It didn't say "they might lay hands on the sick," but "they will." You must stand in faith. You will be in high demand because of the miracles that will come out of your life.

Jesus didn't say wait for the world to come to the church, but He told us to go into all the world and bring the gospel! For too long the church has talked about bringing souls to the kingdom but has not aggressively gone after it. Soul winning simply was preaching and hoping the unsaved would come to the building. The church has spent too much time focusing on the in-house Christians instead of going out and bringing in those who are lost and wounded. God is challenging us. When you go and bring the kingdom to dark places, the Holy Spirit can flow more because He is not hindered by tradition and comfort. Part of this going process is also going to heal the sick. The full power of the Holy Spirit in our life doesn't come with waiting in the four walls, but it comes in going out so He can bring change. We must go out and bring the kingdom of God to the world. We must go out and bring healing in the world.

Don't spend too much time waiting for better conditions. The Holy Spirit thrives in us going forward more than sitting. Some of the church has focused on waiting on the Lord, but it's birthed some laziness. There are far more things God wants you to be doing while you wait for other stuff. The blessing is in going while you wait for other stuff! Christ already told us to go and preach the gospel. We all are preachers. You're a preacher on your job, in your home, grocery store, etc. You don't need to be led to bring the good news to strangers because that's a part of your responsibility.

You don't have to wait to go and heal the sick. Too many have used the phrase "I'm not led to do this or that" based on them not being comfortable more than anything else. Don't confuse being uncomfortable with not being led by God to do something. He often has us to do things that make flesh uncomfortable. It can make the flesh uncomfortable to pray for a stranger who is sick. Yet, it's what we are called to do.

We must first realize that the spirit is above the flesh. You have a responsibility to feed your spirit. If you don't make sure it's fed, you're literally starving yourself. You feed it through prayer and the Word. The miraculous should follow you as a child of God. There are great works we are to do in Jesus's name as the power of God works in us through the anointing on our lives under the guiding of the Holy Spirit. If you believe in Christ through faith, miracles will follow you. More miracles will follow the church when the church gives miracles more to follow. We must go and boldly do the work of the Lord. Too often, we hide behind the comfortable works of being a follower of Christ. Yes, you will be rewarded, but Christ first commanded us to go and bring the kingdom. If people are coming to you, that's the easy part; now the tougher part is going to people! That's where the power will work in you most. There are sick people all around you. Even if you have been attacked with sickness, you can bring shame to the enemy by still going out and praying for the healing of others. God wants to remind you of the power you have access to. Not only do you have access to it, but He expects you to operate in it. God wants to get the glory out of your life. A child of God who does not demonstrate God's power is a child who forgot why God sent them here. Your faith demonstrates the evidence of God at work in your life. This is not a time to shrink back. This is not a time to second guess yourself. It's time to go. It's never a time to look at what you see in the physical, but it's always a time to look at what you see in the spirit. You have the power to cast out demons from your life and the lives of others in Jesus's name! Don't run from something you have power over. We have a responsibility to bring the power of God into the situations others are facing. Don't wait, but go and find them.

Luke 10:1-2, 9, 17: *After these things the Lord appointed seventy others also, and sent them two by two before His face into every city and place where He Himself was about to go. Then He said to them, "The harvest truly is great, but the laborers are few; therefore pray the Lord of the harvest to send out laborers into His harvest...And heal the sick there, and say to them, 'The kingdom of God has come near to you.'"...*

Then the seventy returned with joy, saying, "Lord, even the demons are subject to us in Your name."

So, we see that Jesus appointed seventy more disciples after the original twelve. He sent them together two by two to go into cities and places where He was about to go. God will often send you on assignment to prepare the atmosphere for the arrival of His glory in that place. God is sending you to go and heal the sick in the name of Jesus. It's not just for healing evangelists or those with the gift of healing. All children of God are to heal the sick. It comes with bringing God's kingdom. God never leaves you alone or sends you empty handed. He is sure to give you exactly what you need plus extra. The seventy in this passage did some of the work before Jesus got there. They prepared the way for His entrance and did miracles, signs, and wonders in the name of Jesus. He gave them His power and authority to perform miracles, just as we have today. God may place the miracle someone has been praying for in your hands. Remain obedient to what He's leading you to do. There is a great harvest, but it requires work to get to it. There were not enough laborers who were positioned to walk in the power and authority and to proclaim the kingdom of God. God has a great work for you to accomplish, and your first job is to put your faith to work!

The seventy returned with excitement because they were actually able to go into cities together and demons had to obey them. They went into cities and healed the sick. This was because they were given the authority of Christ. Demons know they must obey you when you walk in the authority of Christ. So, war against them until they release what's yours. The disciples were excited because they had never operated with so much authority. So, Jesus let them know that He gave them authority against Satan, and the enemy could by no means hurt them. This applies to us as well. We are protected when we walk in the power and authority of God. The enemy can never truly harm us because even death has no power over us. God gave you the right to tap into His power and authority, so it's about time you exercise that right and work it on earth. Faith makes the supernatural a reality in your life.

Notice that the key was they were able to perform miracles and cast out demons where they were sent. The key is in being where God sent you. God is sending you on assignment, and no matter how tough it seems, you have the grace to carry it out. Regardless of how tough things may be temporarily, you will always flourish where God plants you. You are to bring light where there is darkness. Sickness is darkness. Faith helps you start and finish the assignment God gave you because it won't always make sense as to why God sent you, but faith goes anyway. The power of God at work in you operates best when you go where God sent you. Faith helps you flourish wherever God sends you. When God's Word goes before you, it will always open doors. Continue speaking His Word, and you will get the rewards attached to it! We can find many other examples in Scripture where the power to heal the sick was evident in the lives of children of God.

Acts 19:11-12: *Now God worked unusual miracles by the hands of Paul, so that even handkerchiefs or aprons were brought from his body to the sick, and the diseases left them and the evil spirits went out of them.*

Here we see that God did unusual miracles through apostle Paul. When you walk in faith, God will do some unusual things through you. It will be unusual in the natural eye, but the usual in the spirit! These healings were done not to glorify Paul, but God did them so that He would be glorified and the people would believe the message in the power of Jesus through the preached word. It was

215

also done so God could confirm publicly to others the ministry God placed in Paul. People don't have to validate you because God already has. Faith takes you from the natural and puts you back in the supernatural where miracles happen. The Holy Spirit anointed the apostle Paul to accomplish all the miracles where he was. The Holy Spirit has anointed you for a specific assignment God has for you. You will be equipped! The anointing is God doing the work through you. This differs from the Glory of God, which is when God does it Himself, independent of using any person. You are anointed to do things you could never accomplish outside of the power of God in you.

Faith helps keep you focused on what's most important. We see that people were healed, and evil spirits left. Faith is your first access point to the supernatural. Faith tells your flesh to get out of the way. Faith gives the Holy Spirit permission to produce miracles through you. Faith in God through Christ is what you will always need to have to be able to get what you need. Your body belongs to God, not to Satan, so if anything is attacking your body or that of another, you can command it to leave in Jesus's name! Yes, it may be stubborn, but you keep praying and warring until you see the results.

Acts 5:12-16: *And through the hands of the apostles many signs and wonders were done among the people. And they were all with one accord in Solomon's Porch. Yet none of the rest dared join them, but the people esteemed them highly. And believers were increasingly added to the Lord, multitudes of both men and women, so that they brought the sick out into the streets and laid them on beds and couches, that at least the shadow of Peter passing by might fall on some of them. Also a multitude gathered from the surrounding cities to Jerusalem, bringing sick people and those who were tormented by unclean spirits, and they were all healed.*

We see that the apostles or leaders in the church accomplished many signs and wonders among the people through the power of God. We know that as children of God, we have this ability through God's power. Miracles, signs, and wonders are to bring glory to God, not to any human. God would love to always use you to bring miracles, signs, and wonders in the lives of others. It's not hard if you have faith! You're a living miracle, and you will be able to produce miracles in the lives of others through the Holy Spirit. Some of the believers of Christ respected them so highly and would not get in their way or say too much because of what happened to Ananias and his wife, Sapphira. They lied to the Holy Spirit and immediately died (Acts 5). The anointing of the Holy Spirit in our lives brings revelation and supernatural increase to any area of lack in our lives.

New converts were added daily because of the power of the message of Jesus Christ and the miracles, signs, and wonders being done through the men and women of God. There are times you don't have to say a word. Simply carrying God's glory brings healing. The power of the Holy Spirit is so strong that if you just show up, something happens in the spirit. Don't take your presence for granted. Some people don't understand who you really are. With what God is birthing out of you, your literal presence will cause healing to manifest because you're carrying God's presence. The people brought those who were sick and sat them in the streets so that even Peter's shadow might pass over them and they might be healed because of the anointing of the Holy Spirit. They also brought the sick to the disciples, and through the power of the Holy Spirit in their lives, the people were healed, and demons left those who were being tormented. When God's Word goes forth, there should be a demonstration of that Word. There is power in God's Word. God didn't send you on earth to look at His power, but He sent you to walk in His power to bring His kingdom on earth. As you continue to press into God, the power of God that will come out of your life in this season will be at levels that will surprise you. It all goes back to faith. Faith thrusts you forward. Faith puts so many things in motion. God never intended for faith to be hard to obtain. He made it easy. If you live by faith, which is attached to God, manifestation must come! It comes with a guarantee. Keep working your faith when problems are trying to work you. Keep chasing after God and the supernatural will not happen sometimes, but it will happen all the time in your life. You are an encounter. When you stand in faith, the glory of God on your life will give those who encounter you a life-changing experience. Of course, it's not to bring glory to you but to God. So, we always point back to Christ. We're a vessel to be used by God. **The world needs an encounter, and that encounter should be with the power of the Holy Spirit living in you.**

We all have prayed for someone's healing and it appeared to not have happened. However, there is not one prayer of faith that you pray that falls to the ground. Remember, your prayers are seeds. Let's say someone you prayed for who was sick died. That seed of prayer your prayed cannot die; it will go to someone else connected to the individual who died. That prayer could have very well blocked some type of sickness the enemy tried to put on someone connected to the individual who passed away.

The enemy wants to make you think your prayers for healing don't work so you stop. They want you to doubt your power. However, you have to keep showing up. I've prayed for healing and saw the physical manifestation of it, and I've prayed for healing and not seen it. Yet, it did not stop me. I used to get frustrated. I would put all this pressure on myself. I would take it personally. However, I was making it about me. I had to put it back on God. I had to know that my seeds of prayer always produce. I had to know that I did my job by attempting. I assure you that the more you attempt, the more you will see results.

I remember when visiting one of our churches in South Africa, we stopped to pray for a group of homeless people we saw standing outside. One particular man was there who wasn't homeless. He just hung out with the homeless. He was blind in one eye. He had lived with it for so long, he didn't think to ask for prayer for his eye. However, we asked him. My wife, son, and I laid hands on him and commanded his eyes to be opened. We prayed the first time, and he saw nothing. We prayed again, and to his amazement, he could see movement, although it was blurry. It shocked him. He would have been content with just that. We prayed again, and his eyesight was completely restored. He was so shocked and amazed. God was glorified.

Imagine if we had never asked him if we could pray for his eyesight to be restored. He would still be walking around being blind in one eye. Imagine if we hadn't kept praying after the first time. He would have still been walking around blind in one eye. We have prayed for blinded eyes to be opened before, and in those moments, nothing happened. Yet, we have prayed for blinded eyes to be opened, as in this case, and it happened. It's your job to keep showing up. It's our job to attempt. Again, the more you attempt to pray for the sick by faith, the more you will begin to see. Don't be discouraged, but be encouraged because you will see more results. We had enough faith for that man's eyesight to be restored. Your faith is big enough, even if the person you're praying for doesn't have faith. Continue to seek God so that you can carry more of His glory. Remember, it's our duty to heal the sick. God wouldn't command us to do something that He didn't equip us to do. Go and pray for the sick, and healing must follow.

Part III. On the Defensive: Assassins Closing Demonic Doors

Chapter 17: The Warfare Over Your Mind

One of the enemy's oldest tricks is to plant a seed of a thought in our mind that's contrary to God's will. You must reject that thought! A lot of warfare begins in the mind. It truly is a battleground. Every word we speak is tied to a seed of a thought, and it's up to you to make sure you speak life to water the good seeds sown. One reason God gave you a mind is to be connected to His mind as a reminder that no thought of God placed in your mind goes to waste.

Adam and Eve were fully connected to the mind of God before sin entered the world. That's why when God had Adam name every animal, all Adam was doing was speaking the mind of God. When you say what God already said or is saying, you are speaking the mind of God, and that's a great gift. You cannot outsmart a demon with your natural mind, but when it is renewed, you can outsmart them with the mind of Christ. This is why our minds must be renewed. The seeds sown in your mind by the enemy are seeds of death, but the seeds sown by God are seeds of life! This is why there is a battle in your mind. This is why the enemy tries all avenues, including dreams, to try to sow seeds of discord in your life, and that's why you should tell the Lord daily to cover you and wash you in the blood of Jesus.

God gave you a mind not for you to solely think independently, but for you not to make a move independent of Him. Think about how strategic God is. He chose to give us a brain. God gave you a memory so you can remind your current and future problems of what God has already done. However, we also have choices. We have free will, so we are not robots. The enemy understands that and tries to get us to make the wrong choice. Satan tries to get in your mind to think like him, but God wants your mind so you can think like Him. God's thoughts help you rule on earth. God's thoughts are never wasted thoughts because if one person does not act on it, God will raise up another who will. The enemy knows that your brain is able to tell other parts of your body what to do. This is why the spirits of stress, depression, rejection, etc., all begin in the mind. Demons try to convince your mind how to feel and respond to feelings, but the Word tells you how to get out of feelings and in the spirit. How you feel about something may cause sad emotions, but the enemy tries to get you to live in them and God desires to set you free! Demons want to turn your mind into a playground because one thought can lead to the next thought if it is not cast down. The spirit of depression and suicide can't show up until other seeds of bad thoughts make room. Pray and cast down every ungodly thought. The enemy even tries to twist imagination. God gave us a creative imagination, but demons try to twist it. I cast down every demonic thought in Jesus's name.

Your mind can hold a lot of information. You must know that you can control your thoughts by refusing to accept any thought that tries to bring you low. Christ came so you can live! The average number of thoughts that humans are believed to experience each day is 70,000. That means that we have the capacity to have 490,000 thoughts a week. Imagine if even half of that was negative: that would be as much as 35,000 negative thoughts a day and 245,000 negative thoughts a week. That's more than enough for the enemy to have a field day and invite more toxic things in our lives.

So, it matters what you say and do. Be careful what you say to people because your words are powerful. One word can create more bad thoughts, or one word can pull them out of darkness. The enemy is crafty and will try to influence others who are already in a bad head space to say or do things to you to get you to say something to them to push them further into darkness and to believe more of those wrong thoughts. You may not be able to change someone's mind, but you have power and authority to cast out demonic spirits that are messing with their mind!

Scripture supports this because Jesus said that one commits adultery by simply looking at another person and thinking about them in a lustful manner because it's already in the heart (Matthew 5:28). The action may not have occurred, but the thought was there with an action played out in the mind. Don't allow bad thoughts to tell you what to do, but let God tell your mind what to do. Think on God, and God thoughts will flow! It's our conscious mind that makes decisions, but it's our subconscious mind that consists of who we are as a person. How we think subconsciously can be hidden from our conscious mind. The enemy knows this. That's where they sow the seeds. That's when you do something that you know better than doing. Our subconscious mind acts based on what it has been taught from our life experiences from as far back as childhood. This is why some struggle to receive love. They know they deserve it, but subconsciously, the enemy is feeding their mind that they don't deserve it. You must pray to God to renew your mind to a place where any thought outside of God won't be able to survive in your mind.

An adult can still be a child in certain areas because they have not been healed from something that happened as far back as childhood. Suppressing something is not healing. God doesn't want just a part of your mind, but He wants to renew your entire mind so you can effectively do His will. As you become an adult, the conscious mind can change its mind about what it told you to believe from past experiences, but the subconscious won't automatically change with it. It now becomes a mind within the mind, and this is how there can be a tug of war. This is where the spirit of confusion operates. This is how you can have mixed feelings and be unsure about things because of the battle between the conscious and subconscious mind. However, you can bring them both under subjection through the Word of God.

If you want to easily cast out a thought the enemy planted in your mind, replace it with the truth of God's Word. When you're out of Christ, you're out of your mind. When you're in Christ, you're in your right mind. God gave us an intellect, but it is supposed to be in subjection to His will. Great intellect will never replace God because He gave intellect! Intellect was created to submit to God's will, not human will. We sometimes spend too much time trying to figure it out. God never once told you to figure anything out. He told you to seek Him in all things, and He will give you instructions. Seek God so He can renew your mind so you can see the situation like He sees it.

The enemy tries to attack your mind because so many decisions are carried out in your mind. Your fleshly mind cannot grasp the deep things of God, but it's your spiritual mind that can. You may have been trapped in an earthly way of thinking, but God is renewing your mind to see it from heaven's perspective. The enemy tries to get in your mind, but when your mind is in Christ, the seeds the enemy sows will die. Demons know your mind is valuable, so they try to get in it. They can't change your mind because you have a made-up mind in Christ. If you're confused, it's the enemy trying to mess with your mind. God is never confused, so ask Him to renew your mind daily. Scripture gives us great insight on the mind and the type of mind we are supposed to have.

1 Corinthians 2:16: *For "who has known the mind of the LORD that he may instruct Him?" But we have the mind of Christ.*

This passage outlines the fact that no human being of themselves can know the mind of God, especially one who has not even accepted Christ. However, we have the mind of Christ. With the mind of Christ, we can know the deep things of God as they are revealed to us. We can get revelation of the things of God because we have the Holy Spirit. When we accept Christ, we get the Holy Spirit, who reveals things to us we would never be able to see outside of Christ. Quite often, the enemy feeds off of our revelation to know what God is up to. The enemy tries to confuse you so you slow down your forward progress in God, but you can confuse the enemy by keeping your faith in God. Demons want you to use common sense by telling your mind to overreact to a bad situation, but common sense to you should be uncommon faith in God. Faith defies the natural. It goes against what appears to be common. When you have the mind of Christ, it defies what seems natural because faith awakens the supernatural in your life. The enemy is afraid of you having more faith in God because they know that with your faith comes more trouble for them!

Philippians 2:5: *Let this mind be in you which was also in Christ Jesus.*

Apostle Paul was reminding the Philippian church, as well as us today, that believers should have this mind in them that was in Jesus. What it means in this passage is to have the same humility as Christ did. The way Christ conducted Himself is how we are to conduct ourselves because we represent Him, and the world needs to see our light shine. Being like Christ is making a choice to be led by God and not by flesh. Your attitude starts with a mind-set. This is why Jesus said we must pick up our cross daily and follow Him (Luke 9:23). Picking up our cross and following Christ is a daily decision, and every day we put it down is a day we give to the enemy! You must show up every day. Your mind is a treasure, and that's why the enemy tries to take it away. God gave you a mind to be trained to do God's will.

Apostle Paul could really relate to the warfare over the mind. We find it in the book of Romans.

Romans 7:21-25: *I find then a law, that evil is present with me, the one who wills to do good. For I delight in the law of God according to the inward man. But I see another law in my members, warring against the law of my mind, and bringing me into captivity to the law of sin which is in my members. O wretched man that I am! Who will deliver me from this body of death? I thank God—through Jesus Christ our Lord!*
So then, with the mind I myself serve the law of God, but with the flesh the law of sin.

Apostle Paul talks about his struggle and struggle we all will face. This is the struggle of doing good when evil is around and distractions are trying to pull us away. In our mind, we know what is right, but our flesh wars against God's will and tries to do what is wrong. This is why our mind must be renewed. So, we must be aware of this battle and, of course, continue to pray. There are many battles the enemy tries to start with you that you never face because they were dead on arrival.

It's a daily process of dying to our flesh and our will and submitting to God's will. Your flesh is in the world and you may feel buried now, but the real you is in Christ. Follow Christ and the real you will be resurrected. In the spirit, Paul was good, but his flesh experienced a war. The war in your flesh began as a war in the spirit. Win the war in the spirit and you will walk in your victory on earth. You can't lose in the natural when you fight and win in the spirit. His soul had to make a choice to go with the spirit or with the flesh. Our soul can take on the character of our spirit or the body.

This is why some proclaimed Christians have no sin conscience and continually live in sin. This is one reason why people can continually lie, steal, and cheat. Their souls have been contaminated and have submitted to their bodies. The soul then creates its own beliefs and doctrine. It has mastered hijacking some things from the spirit and mixing it with the body because the soul then wants to be in control because it's wrapped up in the self-conscious. Apostle Paul talks about this inner struggle of the mind. Your character is not based on who you are in the world's standards, but your character is based on who you are in God's standards! You were one of God's best thoughts, so don't entertain the lie the enemy is trying to get you to believe.

This is why you cannot be moved by what you see or the battle you may face. Don't be shaken by the battle you're in. Be moved by the fact that you can't lose because you've already won in Christ. The battle was so real for apostle Paul that he called it a death. It may feel like you're going through a death, but the only thing dying is flesh. You will bounce back because resurrection power lives in you. This was a battle that began in the mind for Paul. Every decision you make, good or bad, began with a thought. Your

225

thoughts can take you up or bring you down. So, focus on God's thoughts about you in His Word. As we continue to dig in Scripture, we will find more examples of what can happen if our mind is under attack and if we don't do anything about it.

James 1:5-8: *If any of you lacks wisdom, let him ask of God, who gives to all liberally and without reproach, and it will be given to him. But let him ask in faith, with no doubting, for he who doubts is like a wave of the sea driven and tossed by the wind. For let not that man suppose that he will receive anything from the Lord; he is a double-minded man, unstable in all his ways.*

It is believed that the James who wrote this book was the James who was the brother of Jesus. He was talking about us asking God for wisdom and that God generously gives it, but we must ask in faith. It must be pure faith in God with no doubt. Prayer begins with a thought. It's a thought that you will choose to give it all to God and do what He expects you to do. One God idea makes all your flesh ideas look small!

The key here was having faith in prayer. If you are not confident in your prayers to God, you are like a wave in the sea. If we don't ask in faith, we are double minded. Double mindedness is a spirit of Satan that works with the spirit of fear to try to confuse us and pull us away from faith in God through Christ. If influenced by these spirits, it causes one to lose confidence in prayer and themselves. A person goes back and forth, so it's like being lukewarm. Don't let trouble from the enemy tell your mind that there's no use in praying. The enemy knows your prayer life is what keeps you fighting. Your mind needs God in everything. Any independent thought outside of God gets you into trouble.

Our soul is where our free will comes into play. A double-minded man is unstable in all his ways. That's why a person shows up today and they can act like an entirely different person tomorrow. Our soul can choose if it will obey the body or submit to the spirit. This is why prayer and God's Word are so vital. Sometimes you just need to open your mouth and tell the enemy that they will not have your mind or the mind of anyone you're connected to. A renewed mind in Christ takes you from living in what was to living in what will be! Being in your right mind is being clothed with the mind of Christ. Get dressed in Christ. Your old mind couldn't comprehend the new because your mind needs to be renewed and up to date on what God is doing now.

Romans 12:2: *And do not be conformed to this world, but be transformed by the renewing of your mind, that you may prove what is that good and acceptable and perfect will of God.*

You don't conform to the world, but the world must conform to the spirit of God in you. If you fit into the world, you're beginning to look like the world. You weren't sent to fit in as a child of God. You're a light that can't be hidden! You were not sent here to let the world boss you around. You were sent to rule on earth for God. To be transformed from worldly thinking to godly thinking requires a renewed mind. Ask God for a renewed mind. You're in the world to bring change in the world, not for the world to change you.

It's impossible to even begin to know the will of God without a renewed mind in Christ. Don't focus on seeking things in the world. Seek God, and many things will start seeking you. When your mind is not renewed in God, you can call a good thing bad and a bad thing good. That brings confusion, and God never brings confusion. God's will is perfect, and He will perfect it in your life. God's will for your life is not hard to find. If you diligently seek Him, you will find His will. He made it that easy. The key is that we continue to seek Him for the answers. Let's examine one more Scripture that sums it all up.

Mark 12:28-31: *Then one of the scribes came, and having heard them reasoning together, perceiving that He had answered them well, asked Him, "Which is the first commandment of all?"*

Jesus answered him, "The first of all the commandments is: 'Hear, O Israel, the LORD our God, the LORD is one. And you shall love

227

the LORD your God with all your heart, with all your soul, with all your mind, and with all your strength.' This is the first commandment. And the second, like it, is this: 'You shall love your neighbor as yourself.' There is no other commandment greater than these."

In Jesus's answer to a scribe, we see five key things that must be done to love the Lord. I call them the five checkpoints to love God!

1.) Heart –The center. Points to that which gives life.

2.) Soul - Emotions, attitudes, and will of a person. Hence, loving God with all your soul is different from loving God with all your heart.

3.) Mind- Intellect, the place where we analyze, figure out, and plan things; the place where knowledge is processed and stored or cast out.

4.) Strength- Loving God with all your strength is to love God with every part of you. It's to love God with every fiber of your being. It is the outward expression of what is going on within ourselves to the outside world. (Do you look like Christ to others??)

5.) Love neighbor as self

If you're off at one checkpoint and the enemy gets in, it contaminates the word in you. God and evil don't mix. A contaminated word is toxic to you. This is how you can be a good person in the church and still be off and you don't even know it. Light and darkness don't mix, so it's up to you to let your light shine to drive out the darkness. Four out of five is not enough to be fully pleasing to God. We can serve God in four of the areas, but if we don't serve Him in all five, we can miss revelation and can be led astray. God will never lead you astray. Not following His instructions leads us astray!

You can hear a word and it never penetrates and takes root because one of your five checkpoints to love God rejects it. You can be saved and sanctified and still miss it. One rejection of something God is trying to get to you because you don't love Him in all five can lead to years of disappointment and frustration. Send the blood of Jesus to drown out every seed the enemy has sown in an attempt to get you to step outside of Christ. Constipation in the spirit leads to frustration in the natural. Here you are asking God what the holdup is, and you may have missed it when He tried to get it to you in the past. It's not something to beat yourself up about, but it reminds us that we're at war against the enemy.

Satan tried to give Jesus a contaminated word after He came off the fast, but Jesus was able to verbalize the authentic Word. He spent intimate time with God during His fast, so when the enemy came, anything outside of God was rejected. When the Word of God is in you, anything that contradicts His Word will automatically be rejected by you. The enemy will try to change your mind, but when your mind is made up in God, it cannot be changed. When your mind is washed in the blood of Jesus, you won't even entertain things you did in the past. The warfare over your mind is real because it impacts decisions. The decision you make to go with God will impact your life and the lives of all who you come in contact with. When you have the mind of Christ, you won't even waste time giving doubt any place in your life.

Chapter 18: The Weapon of Faith

The enemy is a known thief, and you must have a godly boldness in you to fight and take back what is already yours. There is no other way around it. Some things have just been stolen from you in the spirit realm. The demon that stole from you in the spirit realm is the same demon you fight back in the spirit to take it back. Just because something hasn't manifested in your life yet doesn't mean it's not yours. If God sent it and the enemy stole it, snatch it back! You have all the spiritual weapons you need to ensure victory. You've already been battle tested, and one lesson you've learned is that no matter how wounded you may be, you still have fight in you. Sure, sometimes you get tired of having to fight. Again, the flesh gets tired, not our spirit. However, sometimes we get lackadaisical after we get what was promised. The intensity you use to fight to get the promise is the same level of intensity you need to use to defend the promise!

Don't allow fear to cause you to settle. Fear of disappointment is an attack on your mind in an attempt to get you to step out of faith. You must live in faith. Faith in God is a prerequisite. The enemy knows that they can legally steal from you when you step out of faith and into fear. Fear is a thief, and you must evict it. Faith in God is a requirement if you want to access what God said you can have. You can't reclaim what's yours without faith. This is why the enemy tries to rob you of your faith. The enemy loves stealing things from you, but they're more focused on robbing you of faith because lack of faith equals a lack of God. They want you to be Godless. They want you to be very limited. They know we can't please God without faith. They know it's sin.

You cannot make any transactions from heaven to earth without faith in God. Faith and prayer are the currencies of heaven. You need some level of faith to even pray. In whatever area you find a lack of complete faith in God, that's the area the enemy will try to make their bed in. Spiritual warfare is effective when your faith is tied to God and your sword is drawn against the enemy. So, it's in trusting God and being bold in the spirit to fight against the enemy.

One of the biggest things Satan wants to rob you of is your faith because your faith in God through Christ gives you access to all of heaven. This is why your faith is constantly under attack and constantly on trial. Satan's mission is to deplete you of as much faith as possible and replace it with fear. Essentially, the enemy tries to get us to step out of faith by sending attacks against us. Fear is a spirit sent to attack your faith, and you must build up your faith in God so that fear will be uncomfortable around you. This is why we must always pray that our minds are renewed.

Faith is not hard! Faith is simply a choice to trust God above everything and through everything. As I stated before, faith is trusting God in everything and over everything, no matter what. It is that simple. Your spirit understands that, but you must daily get to the place where your spirit speaks louder than your flesh. Faith gives you access to your God-given territory, and the power and authority of Christ give you the right to rule in your territory. Faith can be increased. So, if faith can be increased, that means there is a higher dimension in faith that we can obtain. However, when you accept Christ, you are given a measure of faith, and that measure is powerful enough to literally move every mountain in your life. God is pushing you to a level of faith you wouldn't imagine you would have been to so soon. He has been pushing us there because it's the only way we will be able to handle the responsibility He's giving unto us. Your faith in God through Christ must have no limitations. The moment you put a limit on faith, you limit yourself. Faith rarely makes sense to your flesh because it's none of your flesh's business unless it's needed to get your flesh in order with God's will.

Faith is not bound by time, but faith in God through Christ is saying you will trust Him no matter how long it may seem to take. God may wait for what seems like the last minute, not to scare you, but to remind you that faith is not moved by time and you shouldn't be either. There was nothing lacking in Jesus when He walked the earth, so nothing should be lacking in us because He still walks the earth through us. Faith allows you to see it like God sees it, and it always looks better from God's perspective. You put

231

faith in whatever you believe and give attention to. Place your faith in God, not the problem, and give God your attention.

Not only is faith a spirit and a mind-set, but faith is alive. It wakes up in you what seemed to have been dead. Faith frees you up for the Holy Spirit to have full residence in your life. God wants you to live in faith for the rest of your life because it's how He always intended for it to be. Faith is spiritual, and you can only understand faith in the spirit. When you live from the flesh, you see the world's view, but when you live from faith, you see heaven's view of the matter.

Some may think you're crazy for believing God for what appears impossible, but God wants you to be faith crazy. I remember the date: September 17, 2009. God told me to come off my job. I thought I was going to be making all this money in business, but that's not what took place at that time. Little did I know, it was going to be a three-and-a half-year journey of trusting God in ways I had never trusted Him before. Not only did He tell me to come off my job, but He told me not to get another job until He told me. Plus, I knew by that point that I would only take a job that was an assignment from God.

Everyone didn't understand why I wasn't working. I went from helping pay bills of others to wondering how my bills would be paid. I was also in the process of searching for a home to buy. I had moved in with a family member temporarily as I was in the process of purchasing a home. Little did I know that home was not about to be purchased. Now I had no income. My faith did not waver, but I was asking God what was going on. I was tired of not going to gatherings because I didn't have money to pay for the food. I was tired of people wanting to do lunch meetings with me. So, I found myself on involuntary fasts.

God deals with all His children a certain way. Every time I even thought about having a pity party, the Holy Spirit would tell me to get it together. It's like the moment I even considered feeling bad, those thoughts were arrested. I remember standing in the kitchen one day, and the Lord told me, "I will trust you with more money

232

when you can trust me with no money." Those statements forever changed me. He reminded me that although I wasn't working and had no income coming in, I was still in a good position considering what my account looked like.

I still remember going to the bank to deposit $1. Think about the embarrassment of that. However, I actually found it funny. I took a picture of it to remember that day because I knew it would one day change. The reason I deposited that $1 is because I needed gas, and during that time, I was able to use my card and go over $1 and pray that I would get the money in enough time to deposit to avoid being overdrawn. That same day, someone was led to give me some money. Yes, I had times where my account was overdrawn. Too many times than I care to remember, but God always made a way. God sustained me, and it was during that season my prayer life began to change, and my faith went to new levels.
Everyone didn't understand. Some thought it didn't make sense. Some thought God wouldn't tell me to come off a job without another job. Some were naturally worried about my well-being. All in all, I still had to have faith, even in the parts I didn't understand. I knew I had to trust God, and that would not be shaken. God processed me through it, and I came out with faith strong enough to carry many others. Yes, God gives us wisdom and understanding. However, common sense is man's view of how something should be done; faith is God's view of how it should be done! Faith is not common. God is emphasizing the importance of unlimited faith because it's what you will need to please Him on the level He has you on. God is getting us back to the place where the supernatural becomes natural. Faith will be your key, and if you keep using it, it will keep unlocking doors. There are opportunities that God is sending that you may not feel as qualified for, but God will give you the wisdom to handle it.

Things are speeding up and will manifest rapidly. Stop trying to limit God to how you think things should be, or how things should go. Trust Him in it all. Yes, the enemy tries to disrupt your faith, but God is looking for your faith. You must surrender your will to God. Every area of your life in this season will experience rapid

acceleration! God wants you to trust Him when it appears nothing is changing. God is going to change it suddenly. You are entering into the highest level of faith you have ever walked in before. Your faith will be pushed like it's never been pushed before. Faith loves challenges, and it will produce what you've never had before.
Don't try to figure out what God is doing because your mind won't get it. Stay in faith because it makes sense to faith. The time in life where you're moved by what you see or don't see should come to an end. Faith is on display, and it's moved by what God sees. Take the limits off of faith. God wants to give you a new set of eyes, and it's the eyes of faith There's no room to panic anymore because you will see it like God sees it.

When you tie your faith to God, miracles are created. We're reminded that we're in the world but not of the world. You were birthed out of the supernatural, so you have an all-access pass to live in the supernatural. Faith allows you to continue to walk in it. The enemy will always try to get you to walk in fear, but faith kicks fear out. We were sent to the world to bring the supernatural, but for some reason, we got too comfortable in the world system. The supernatural is above the world system. The supernatural comes with the kingdom of God, and you are to bring the supernatural on earth! Faith plays a big role in this process. The supernatural doesn't have to make sense to the flesh. Faith doesn't come for you to adjust to the world, but faith comes to make the world adjust to you. The world is not our home. You are out of order and out of place to conform to the thing that is supposed to conform to the God in you.

We limit the supernatural from coming in our lives when we don't live in faith. You were sent on earth to make a change in the world around you, no matter how things might look or what your brain might think. The job of faith is not to make things make sense in your brain; faith puts you back in your right mind in Christ. God wants to get your faith to a place where miracles are no longer big events, but they are part of your everyday life. They are what you expect. So often, miracles are few and far between for us, so they become big events. We are shocked when one happens, but if you catch on to this, you will be shocked when miracles don't happen at a high level in your life.

You are wired to walk in the supernatural power of God, and anything below that is a problem that must be corrected. There should be an obvious difference between Christians and those who are in the world because we are to let our light shine! Your faith helps your light shine brighter in the world because what the world's faith produces is no match for what faith in Christ produces. The world tends to operate in their own idea of faith, but it's not faith in Christ. So, it's our job to bring the supernatural in this natural world. No matter how crazy the vision or instructions God gave you may seem, it always makes sense when you walk by faith.

You must get reacquainted with the lifestyle of faith. It requires being detoxed of old habits. It requires a complete healing and renewal of your soul, and you can pray for that. Faith doesn't share the credit with anything else. That's why faith loves taking on the most challenging jobs, so you'll know it was all God! Miracles, signs, and wonders are supposed to be produced out of your life. You are supposed to also help bring them in the lives of others. Faith in God through Christ is your starting point because without it, God is not pleased. God created us, and He placed His creative power in us so that we can produce things on earth on His behalf. God is the Creator, and we are creators since He gave us power to create. We must start creating while on earth, because it brings His kingdom. These things can only be done in the supernatural, and we must be reminded that, every time we pray in faith, we always produce.

You cannot take yourself lightly. The power of the Holy Spirit in you can literally transform the entire world. Change the world around you! The supernatural should be natural to you. When you have faith in God, it's a faith deposit that gives you continuous returns on investment. Faith must be your food. Faith must be a part of who you are. God put faith in you, and all you need to do is use it! When you walk in faith, you will find that challenges won't appear as challenges as much anymore. You will see them as opportunities. That's the power of faith. That's the lifestyle of faith. Faith changes how you see things. This is why we need to look through the lens of faith.

Faith gives your problems a problem because faith has never seen a problem that it could not take to heaven to get solved. Regardless of what the situation may look like, you must remember that faith still works, and it will produce. We must remember that your faith is like sowing a seed. That seed will grow, and it will produce a harvest. Some seeds may grow faster than others, but they still grow. Faith guarantees results because your faith pleases God. It's never a time to get down on your faith, but it's time to raise your faith up. You are gaining momentum in the spirit realm. Your faith is knocking down the walls that fear put up to hinder manifestation, and you can go in and get what's yours plus interest. Faith still works, and it still works in your life. Don't stop trusting God in the situation by making a move that is outside of faith. The greatest threat to you is if you take matters into your own hands because you get frustrated with God! Keep the faith. You either believe God or you don't. Your faith will not only produce, but it has already produced in your life. Don't forget what God has already done just because you're focusing on what hasn't manifested yet. Remember that when you walk in faith, you're sowing seeds in your life. You're not getting close, but you're already there. Don't stop and look at the situation, but keep walking by faith to the other side. Fear and doubt are terrible drivers in your life that lead you the wrong way, but your faith in God has never made a wrong turn. God is building your faith. Don't waver. Don't look the other way. God is building your faith because it will take great faith to participate in this great move of God.

It's an honor to be in the will of God. Your faith should be so persistent that the idea of failure or that manifestation won't come won't have room to even enter your mind. Remember that faith is easy. It was never meant to be hard, especially when God placed faith in us. You are wired to walk in faith because you came out of

God. Anything outside of faith is your enemy! Faith still works. Faith is alive and well, and it will do for you more than you even realize it's capable of doing. You're on center stage, and your faith is playing a leading role. So much has been built up in the spirit, and it's going to come rushing into your life, but the enemy wants you to step out of faith so that the blessings of God can't overtake you.

Don't allow frustration to fool you into thinking that things won't change. Faith will help you see that things are already changing! This is why we are supposed to walk by faith and not by sight. More is happening in your life than you have acknowledged because it's hard to see it when you're in it. However, faith can always see it. Your life is changing before your very eyes, and you haven't seen all the pieces. You're progressing, and it's happening at a rapid pace. It's already happened in the spirit, and it's coming due to manifest in the natural. This is why blessings will overtake you! Things are accelerating in the spirit, and that means that blessings are building up at a much faster pace than your flesh has been accustomed to. That creates an overflow.

The enemy will try to get you to worry, but when worry enters, don't give in to those feelings. Put the pressure back on your faith. Some of you have been looking at it the wrong way. God wants us to address that frustration head on. That is an enemy of God! It's an enemy that has caused too many of His children to blame Him for something He had nothing to do with. You don't have a God problem, but you have an enemy problem. Don't get mad at God for something He gave you the power to handle. We've all experienced frustration. Sometimes the easiest person to get mad at is God because we want someone to blame, but He's on your side! He has opened doors. What if God already released it and the enemy is legally blocking it? If God hasn't released it, you just need more patience. If God has released it, you need more fight in you. One way to know God has released it is when the enemy fights you hard in that area and there seems to be no movement in that area. The key is to continue to seek God to get the answer. Faith doesn't get frustrated with God because faith knows that God always takes care of His children. Faith is truly a weapon in spiritual warfare. Scripture tells us that the shield of faith quenches the fiery darts of the enemy (Ephesians 6:16).

So, we must seek God diligently by faith. When you consistently seek God by faith, God promises to reward you. What you do in the natural impacts what happens in the spirit, and what you do in the spirit impacts what happens in the natural. That's warfare! The enemy wants you to focus on the natural in an attempt to keep you from fighting in the spirit because it's in the spirit where we get results. You need faith to fight. **Faith is a weapon that is often overlooked because it's not seen as a weapon by many. However, faith reminds trouble about God.** Faith is what you send ahead of you. We can't physically get to heaven while on earth, but our faith can travel. Our faith speaks louder to God than our words. This is why faith is evidence. Your faith in God presents evidence to the enemy during warfare that you still belong to God and the enemy cannot have you.

We must understand that faith really does fight for us as well. We see it clearly in Scripture in 1 Timothy.

1 Timothy 6:12: *Fight the good fight of faith, lay hold on eternal life, to which you were also called and have confessed the good confession in the presence of many witnesses.*

Here we find the apostle Paul talking to his spiritual son Timothy. He was reminding him that trials will come as he proclaims the gospel, but he must keep the faith. Trials may present themselves in your life, but you're above it when you live by faith. Faith puts you above problems you face because faith is greater than any problem that comes your way. Your faith confuses the enemy because they don't understand why you won't just quit.
Paul also reminded Timothy how Timothy confessed his faith in God through Christ in the presence of many witnesses. In other words, others were watching. Your faith is on display, and you can't afford to step back because your faith is being witnessed by others. Don't panic when it feels like time is running out. Time

238

can't go faster than your faith. Faith is a fight because demons are always trying to pull you away from it! Your faith is strong enough not to get pulled away. You should prefer to stand alone in faith than to stand with a crowd in fear. Your faith sends fear back to hell. The beauty in it is that you're never truly alone. Keep fighting the good fight of faith. Faith still works. Faith in God will work every time if you just give it time. There has never been a time when faith has not produced. What faith has produced will manifest in your life at the perfect time. Fight with your faith because faith is undefeated against every obstacle the enemy tries to send. The enemy wants to get you out of faith so that they can sift you.

Luke 22:31-32: *And the Lord said, "Simon, Simon! Indeed, Satan has asked for you, that he may sift you as wheat. But I have prayed for you, that your faith should not fail; and when you have returned to Me, strengthen your brethren."*

The one in this passage referred to as Simon is Peter. His name was Simon Peter. Notice that Satan had to ask God for permission to sift Peter as wheat. The enemy was trying to find a legal right to attack Peter. That legal right was through a lack of faith. Sifting is a gradual process. The enemy has been trying to wear you down, but you wear the enemy down with your faith. Your faith in God is a threat to the enemy, so don't step out of faith because faith gives you a great advantage. Don't step out of faith because faith has never failed. Again, demons aren't afraid of you in your flesh, but they are very afraid of who you are when you walk in faith. Faith never fails us, but flesh will fail faith. Don't operate by what you see—operate by what God said!

Jesus told Peter that He would pray for him that his faith would not fail. We overcome Satan's attacks through our faith in God. Faith is a weapon in warfare because it's your faith that shields you from the darts the enemy tries to throw at you. If Jesus prayed for Peter's faith not to fail, we should also pray for our faith and others' faith not to fail. Demons can't break through your shield of faith. They only hope you lower it enough so that they can get to you. Faith in God never fails, but sometimes people fail to keep the faith!

After we have come through a storm, we should always strengthen others. The ministry of experience is a powerful ministry, and you should share your experiences and set others free. Your faith is an open invitation for heaven's storehouse to invade your life. Ask in faith. Others will be looking at you and your faith. Keep the faith, and faith will shine a great light on you. Faith is so important that if we don't have it, we are actually in sin, and sin obviously gives the enemy a legal right to steal.

Romans 14:23: *But he who doubts is condemned if he eats, because he does not eat from faith; for whatever is not from faith is sin.*

In this passage, the apostle Paul was speaking of those who were weak in faith and those who were strong in faith. He was addressing things like those who choose to eat meat and those who choose not to eat meat; those who choose to drink wine and those who do not; and those who believe one day is more sacred than another and those who see all days as the same. Apostle Paul was saying that while none of those is wrong in itself, if a person does it, they need to do it without any doubt. Where there is doubt, there is no faith. Where there is no faith, it is sin! Faith was placed in us because we need it to please God. God didn't make it hard because He placed faith in us to start with. What you do outside of faith is sin!

Whatever area in your life has any unbelief or doubt is the area that needs to be replaced with faith. Faith will make your obstacles obey you. Faith was meant to grow and be stretched. It helped grow you up. Your spirit is big enough to contain limitless faith. Apostle Paul was urging the people not to get caught up on debates about eating and drinking. He said the kingdom of God is much more than eating and drinking. It is living a righteous life, a life of peace and joy in the Holy Spirit, not being legalistic. Don't allow opinions of others to shake your faith. The world has it backwards.

Faith doesn't make you look crazy, but not keeping the faith makes you look crazy. Faith is stronger than an opinion because faith produces facts. Faith doesn't suggest something might happen, but faith says it will happen. The Holy Spirit helps you do the will of God, and faith helps to position you so the Holy Spirit can work through you. Faith helps you get what God said, and it helps you keep what God sent.

If you lack faith, deliverance is needed because faith is the prerequisite to have any chance at pleasing God. Faith is a must have. Just like you need air to breathe, you need faith to breathe in the spirit. A lack of faith begins to starve your spirit. Your spirit thrives when it is walking in faith. Faith has never been a natural thing, but it has always been supernatural. If we don't have faith in God in all things, no matter how big or small, we have sinned and need the key of faith through Christ to free us. This is one reason the enemy tries to sow seeds of doubt in your mind. If you doubt what God has said, that's sin because doubt is an enemy of faith. Fear brings bondage, but faith brings freedom. God wants you to live in freedom. Faith causes heaven to act on your behalf! God is looking for your faith because the more faith He sees, the more His presence will dwell. Doubt is a seed sowed by the enemy that tries to invite other demons to the party. Doubt is Satan's opinion about a matter. If you doubt God in any way, you need quick deliverance from Satan's opinion so it doesn't grow! When faith grows in your life, a problem that would normally bother you will excite you because faith has another chance to shine in your life.

Faith doesn't make you crazy; faith makes you sane in God. Faith is waiting for the opportunity to do what others thought would not happen in your life. Your faith frightens the impossible. Again, all have been given a measure of faith, and that measure alone is enough to move any obstacle demons place in front of us, but you must use that faith. Faith is your choice to trust God in all things, and it's the best choice! Your faith doesn't need anyone to celebrate it because when faith produces, it throws its own party on your behalf. When you live in faith, faith produces the evidence you've been waiting for. Faith also presents you with opportunities to go to new levels in God. Peter had this opportunity, and the enemy tried to snatch it away with fear.

Matthew 14:27-32: *But immediately Jesus spoke to them, saying, "Be of good cheer! It is I; do not be afraid." And Peter answered Him and said, "Lord, if it is You, command me to come to You on the water." So He said, "Come." And when Peter had come down out of the boat, he walked on the water to go to Jesus. But when he saw that the wind was boisterous, he was afraid; and beginning to sink he cried out, saying, "Lord, save me!" And immediately Jesus stretched out His hand and caught him, and said to him, "O you of little faith, why did you doubt?" And when they got into the boat, the wind ceased.*

Here we see Jesus was walking on water. In this passage, we see three of seven ways to access the supernatural being demonstrated: Jesus, faith, and obedience.

How to Access the Supernatural

1.) **Jesus-**Only way to God.

2.) **Holy Spirit-**Only way to Jesus.

3.) **Word of God-** Word gives life to our spirit.

4.) **Prayer-**How we communicate with heaven. Language of heaven. Currency of heaven.

5.) **Faith-** Cannot please God without it and a currency of heaven.

6.) **Praise and Worship-**Sets the atmosphere for God's glory to enter.

7.) **Obedience-** It's what God requires. It separates us from the enemy. Disobedience is an enemy of God.

Peter had faith to walk on the water, and he was obedient to Jesus's commands to come and walk on the water. Faith and obedience go hand in hand. You must have both when serving God! The supernatural became natural to Peter. The supernatural is what should be natural to us. Faith puts a command on heaven to release what's already been promised to you. It's where we should be most comfortable since we're spirit beings living in a physical body. However, our life is hidden in Christ who is our life. So, we're seated in Christ. Your faith in God can do what faith in man can never do.

Peter walking on water was not safe from the natural mind's view. It was dangerous as well because of the storm. Faith isn't safe to the natural mind because it seems too risky, but it's very safe in the spirit because it gives the best return on investments. Peter walked on something that could have drowned him. Faith allows you to walk on the very thing the enemy sent to drown you. We can also learn another principle here. Fear will immediately take us out of the supernatural. Peter was walking on water, which was supernatural, but when the wind became strong and he became afraid, he was immediately back in the natural. Jesus let us know why Peter was taken out of the supernatural, and it was because he had little faith and began to doubt. You were sent to do work in the natural but still be able to live in the supernatural. Fear holds you back in bondage, but faith pushes you forward and breaks you free. The enemy wants us to doubt and be unstable in our faith in God because he knows it will lower us below our potential and power. This is why God lets us know that He did not give us a spirit of fear (2 Timothy 1:7).

Fear and doubt are two of the biggest obstacles in the body of Christ when it comes to the supernatural. We must overcome them to continuously access the supernatural. Faith opens doors that we cannot see because they can only be seen in the spirit. If you ever want a glimpse of some of what's to come in your life, just look through the lens of faith. Fear says to wait and wait, but faith says you can have it right now. Faith can also be passed down.

2 Timothy 1:5-7: *When I call to remembrance the genuine faith that is in you, which dwelt first in your grandmother Lois and your mother Eunice, and I am persuaded is in you also. Therefore I remind you to stir up the gift of God which is in you through the laying on of my hands. For God has not given us a spirit of fear, but of power and of love and of a sound mind.*

Apostle Paul also wrote this letter to Timothy. He wastes no time getting to the point. He said he was reminded of Timothy's faith, which was also seen in Timothy's grandmother and his mother. This lets us know that faith is noticeable. Your faith cannot only be seen in the spirit realm, but it can also be seen in the natural. Others are encouraged because of your faith! Notice Paul said it dwelt in them. You must have faith. It is a requirement for the things of God. Faith is contagious. Your faith is not just for you, but it's also for those who are watching. Your faith can increase someone else's faith. Stay in faith because someone is watching to see how you handle it and the results that come with it. You can have enough faith for someone else for something to happen in their life, and your faith in God can cause it to manifest. This is why you must take your assignment in your God-given territory seriously. God expects you to have influence there.

Paul urges Timothy to begin to operate in his gifts. He told him to stir up the gift or to rekindle or start up the fire of his gift. He knew he had power to heal the sick, cast out demons, etc., because it's what God left us with. Faith comes with the guarantee that it will produce miracles in your life if you give it time to finish the job. If you are looking for a miracle, the first place to start is faith through Christ.

From this passage, we see that faith can also be generational. Faith can be passed down. Therefore, faith is transferable in the spirit. A bloodline can have a history of fear or a history of great faith. You can make sure that faith is passed on to generations in your family. Faith can be taught, but for it to be most effective in your life, it must be caught! We can pray for faith to be increased in others. Fear is a demonic spirit, but faith is a godly spirit. Fear is your enemy, and faith is your friend. If demonic spirits can be

244

transferred, we know that godly spirits can be transferred because Satan only tries to duplicate what God does. The enemy doesn't attack your faith to try to stop only you, but they do it to try to stop you from igniting faith in others. The enemy tries to get you tired and frustrated with not seeing manifestation so they can steal from you. No matter what, don't step out of faith!

God gave us His power and authority so that we may walk boldly in the supernatural and wipe out darkness and replace it with light. He gave us the spirit of power, as His power is spiritual/supernatural power that can impact the natural. According to Strong's Concordance, one of the definitions for power in this verse is "power for performing miracles." We know that it applies here because in verse 6, Paul spoke of how he had laid hands on Timothy, which originally stirred up his gifts. We know as children of God that we have this power to perform miracles in the name of Jesus. It's our responsibility to bring the supernatural to earth. Miracles, signs, and wonders should be a part of our lives because we are spirit. Your faith can be big enough to set others free! It will be battle tested, but you will be victorious if you stay in faith.

James 1:2-4: *My brethren, count it all joy when you fall into various trials, knowing that the testing of your faith produces patience. But let patience have its perfect work, that you may be perfect and complete, lacking nothing.*

What James was saying doesn't make sense on the surface because who really feels they should have joy when they are going through a tough time? However, he tells us why we should have joy. We should have joy in knowing that as our faith is tested, it will produce patience or endurance. You should have joy when your faith is tested because faith has never failed a test! The enemy will try to test your faith. They will try to test your authority. We just need to let faith go to work. One of the biggest mistakes the enemy makes is to challenge your faith because it will only make it grow in the long run. Once patience does its work, we will be mature and complete, lacking nothing. This is a promise. We see here that when we are tested, our faith is tested. When your faith is tested, it produces patience/endurance over time. As you become more patient and stronger, you will mature. Faith builds you up when it seems like everything around you is trying to bring you down. Faith is not found in the problem, but faith looks at the problem and produces the solution. You will become complete for the task at hand, and you will lack nothing. You will have everything you need. Faith is connected to a process that will leave you lacking nothing when it's completed. Faith in God never lacks, and as you activate it, it will make sure you never lack.

So, you can have joy in the midst of your test, because your test has nothing to do with your joy. You have a right to joy, and if something takes it, faith in God through Christ can help you find it. So, count this as joy because the test comes with the level you're on. Just like certain jobs require random testing or testing to make sure you are up to date on everything, God will allow tests to accomplish a similar thing in the spirit.

Sometimes it could be a risk for God to trust you, but He does! So, there is absolutely no reason for you not to trust Him. God took the risk to trust you, so you should have enough sense to trust Him with everything. What you had to do the last time may be different this time, although the situation may look familiar. However, your response should always be in faith, and after you receive instructions, you should respond with obedience to God. Faith is not waiting for something to happen, but faith makes it happen now. At the end of the day, God expects us to live from faith forever.

Hebrews 10:38: *Now the just shall live by faith;*
But if anyone draws back,
My soul has no pleasure in him.

Faith cannot be seen. Faith is a spiritual deposit. There is a difference between having faith and living by faith. God says we must live by faith. Not only that, but He also said that it's impossible to please Him without it. Faith is not an option, but it's what we must live by as a child of God. Faith is a heavy meal in the spirit, and your spirit needs it to thrive. Faith is not some theory; as a child of God, it is a way of life. Faith believes what seems impossible in the flesh, because faith knows that nothing is impossible in the spirit with God. When you look back over the chapters of your life so far, you can look back and see a life of faith. It doesn't mean you got it right all the time, but you eventually knew that trusting God was the best way. Faith doesn't get caught up in the problem, but it gets caught up in the solution!

Fear is tied to who Satan wants you to become, but faith is tied to who you really are in God. When we draw back or replace faith with fear or don't put our faith in God, He is not pleased. He takes no pleasure in that because fear is an enemy of the kingdom of God. Therefore, fear is your enemy. Doubt is your enemy. Sickness is your enemy. Stress and depression are your enemy. Rejection is your enemy. All of those are spirits contrary to God. This is why you must walk by faith. Your faith in God will put doubt to shame!

Your faith helps to activate the supernatural power of God in your life. It helps produce miracles. When faith in Christ produces what seemed impossible, it's just a normal day at the office. Faith doesn't compete because faith eliminates competition. Your flesh may live on earth, but your spirit should live in faith. Faith is necessary, and God requires it. God wants you to a place in faith where you know no other way. Your spirit knows no other way except faith because it knows that it is the only way. Your faith has made a way for you in the wilderness, and it is giving you access to what you didn't think you deserved. When you completely live by faith, nothing will seem impossible to you.

We can identify at least four levels of faith in Scripture:

    1.) No Faith

    2.) Little (Weak) Faith

    3.) Great (Strong) Faith

4.) Beyond Measure (Increase Exceedingly)

2 Thessalonians 1:3-4: *We are bound to thank God always for you, brethren, as it is fitting, because your faith grows exceedingly, and the love of every one of you all abounds toward each other, so that we ourselves boast of you among the churches of God for your patience and faith in all your persecutions and tribulations that you endure.*

Apostle Paul was talking about the faith of those in the church of Thessalonica. It was growing exceedingly. According to Strong's Concordance, the Greek word for exceedingly in this passage is "huperauxanó," which means increase exceedingly or to increase beyond measure. They had faith beyond measure.

When you're swimming in faith, when your house/temple is filled with faith, it's hard to step out of faith. When people come in your home, faith should get on them. It should be contagious. God wants you to have so much faith that it overflows and jumps on others. Remember, faith is a spirit. The enemy can put fear and doubt on people, but we can ignite faith in people. We can transfer it. Faith is transferable. Your faith is a game changer. Your faith is a legacy changer. Your faith is a generation changer. Think about going in a house where someone is frying chicken or fish. It doesn't take too long before that smell will get on your clothes because it's flowing throughout the house. You don't smoke, but if you go in a house where it's filled with smoke from a smoker, you will leave smelling like smoke. The smell gets in your clothes and in your hair. Your faith should get on others when they come in your space. It should get all over them and they won't know what got into them, but they will feel so much better. They will be rejuvenated. You gave them a shot and a boost of faith!

The smoke alarm goes off if it detects too much smoke. A faith alarm should go off in the spirit when you show up because you aren't bringing faith just for yourself, but you're bringing it for others, too. You can have enough faith for others, too. You can have faith for someone else's healing, deliverance, breakthrough, etc. God wants you to have faith in the overflow so you can pass it around. Let it get all over them in Jesus's name!

Chapter 19: Relationships: Destroying Covenant-Breaking and Sex Demons

The enemy wants to break godly covenant and prevent you from getting in godly covenant, but you have the power to break the enemy! There are marriage covenants, friendship covenants, business covenants, etc. If God brings it together, it is a divine connection. Divine connections are important because God makes the connections. It goes far beyond just romantic relationships. God connects you with certain people in life because there is something they have that you need and that you have that they need. God is the most resourceful manager there is! Everything God joins together, demons try to pull apart. When you know it's a God thing, you need to fight back. You have all of heaven's defense at the tip of your fingers. It's one thing if demons came and caused havoc in your life, but it's another thing if you let them get away with it. God is not connecting you with the right people only for you to sit back and watch the enemy take it all away. Fight back!

Covenant-breaking demons hate godly covenant. They want you to be in covenant with them. This is why they will do everything in their power to keep you in chains. When these demons oppress people, they may give some freedom, but it's a game to them. They give and snatch away. Covenant-breaking demons want you to want what's not good for you because it allows them to stay around. You must evict them! This is why it's even difficult to walk away from something you know is not good for you. Beware of the tricks of the enemy: these demons make wrong feel right and make right feel wrong. This is why relationship with God is so important. This is why prayer is so important. We all could potentially be fooled by the enemy if we don't watch and pray. They are looking for an opportunity to break up what God set up. But God's name is in you, and that outranks the attack.

These covenant-breaking demons' favorite entry point is through illegal sex, which is sex while not married or sex with a person who is not your spouse. They also love to enter through your family bloodline, and some of these spirits have been living in your bloodline for centuries, known as generational curses, which we have already discussed. Covenant-breaking demons also love to enter through relationships that were not ordained by God. Ask the Holy Spirit for instructions before you enter any relationship and even after you're in it. God-ordained relationships still require God to keep it.

God is a God of His people. So, He is always connecting people together to accomplish various things in the earth. You are living in a lie if you believe you will go through life without God using people to help you along the way! We need people used by God to help us get to where God is sending us. The greatest form of wealth is found through God connecting you with the right people on the journey. Demons know this, and that's why they constantly want you connected with the wrong people. This is why they are always sending the wrong people in the midst of the right people to try to throw you off. It's not even that the people are necessarily bad people, but they may just not be connected to your destiny. They aren't a part of God's will for your life. **Satan is a covenant breaker, but God is a covenant keeper!** Let's explore some Scriptures to give us deeper insight.

Jeremiah 3:6-9: *The LORD said also to me in the days of Josiah the king: "Have you seen what backsliding Israel has done? She has gone up on every high mountain and under every green tree, and there played the harlot. And I said, after she had done all these things, 'Return to Me.' But she did not return. And her treacherous sister Judah saw it. Then I saw that for all the causes for which backsliding Israel had committed adultery, I had put her away and given her a certificate of divorce; yet her treacherous sister Judah did not fear, but went and played the harlot also. So it came to pass, through her casual harlotry, that she defiled the land and committed adultery with stones and trees."*

Here we find God speaking to the prophet Jeremiah. Israel committed adultery against God by worshipping idols and partaking in sex orgies practiced by the worshippers of these idols. False gods had their own priests, who had women servants of these idols who would tempt men to convert through the sex orgies attached to this type of worship. This type of activity still goes on today with sex orgies. The people participating in these orgies today may not even know that they are a part of a demonic initiation process. This setup was similar to pimps and prostitutes. This type of activity opened more demonic portals on earth. Sexual intercourse in itself is not bad. God intended for it to be enjoyed in marriage. Satan will try to use what God meant for good to try to twist it, but you can change that by walking in obedience to God! This is why repenting of our sins is also important. You must renounce what you have done that displeased God, leave it in the past, and move forward in obedience to God. God sent Jeremiah to warn the people, but during this time more false prophets were on the rise and gave false prophecies against what God gave to Jeremiah. The false prophets convinced the people that all was well and they could continue doing what they were doing. Yet, God was not pleased. Jeremiah felt isolated for being given such a tough assignment, but God strengthened him. You may feel isolated for doing what's right, but I assure you that the rewards for righteousness always outweigh temporary gratification. Today, there are still occult practices in which they try to get young people addicted to drugs so they can prostitute them for these demonic organizations. Since God has raised us up as part of a remnant generation that will usher in the supernatural power of God and walk in great deliverance, we must know what is going on and what type of portals are being opened.

Demons will try to use any sin we commit to gain access. They will even use the sins of those you're connected with. Watch your circle! Bad soul ties can cause your entire attitude to change. They can cause you to act outside of your normal character. Bad soul ties are not always with bad people, but they can just be people who are bad for you. There may be times when you are not with that individual anymore, but you cannot get them out of your mind.

This is a result of a soul tie. You can repent to God for the sin, and that puts you back in right standing with God. However, it doesn't automatically cancel a soul tie that may have been formed. You must also renounce the soul tie.

Contrary to popular belief, soul ties do not even require sex. However, sex makes it much more complex because the two are literally becoming one flesh, as Scripture tells us. This is when your soul becomes tied together with another. It is like you are bonded together as one. The soul is simply the inner part of humans that is the seat of human feelings, desires, passions, appetites, and emotions. In knowing the definition, we understand what it means when your soul is tied to or connected to another. When we hear of soul ties, it is often referencing sex. However, it can also be formed through close relationships. Demons try to make you feel a connection to someone you know you shouldn't be connected to in order to try to keep you in bondage. Be free! All soul ties are not bad. There are godly soul ties and ungodly soul ties. Good soul ties can be found in healthy relationships with your parents, siblings, children, other family members, God-ordained relationships, and the right friends. There can also be bad soul ties among those individuals, and all bad soul ties must be broken so you don't continue in that unhealthy pattern. You must first pray that any ungodly soul tie be broken. Speak over your life and declare that whatever is attached to you that's not from God must leave in the name of Jesus! Command them to leave. Continue to pray and speak that over your life until you see and sense the change. This is important because you cannot effectively move on until that is severed or it will definitely impact future relationships.

It's almost like carrying around bed bugs. They can be difficult to detect, and they can be a pain to get rid of. If they get on your clothes, they will travel with you and will attach themselves to the next place you lay your head, which is home. The demonic spirits attached to ungodly soul ties attempt to travel with you in an attempt to keep you in bondage and to connect you with someone else, to either keep you going through the same cycle or to cause havoc in the next relationship, whether the person was sent by God or by Satan. There are some people who you just have to let go because it will cost you far more to keep them around than if you let them go. We must also be aware that the enemy uses any open door to gain ground. Sexual immorality in a city can give demons so much more room to run wild because they have so many doors they can enter into. They use these opportunities to take over entire communities and cities. We find this in Scripture.

Revelation 2:12-16: *"And to the angel of the church in Pergamos write,*

'These things says He who has the sharp two-edged sword: "I know your works, and where you dwell, where Satan's throne is. And you hold fast to My name, and did not deny My faith even in the days in which Antipas was My faithful martyr, who was killed among you, where Satan dwells. But I have a few things against you, because you have there those who hold the doctrine of Balaam, who taught Balak to put a stumbling block before the children of Israel, to eat things sacrificed to idols, and to commit sexual immorality. Thus you also have those who hold the doctrine of the Nicolaitans, which thing I hate. Repent, or else I will come to you quickly and will fight against them with the sword of My mouth."'"

Here we find John's revelation. Christ addressed seven churches during this time, and it is also a sign to us today. He addressed it to the angel or spiritual human leader of the church at Pergamos. Evil was all around the people there because of great sin and worshipping of idols. It was so bad that Satan had set up his throne there and dwelled there. Now, if Satan could set up his throne there, we know how many legal rights he had there. We know how much access he and his workers had. Persecution of Christians was bad there. Christ commended the people for keeping the faith in the midst of persecution. Satan had gained great influence in this city. The enemy wants to gain influence in the place God has planted you. You must walk in your kingdom authority to show that you're the boss.

There is no question that demonic portals had been opened up in this city. So, it is obvious the church was not fully doing its part. We see in verse 14 that Christ had a few things against the church at Pergamos. We cannot afford to sit back and pretend we're asleep when the enemy boldly comes on our territory trying to bully us. Fight back. I discussed in chapter 9 about demonic altars, and how Balaam was a perfect example of a prophet of God going bad for the sake of money and greed. Balak, the king of Moab, was afraid that the Israelites might destroy him and his city, so he called Balaam to curse the people so that he could defeat them. Nicolaitans did the same thing. They tempted God's people to commit idolatry and fornication, which was most often tied to idol worship. Sexual immorality is one way to open up demonic portals. This is why we see such a rise in homosexual behavior and acceptance of it in our culture. It is a spirit. However, homosexuality is only one manifested sexual spirit. That unclean spirit can manifest in many ways.

This is why thoughts are powerful. Reject the thought of the enemy in your mind, and accept the thought of God. A demonic portal can be opened over a city through something such as sexual immorality. It invites demons in. This is why laws that are passed in whatever country or state you live in are very important. Principalities try to influence politicians and legislators to create laws that oppose God's will. We have a responsibility to overturn demonic systems set up in our God-given territory.

There are three main areas the enemy loves to attack the body of Christ in heavily: health, wealth, and relationships (intimate and family and friends). I call them the Big Three. There are demons working against you trying to rob you of your peace and joy and trying to prevent you from getting to who and what God has for you. The enemy tries to attack your desire to love and be loved, but you must hold to the promise of God. If you know God's love, you will not accept anything that is beneath that love! Demonic spirits will attempt to get you to go for less than what God has. God's love attracts God's love. If you're considering someone whose love doesn't come close to what you know God has, don't entertain it.

Incubus (husband spirit): An evil spirit that has sexual intercourse with women while they are sleeping. Demonic sexual attack on females may be caused by sexual sins, witchcraft spells, curses of lust, or inherited curses. It can also attack children. It is an unclean spirit that defiles you in the night.

Succubus (wife spirit): A demon assuming female form to have sexual intercourse with men in their sleep.

These spirits can show up in your dreams and often may come as someone you know or have fantasized about. The demon MARE works with the incubus and succubus demons. This demon can cause dreams of sexual content coupled with those evil spirits. The dream itself is called a NightMare. These sexual spirits are tormenting and can feel as though you are being molested. Most attacks are at night, and the individual may be awakened by fondling hands, caressing hot lips and tongue, and other forms of lust-inducing stimulation. Every kind of abnormal and deviant sexual experience can be generated by these evil spirits, which are unclean spirits. They deal with married couples, too. Someone can be married and dreaming about having sex with someone else. Why does this happen? This happens because of an open door from:

- Masturbation
- Sexual abuse
- Reading or watching pornography
- Internet sex
- Sex outside a marriage
- Didn't take control of sexual thoughts
- House being out of order
- Something in your bloodline that had nothing to do with you, but they gained access through it.

Spiritual husbands and wives feel they're in covenant with you so they feel they can steal your husband or steal your wife, money, etc. They are very jealous because they feel you belong to them. These spirits do not want you to get married, and if you do, they try to set you up to marry someone they can continue the same cycle with. They try to bankrupt you emotionally and spiritually, and sometimes they will let someone get money if they're in love with it just so they can invite the demon known as mammon. Scripture says you can't serve God and mammon.

A spiritual husband also causes fertility issues. If you have ever been told you won't be able to have kids, that could be an attack on your body by a spiritual husband. The spirit wife also deals with the male genitalia. You're not a bad person just because these spirits attack. That's just what it is, an attack, and you can do something about it. **Just because a demon attacks doesn't mean that you did something; oftentimes it's because of what they're afraid you will do to them!** Lust can produce more than just sex. Lust is a desire, longing, and craving for something that is forbidden. I had a spirit spouse for a long time and did not know it until I understood more about spiritual warfare and how demons operate. There was this woman who would always come to me in my dreams and kiss me when I was a child. I would always wake up with this nasty taste in my mouth after she kissed me. As I got a little older in high school, she would have sex with me in my dreams, and sometimes I would wake up with wet dreams. This spirit wife was with me even into adulthood. When I gained more understanding, I started coming against it. One night in my dream, I was riding on a motorcycle, and a woman with long hair was behind me. She was wearing a helmet. I lifted up the visor of the helmet, and in my spirit, I knew it was the spirit wife who was there. I evicted her off the motorcycle, and she started screaming very loudly because she was found out and kicked out of my life. Yes, years later, she still made attempts to try to enter back in with crafty strategy in my dreams, but she was still caught.

This spirit caused a lot of problems in relationships. I was never in a bad relationship, but this spirit still fought me hard when it came to getting married. There were three different times that I knew beyond a shadow of a doubt I was supposed to be married before I met my wife Donna, and that spirit spouse always caused issues to prevent it. Honestly, the reason Donna and I got married is because we understood what we were up against because the enemy fought us very hard before marriage and in marriage. That was my experience and deliverance from a spiritual wife that was married to me. I had to issue a divorce decree in the spirit. I had to pray and war until it was evicted for good.

Here are two examples of activities the enemy has led some people to believe are not sin outside of marriage. When I had the spirit wife, they used these things as an open door in my life to strengthen them to be able to stay longer.

Masturbation- Some believe that this is ok, but masturbation is still sin. It is still sexual immorality that is a direct result of lust. When you look up the word self-abuse on dictionary.com, masturbation is one of the definitions, even in the medical dictionary cited. It began to show up in the dictionary as a synonym in 1728, according to etymonline.com. Well, certainly most who perform the act of masturbation are not attempting to abuse themselves, but even though it's temporary pleasure, it is really just serving as a substitute for sex. So, it's like abusing yourself because you cannot have what you truly desire at that moment.

Oral Sex- Again, this is yet another substitute for sex. This is still sexual contact that should be avoided when not married.
Every sin begins with a seed, and that seed is usually a thought. Sometimes, you may have a thought from a past experience that triggers it. You may smell a cologne or perfume that reminds you of someone in your past. A number of things can trigger thought. Those thoughts can lead to real action if they are not brought under subjection.

1 Corinthians 6:15-20: *Do you not know that your bodies are members of Christ? Shall I then take the members of Christ and* *make them members of a harlot? Certainly not! Or do you not know that he who is joined to a harlot is one body with her? For "the two," He says, "shall become one flesh." But he who is joined to the Lord is one spirit with Him.*

Flee sexual immorality. Every sin that a man does is outside the body, but he who commits sexual immorality sins against his own body. Or do you not know that your body is the temple of the Holy Spirit who is in you, whom you have from God, and you are not your own? For you were bought at a price; therefore glorify God in your body and in your spirit, which are God's.

We must understand that though we are here on earth, our bodies do not belong to ourselves. They belong to Christ because when Jesus died on the cross for our sins, He paid the ultimate price for us. So, when we accept Christ, we no longer belong to ourselves. Our bodies belong to Christ, which is why we are also known as the body of Christ. That applies physically and spiritually. As the church as a whole, we are the body of Christ. As an individual, we are also the body of Christ. So, if we are the body of Christ, we cannot do just anything we want with our bodies. Your body belongs to God, not you, and if you recognize that, you would know the gift that you truly are.

If you have sex with someone, the two of you become one. So, would it be good to take Christ's body, which we have, and attach it to a prostitute? Absolutely not. Would it be good to take Christ's body and have sex with someone who is not your spouse? Absolutely not. The two of you become one flesh. We are joined to God, which makes us one in the spirit with Him. This is why we must flee or run from fornication. Every other sin is committed outside of our body, but fornication is sinning against our own bodies, because we are the body of Christ. So, that's why ungodly soul ties must be broken. Demons are looking for a free attack. Do your best to avoid giving them access for a cheap shot.

Not only are our bodies the body of Christ, but our body also serves as the temple for the Holy Spirit that is within us. If the enemy can gain access to a child of God to have sex with them or get them to sin by having illegal sex, the enemy can use semen or the bodily fluids/blood from a woman to create spiritual children in the demonic realm. This is similar to how the angels who had sex with women created Nephilim, which was a half breed of human and angel. These Nephilim were giants, and after all the detestable things they did, God sent the flood (Genesis 6:1-4). However, the spirits of the Nephilim roamed the earth after they drowned in the flood, and those are demons. They are disembodied spirits who are looking for a body or thing to dwell in. They, along with witches and warlocks, can use semen and bodily fluids to create spiritual babies with a human to keep them in bondage. They even use blood from abortions to create a covenant with an individual. Through prayer and warfare, those demonic babies can be destroyed. The enemy is looking for any way to legally come in covenant with us. What makes it a bit easier is when there were old covenants on the bloodline and continual sin is committed to give them access to reestablish an old covenant that was broken on the bloodline. Not only should we repent of our sin, but we should repent for the sins of our ancestors and anyone on our bloodline. We have such a precious gift in us in the Holy Spirit that we would not want to attempt to commit sexual sins knowing such a powerful gift is in us. If the sin is committed, sincere repentance to God is needed. Don't beat yourself up about what happened in the past, but repent to God and look forward to the joys of the future. You are more than able to overcome every trap of the enemy. The enemy has power, but you have more power!

Warfare against Godly Covenant: The Relationship Fruit

God created man and woman to be together. Everyone has a story to tell. Everyone has history. Everyone has had some type of relationship with the opposite sex, whether you were actually with them or just really liked them. This begins at a very early age. Children don't always understand the dynamics between male and female. So, this is why many of you were in the situation as a child where someone of the opposite sex would hit you and pick on you. In most cases, it was because they liked you, but they did not understand the proper process of how that works. However, it shows that something went off in our minds even as a child.

Some of the media has not helped with this process. There was a time when one did not have to worry about messages in cartoons. Now, parents must even censor cartoons to make sure they are appropriate for their children. We see commercials, cartoons, and what are supposed to be children-friendly shows insinuating inappropriate behavior between youth. There is now more sexual content on these cartoons than violence. The Parents Television Council® released the results of their study, "Cartoons Are No Laughing Matter," documenting shocking levels of adult content on networks with the highest-rated primetime animated cable shows among children ages 12-17, according to Nielsen data. Based on the Nielsen findings, the PTC examined 123 episodes of animated programming that aired on Adult Swim, Cartoon Network, Disney Channel, and Nick at Nite for the presence of sexual content, violence, drugs, and explicit language between March 21 and April 14, 2011.

Parents Television Council researchers documented 1,487 incidents of explicit language, drugs, and sexual content during the four-week study period. On average, young viewers were exposed to adult content once every two minutes and 19 seconds. TV-PG-rated animation featured sex, drugs, or profanity every two minutes and 31 seconds. Adult Swim, which used to begin airing at 11 p.m. ET and now begins at 9 p.m., included some of the highest-rated animated shows among ages 12-17 and the highest levels of explicit content.

We were all programmed as children, and now our youths of today are being programmed with the aid of television. This shows us how much influence the media has. We also know that Satan can sow seeds through the media in a very subtle way. You have eye gates and ear gates. What enters your eyes through what you see and what enters your ears through what you hear are seeds. There are either good seeds or bad seeds. What you expose yourself to that is not of God can give demons legal rights to you or your children. These small seeds can grow and become a far bigger problem if they're not uprooted. For some of you, it began as a child. It wasn't anything you did, but it was likely something on your bloodline or something that you or the violator were exposed to early on.

From our countless deliverance sessions and deliverance assessments, we have found approximately 70% of those seeking help have experienced some type of molestation or illegal and uninvited sexual contact from someone else as a child. This could have been an older family member, classmate, neighbor, babysitter, etc. We have also seen many cases where all the kids in the family would just experiment with each other sexually as little kids, whether it be through touching or actually committing a sexual act. Those seeds were planted young, whether through exposure or something that was passed down on the bloodline. There have been examples where every sibling had been sexually violated as a child. This simply carries over into adulthood if it's not dealt with spiritually and emotionally. Spiritual seeds are very real whether they are good seeds or bad seeds.

As a woman, you may have been programmed to believe that a man would come along and take care of you. However, over time, you may have realized that you cannot sit around and wait for a man to come and rescue you. So, over time, we have seen the Independent Women Movement. You may have not had your father active in your life, so you did not really know what a good man looked like. Perhaps you did have your father around, so you had every reason in the world to trust men because of Daddy. Surely, all men who are interested in you would have your best interest at heart, right? However, some of the men you encountered did not seem to be as loving and caring as Daddy. So, some of you began to think, "Is something wrong with me?" So, maybe you began to change your look, change what you said, and even went against the good qualities you were taught because you were reprogrammed to think that in order to get a good man, you had to compromise who you were. Of course, something did not feel right because it went against what you were taught or what you believed. Over time, some women have been reprogrammed and do not recognize it because they no longer recognize themselves. I mean, of course they did not think they changed because they began to accept anything in relationships and doing things the wrong way became normal.

Men, some of you may have been taught that you need to find a good woman who will cook and clean for you. Perhaps you were taught that you should find a good woman just like your mom. Some of you misinterpreted that to mean that you had to go and find a woman to be your mother. You may have gone through life looking for that woman who would wait on you hand and foot. Mom may have spoiled you, so women should spoil you, right? So, some men missed the target and figured they would just go around and deal with a lot of women until that void of finding another mother figure was filled. You may not have been programmed that way, but many men were reprogrammed when a woman did not do everything they asked.

So, many men and women have gone through life living through trial and error in search for what they believe is love to the best of their knowledge. Some began earlier than others, but it has often been triggered by disappointment by the opposite sex. When expectations were not met, some compromised and changed to try to create a better situation, while others capitalized on the opportunity to take advantage. Men and women in these situations have taken advantage of the disappointment. Some men tell women whatever they want to hear so they can get whatever they want. Some women play along with the man so that he can give her whatever she wants. What ultimately happens in a lot of cases is that one of the parties involved does most of the giving while the other does most of the taking.

Where did we go wrong? What happened? What changed? Many of us were taught good morals. In order to diagnose a problem and to see how far we have come or how far we have strayed away, history is very important. So, let us take a look at the first man and woman and how they were created by God.

Genesis 1:27-28: *So God created man in His own image; in the image of God He created him; male and female He created them. Then God blessed them, and God said to them, "Be fruitful and multiply; fill the earth and subdue it; have dominion over the fish of the sea, over the birds of the air, and over every living thing that moves on the earth."*

So, we see that God created man and woman to rule on the earth and do be fruitful (have children) and fill the earth with those children. We also see that man and woman were originally created in the image of God. So, we are not God, but have God-like qualities. In other words, God gave man and woman power and authority on earth. We get to the second account of man and woman in more detail in the next chapter.

Genesis 2:21-22: *And the LORD God caused a deep sleep to fall on Adam, and he slept; and He took one of his ribs, and closed up the flesh in its place. Then the rib which the LORD God had taken from man He made into a woman, and He brought her to the man.*

God put the man into a deep sleep and pulled a rib out of the man and created the first woman. This does not mean that the man is superior to the woman; this simply means that man and woman are a part of each other. You are a part of the one God has ordained for you to be with.

Now everything was fine. Expectations were met for both man and woman. They lived peacefully with each other. They went about their daily lives in relationship with God and one another. There was no compromise until the next chapter.

Genesis 3:1-13: *Now the serpent was more cunning than any beast of the field which the LORD God had made. And he said to the woman, "Has God indeed said, 'You shall not eat of every tree of the garden'?"*

And the woman said to the serpent, "We may eat the fruit of the trees of the garden; but of the fruit of the tree which is in the midst of the garden, God has said, 'You shall not eat it, nor shall you touch it, lest you die.'"

Then the serpent said to the woman, "You will not surely die. For God knows that in the day you eat of it your eyes will be opened, and you will be like God, knowing good and evil."

So when the woman saw that the tree was good for food, that it was pleasant to the eyes, and a tree desirable to make one wise, she took of its fruit and ate. She also gave to her husband with her, and he ate. Then the eyes of both of them were opened, and they knew that they were naked; and they sewed fig leaves together and made themselves coverings.

And they heard the sound of the LORD God walking in the garden in the cool of the day, and Adam and his wife hid themselves from the presence of the LORD God among the trees of the garden.

Then the LORD God called to Adam and said to him, "Where are you?"

So he said, "I heard Your voice in the garden, and I was afraid because I was naked; and I hid myself."

And He said, "Who told you that you were naked? Have you eaten from the tree of which I commanded you that you should not eat?"

Then the man said, "The woman whom You gave to be with me, she gave me of the tree, and I ate."

And the LORD God said to the woman, "What is this you have done?" The woman said, "The serpent deceived me, and I ate."

Adam and Eve were programmed to think like God, but the serpent came along and distorted that by planting a negative thought in their minds. Yes, the serpent was a trickster, but both Adam and Eve knew better than to eat what I call the "relationship fruit." I call it the relationship fruit because eating from that tree caused major issues with Adam and Eve's relationship and their relationship with God. They both had a choice to obey God or disobey. They both chose to disobey. Now, they were reprogrammed to act and think outside of what they had been taught. They compromised. The moment they compromised is when everything changed.

Eve may have eaten the fruit first, but Adam was with her. They were both responsible. However, God first told Adam, who in turn told Eve, what trees they could and could not eat from. They were both responsible because they both received the same instructions. Verse 7 lets us know that both of their eyes were opened, and they saw that they were naked and sewed fig leaves together to cover their nakedness. Prior to this, they did not even know they were naked. **The first attack in spiritual warfare on earth in Scripture is an attack on covenant!** It was the covenant between Adam and Eve, and their covenant with God.

Many men and women today need to be reprogrammed to go back to the place where we are truly walking with God as Adam and Eve did before they went against God's instructions. Because Adam and Eve opened themselves up to another way of thinking, they made things harder on themselves. They compromised, and it caused a division among them. We see this division among many men and women today. Each side is blaming the other or has something negative to say about the other side. Adam and Eve were created to team up together to produce more generations who walked with God. The same applies today. Men and women are to team up to produce generations who also walk with God. Men and women are to team up to continue to honor the union God established from the beginning. Even if you may not have children or desire to have children, men and women were still created to work hand in hand.

God called the man first because he represented the head of the household. Adam tried to hide because he heard God coming and knew he was now naked. God responded, "Who told you that you were naked?" God never programmed man or woman to know that. Instead of asking for forgiveness, Adam went into subtly passing blame on God. So, Adam tried to put the blame on God for giving him Eve, and Eve tried to put the blame on the serpent for telling her about the tree. No one wanted to take responsibility. Who knows what may have happened if they were willing to talk about it and admit their fault rather than finding someone else to blame? You know how some individuals try to blame others for their actions. They try to make excuses and blame different life experiences as to why they sleep around or cannot commit. They make excuses for why they settled, even though not many are willing to admit that they settled. If they are able to diagnose the problem, certainly they can seek a solution. Men and women must take responsibility for their actions and not come up with a list of excuses. When you become an adult and know right from wrong, there is no room for excuses. Men and women must take responsibility for how we treat one another.

God created man. Then God planted a garden in Eden to be man's home. Then God created trees to produce food. He had the rivers flowing to bring water to the garden and provide drink. So, we see a process: A man was given shelter, food, water, placed within a governmental system to rule in (God's government), given laws to abide by to remain in rulership in the government, and then God gave him a wife so they could rule together on earth.

In the beginning, Adam was alone with God, then Eve came along and Adam and Eve were in covenant with God. Adam followed God; Eve followed Adam. This was how the order was set. However, in the end, Eve followed the serpent, Adam followed Eve, and they all had to answer to God. A woman has no problem following a man as long as the man can lead. A man can only truly lead when he is following God. We find a fatal flaw in the first man, Adam. He only wanted to take responsibility when it was convenient. God didn't create him to think this way, but Adam used his free will to think independent of God. Adam had no problem naming animals and having dominion over the sea and every living creature because it demonstrated the power and authority God gave him. He had no problem when he was presented with a wonderful gift named Eve. He was excited that God pulled Eve from him and said this is "bone of my bone and flesh of my flesh." Eve was a blessing and a gift that God gave to Adam. He gave Adam and Eve the task to replenish the earth and to rule.

However, instead of taking the responsibility as the head of the house and covering his wife, he did not want anything to do with what happened. Not only did Adam not take responsibility, but he even allowed Eve to eat the fruit first, knowing it was wrong. That was almost equivalent to someone breaking in your house, and you, as the man, telling your wife to go in front of you to see what's going on. Adam was practically saying, "I don't know what will happen, Eve, so you go first just in case." Yes, they were to rule together, but Adam was to cover and protect her. Man and woman had free will from the beginning. They had a mind to make decisions.

Adam chose not to step up and be the man of the house. He was not willing to put everything on the line for his wife. There is no question that Eve trusted Adam as her husband. Adam told Eve everything God told him. Not only that, but because Eve was a part of Adam, she had his DNA, which was the spiritual DNA of God. She trusted Adam as the head of the household. Adam was with her when the serpent told Eve about the tree. What happened? Adam sat there and did not say anything to Eve or the serpent. So, it's safe to say that Eve likely also thought it must be ok because Adam remained silent. I believe that if Adam had spoken up, Eve would have dismissed the serpent. Even if Eve had reservations about listening to the serpent, she dismissed them because Adam was standing by her side in silence.

Something apparently happened between Adam and Eve after the serpent arrived. Why did the serpent talk to Eve and not Adam? Was Eve Ms. Independent Woman? Was Eve now the head of the household? Was Eve the sole decision maker? I say no to all of the above. Eve did not have to consult Adam about the decision because he was right there with her. I can imagine that she looked at Adam, but he gave no indication that something was wrong. His silence was consent.

A woman wants a man who will take a stand and a man who will lead. Adam did not lead in this situation. Eve went through the entire process with the serpent and even told the serpent what God said. Eve did all of the talking and debating because Adam stopped leading. How could he stand there in silence? How could Adam allow the enemy to come on his family's territory with him present? It is evident that Adam stopped leading during the time when they ate the relationship fruit. Adam sowed a seed of doubt right before the relationship fruit was eaten. I see it as a seed that grew and grew, but the eating of the fruit was just the climax of a problem that had already begun. They always had free will. We could speculate all day, but we do not know what happened before the serpent came along. However, we see what happened after and how Adam stopped leading.

Genesis 2:19: *Out of the ground the LORD God formed every beast of the field and every bird of the air, and brought them to Adam to see what he would call them. And whatever Adam called each living creature, that was its name.*

I mentioned earlier that Adam named every animal. Guess what? Adam even named the serpent. So, he saw this serpent before Eve ever came on the scene. Granted, this serpent was used by Satan, but he still showed up in the form of something Adam was familiar with. If that is not enough, I will give you one more Scripture.

Genesis 3:20: *And Adam called his wife's name Eve, because she was the mother of all living.*

Yes, Adam was even given the honor to name his wife. He had all of this wonderful responsibility, but because he did not continue to lead, we find the consequence of it.

Genesis 3:21-24: *Also for Adam and his wife the LORD God made tunics of skin, and clothed them. Then the LORD God said, "Behold, the man has become like one of Us, to know good and evil. And now, lest he put out his hand and take also of the tree of life, and eat, and live forever"—therefore the LORD God sent him out of the garden of Eden to till the ground from which he was taken. So He drove out the man; and He placed cherubim at the* *east of the garden of Eden, and a flaming sword which turned every way, to guard the way to the tree of life.*

In verse 21, Adam and Eve are mentioned together and God clothed them. However, verses 22-24 only reference the man. Because Adam did not lead and was silent when the serpent came around, he was the main reason that he and his wife were evicted from the Garden of Eden. Yes, Eve played her part and received her punishment as well, but God held Adam most responsible. Now, we have a snapshot of the first man and woman. We see the consequences when a man stops leading. The man played a pivotal role in the family unit in ancient Israel. Although the women typically performed the cooking of the meals and tending to day-to-day needs of the children, men still went out and brought in the food and were also responsible for teaching children. The men also cooked a lot of the meat. The women's role in the home was also vital. The women also had to determine the best ways to ration food.

Men, it is critical that you take on responsibility. If you have children and you are not with your children's mother, I urge you to make sure that you still take on the responsibility of making sure you take care of your children more than just financially. Financial stability is not the same as emotional stability. Providing for the needs of a child does not replace the providing of guidance, nor does it replace your presence.

Back to the Basics for Singles

It appears that society today is not so far removed from the relationship fruit. We can look all around society and see that women are the head of many households. Too many men have become too dependent on women to where many women feel they don't need a man. We hear clichés such as, "I can do bad all by myself." There are men going around talking about how many options they have. All of this is going on, but not enough dialogue is going on between men and women. We have women telling their female friends about men and men telling their male friends about women, and not enough talking is going on between the men and the women. Too many men are putting up walls the minute a woman appears to not conform to their ways, and women are putting up walls the minute a man does not fall in line with their ways.

When did society take a turn? When did the simple things become so complex? When did men stop approaching women and women start approaching men? When did that become a norm in our society? When did a man begin to think that a woman was supposed to roll out the red carpet for him when he has not proven himself? When did a woman become convinced that she had to lower her standards just to get a man? We may not know exactly when this all began to be pumped into society so it has become a norm as opposed to the exception. However, it began with subtle changes, and over time, it has become blatantly obvious.

Nevertheless, we have to get back to the basics. The basics are the simple things. It is like Relationship 101. The problem is that too many individuals are trying to skip to the advanced level without first mastering the basics. One must first learn to count before they can complete any math formula. **Stop allowing people to graduate in your life when they never passed the test!** That means that they will not be equipped when you run into real challenges. Get back to the basics.

I will outline a few basic principles that we must keep in mind on our journey toward healthy relationships and marriage.

1.) **A Man Pursues a Woman-** Well, this is about as basic as it comes. However, this first principle alone has become unnecessarily complex. I have lost count of how many women I have consulted who are frustrated that men find them intimidating. To make matters worse, it's true that some men are intimidated by certain women. Since when did having standards, serving God, being about your business, pursuing your goals, and just being a flat-out great package become intimidating? Since when did a woman have to apologize for being who God made her to be? This should be seen as a great opportunity to potentially connect with a woman who is not looking for a bailout, which is simply for a man to come along and rescue them.

You shouldn't want a spouse to complete you; you need them to complement you. Complete means a finished product, and no more learning or changing can occur. If you can't find comfort and peace in God alone, can't no man fill that void. Only God has the ability to fill voids. He does not send people to fill voids; He sends people so you can have more of what you need to fulfill His will. The problem is that a strong person can unintentionally shine a light on someone else's insecurities. When someone intimidates you, it means that they frighten or threaten you. The last thing you want in a relationship is competition between each other. That could never work because in marriage two are becoming one. You cannot be with someone who is jealous of your successes. If nothing else, the higher one goes, the higher the other goes because you are supposed to be in it together. Men, I submit to you that **you should not want a woman who only takes away, you should want a woman who adds on!** Let the ego go. You both should be able to add on to each other.

Women, do not water yourself down for the sake of just getting a man. Adam was blown away when he first saw Eve. So, men, it's ok if she is breathtaking, but get yourself together and pursue. A woman does not find great joy when you say things to her like: You must have a boyfriend; you are too pretty to be single; you're too intelligent to be alone, etc. That is not a compliment. If nothing else, it is frustrating and makes you sound insecure. If any of those were true for the current moment, why would you be attempting to have a conversation with her? Don't strike out before you even start.

Women, stop thinking that you need to help a man say what is on his mind in reference to how you think he feels about you or what you think he wants to say. Better yet, stop thinking you can read a man's mind. He should not need his hands to be held. He is no longer a child, not on a bottle, not on training wheels, and does not need you to be his mother. You should not want to be his mother, nor can you be. If that's what it appears he is asking for, send him back home to his mama. A wife needs a man to be her husband, not her child. A man needs a wife, not another mother. If he cannot step up to the plate, then he is just not the one or is just not ready. As I say time and time again, a man knows what he wants and will go after it. You won't have to do any guessing.

2.) Know Yourself- Sure, everyone under the sun thinks they know who they are. However, when certain circumstances arise and you are tested, that helps you see where you really are. If you don't know enough about you, how can you attempt to build a relationship with someone else for the long term? There is no need to waste someone else's time when you already know they don't possess most of what it is that you desire. The old saying goes, "If it don't fit, don't force it." Too many broken relationships are a direct result of trying to make something work when you see all the signs as to why it will not work. Remember these two simple rules, and it will save you a lot of time: You cannot change anyone, and you cannot make anyone love you unconditionally no matter how hard you try or how much you do.

The key is being confident in who you are. You are who you are, and there is no one else in the entire world who is exactly like you. That automatically makes you unique. Stop apologizing for who you are. You may not apologize through your words for who you are, but too many are doing it by changing who they are to try to make a relationship work that wasn't supposed to work to begin with. **The moment you lower your standard is the moment you cheapen your worth!** You can make all the excuses in the world for why you did it, but the only person in the mirror looking back at you is you. Here is another formula that is proven: Eventually, you will get back what you expect, and you will only put up with what you allow. Know yourself!

3.) Don't Complicate Things- It either is or it isn't. Anything after that complicates things. The man wants to be with the woman, and the woman wants to be with the man. If both are not on the same page, that equals instant complication. Sitting around guessing what the other person is thinking creates complications. Sure, when feelings are involved, things have the potential to get complicated. Communication is key. I am talking about verbal communication backed by action. You cannot just go by what someone says unless they have a proven track record with you. Words must be backed by action. You complicate things when you hear one thing, but you see another and ignore it. Whenever you pretend not to see certain signs, you are saying that you choose to ignore them. That's when excuses begin to come into play. Things get complicated when you hang on to words and hope that eventually the actions will line up.

Everything will not always be easy, but if you are going to go to war, make sure that you are going to war with someone who is willing to fight with you. It is difficult to walk away, but there's much more pain if you stay around and leave your heart exposed to someone who is just not on the same page with you. You deserve the best that is for you, and you have to demand the best. **I would rather wait for a season for the right one rather than to sacrifice a lifetime with the wrong one!** Don't live below your potential, no matter what has happened or what is happening right now. It does not matter if it appears no one is in sight, and you don't even see a potential mate. God specializes in overnight deliveries. What took years can literally change overnight. God has you covered.

Overcoming Your Past

There are still too many men and women eating the relationship fruit. The relationship fruit has broken up many marriages. The relationship fruit has created a lot of single-parent homes. The relationship fruit has created some women trying to be men and some men trying to be women. The relationship fruit has created lack of commitment in relationships. Who are you listening to? Who has your ear? What do you truly want? We have diagnosed the problem; now we can dig deeper. To embrace your future, you sometimes have to survey your past to make sure it is really in the past.

Everyone began somewhere. Everyone must travel on their own journey. You have been and are on a journey. This requires you to remember things from your past. It is not intended to take you back to your past, but to make sure you understand how you have grown from your past and how your past has molded you into who you are and who you are becoming. You may not care to travel down memory lane, but all of your past was not negative. Yes, some parts may have been bad, but they all were not bad, even if sometimes that is how you felt.

Too often, old baggage from past relationships is carried into new ones, which causes problems in the new relationships. You must face it and fight it. You're fighting against what the enemy is throwing at you. We all have a little fight in us. Some may seem stronger than another, but God has given us all the ability to fight in the spirit. All of us have gone through tests and trials along the way that required us to fight to get through them. For some of you, it has felt like you have had to fight all your life. It may feel like you had to fight for everything you have. At times, as you look around, it may seem as though others who aren't committed to serving the Lord and others who aren't committed to dating God's way don't seem to have had to fight as hard as you have fought and are fighting right now. You may have had thoughts along the way that it was no longer worth the fight, and that you may as well just lower your standards for a piece of a relationship.

The enemy may have whispered in your ear saying that something is wrong with you. The enemy influenced others you dated or who appeared interested in you to say things that cut you deep. You tried to be tough, but deep down, those words cut. The enemy was trying to convince you to believe a lie by whispering things like: you're not pretty enough…you're not smart enough…you're too strong willed… you're too independent…you're too big…you're too small… don't no man want a woman with a kid, let alone more than one child… you're asking for too much. The list of lies could go on and on. However, for far too long you've asked for too little. Yes, you should have godly standards when it comes to dating and relationships. Yes, you should have expectations! Your expectations for your mate will never be able to exceed God's expectations for your mate.

Marriage was not your idea, but it was God's idea! Over the years, your list seemed to grow shorter and shorter, and it may be frustrating because the statistics will lead you to believe one thing. They'll say there are more men in your area compared to women. I once read an article how in many big cities, there are far more unemployed men as compared to woman. There are all types of articles citing all types of numbers using all types of data. Some of it may warrant a second glance, but the last time I checked, no one was better at math than God.

All you need is the right one. You+them=2. But when God is in it: You+Them+God=1. Only God can do that kind of math. You have gotten frustrated along the way, but God is great at math. This is the same God who took two fish and five loaves of bread and fed a multitude. This is the same God who, when there was no food in the wilderness, fed the children of Israel more food than they could handle. This is the same God who turned water into wine when Jesus attended a wedding at Cana and they ran out of wine. God is great at math. So, this is the same God who can take you and connect you with the one He has regardless of what it looks like right now.

The enemy has fought against you, picked on you, and bullied you, but at the same time, they underestimated you. Well, I firmly believe that the enemy picked the wrong one to start a fight with in you! For some of you, your prayer for your God-ordained mate was not held up for three weeks, but it's been three years, ten years, twenty years. The only problem is perhaps you were low-key putting the blame on God, and God was actually putting it on you because one of two things happened: God hasn't released them yet and it's in His timing, or God has released them and the enemy has been blocking you and them coming together.

I submit to you that most of your delayed manifestations have less to do with God's timing and more to do with an enemy trying to stop it. There are laws governing the heavens, and our prayer or lack of prayer impacts delivery dates. You've been given power and authority over every problem the enemy sends! God has assigned angels to defend you as you war against the enemy who is trying to steal your relationships. There are demons working against you trying to steal your peace and joy and trying to prevent you from getting to your mate. The enemy tries to attack your desire to love and be loved.

God is love, and people say they know God loves them and that they're in relationship with Him. However, if you knew His love, you wouldn't have settled for some of the relationships you've been in. If you know God's love and understand that God will love you through the one He sends, then you will not accept anything that is beneath that love. God will love you in greater ways through the right one. No love is greater than God's love, and so if someone who comes in your life does not show the love God has already shown you, they're not it. Don't give up. Again, keep praying and warring until you see the results.

Chapter 20: Regaining Control of Spiritual Gates

We must understand the importance of spiritual gates. These are very important because the enemy tries to take over our gates to prevent certain things from getting to us, which is why persistence in prayer is so vital. There are gates to a person's body and soul, through which the enemy can attack. Once a gate has been breached, which is usually through sin, disobedience, stress, doubt, worry, etc., the enemy has some access. There are gates in each person such as eyes, ears, mind, mouth, feet, hand, skin, and sexual organs. One way the enemy can block you from getting into position to ascend into God's glory is if they control gates in your life.

God has much more He wants to say to you, and He is calling you to press in and spend time with Him to find out what it is. Demons can do nothing when you get into God's glory because they can't come that high, so they try to prevent you from going deeper in prayer. You must control the gates in your life because if you don't, the enemy will! God has given us the power and authority to take control of our spiritual gates. You are God's field, and no demon should be playing around in it. So, they must be evicted. Oftentimes, God already answered your prayer and either wants you to come higher so you can hear or it got held up in warfare. Getting answers from God is never the problem. The issue is in being persistent until you hear them or fighting the enemy who is blocking you!

Now that we have established that, we can look into why we don't always get the answers at the rate we want. If God is pushing you to seek Him on a deeper level, it will seem like you're not hearing Him because it's too loud on the level you're on. You must go deeper in Him. You must remain persistent and consistent. You must develop the lifestyle of prayer and study of His Word. When your spirit starts feeding on a higher level, you will get spiritually frustrated if you're not giving it what it needs as it grows. Some of you are frustrated because you feel you have prayed and fasted and warred, but the results are not what you desire. Not only that, but you feel like you're just not hearing God. Your spirit is crying out while your flesh is trying to act out. When your spirit cries out for more of God, your flesh acts up! So, you must shut in with God and tell your flesh to shut up. Let me make it clear to you right now: **God is not silent!**

The enemy attempts to block the manifestation of our prayers. They try to sow all types of seeds in your mind and have your mind all over the place to try to distract you from hearing. Of course, that could be from wounds in your soul. They can use the wounds in your soul to block things. It could also be from witchcraft in operation trying to cause issues. Keep in mind that the enemy always plans to try to attack, so we must plan to counterattack. We must also be on the offensive. Rather than waiting for the enemy to do something, we can anticipate what the enemy will try to do and be proactive in blocking it.

Witchcraft being sent your way can cause you to get sleepy in prayer. If you tend to get sleepy in prayer often, witchcraft is at work trying to make you so tired that you don't consistently spend time with God. I'm not talking about after you've had a long day and then try to pray when you get in the bed after already being tired. I'm talking about if you notice a pattern that you get sleepy often during prayer even if you are rested. If so, it's a sure fact that human agents of Satan operating in witchcraft are sending curses to try to prevent you from getting closer to God. You must war against it. If you can stay up and watch TV and not get sleepy but the moment you go into prayer, heavy sleep suddenly comes upon you, the enemy is at work behind the scenes.

One good example is in the movie *The Wizard of Oz*. The witch said, "Something with poison in it, but it's pleasant to the eyes and soothing to the smell. Poppies will put them to sleep." She put a spell on the flowers, and when Dorothy and the others ran through the field, it put her and the Lion and her dog into a deep sleep. Yes, witchcraft was in that movie. The enemy works in that way. Everything that looks good isn't good for you. The Scarecrow said that it was a spell. Witches can try to send spells to make you get sleepy often in prayer. They also try to send demonic fog to make you feel scatterbrained or that you're all over the place. It starts with demonic chatter where all the thoughts are going through your mind. That's when you're still in the flesh trying to pray. However, demonic fog will cause you to not hear or perceive clearly in prayer. It's like you can feel a wall up when you pray. It's like you can tell something is getting in the way. The enemy is most threatened by you when you pray. So, you ought to make them feel threatened every day.

We can see in Scripture how important the gates of a city were.

Nehemiah 2:11-13, 17-20: *So I came to Jerusalem and was there three days. Then I arose in the night, I and a few men with me; I told no one what my God had put in my heart to do at Jerusalem; nor was there any animal with me, except the one on which I rode. And I went out by night through the Valley Gate to the Serpent Well and the Refuse Gate, and viewed the walls of Jerusalem which were broken down and its gates which were burned with fire...*

Then I said to them, "You see the distress that we are in, how Jerusalem lies waste, and its gates are burned with fire. Come and let us build the wall of Jerusalem, that we may no longer be a reproach." And I told them of the hand of my God which had been good upon me, and also of the king's words that he had spoken to me.

So they said, "Let us rise up and build." Then they set their hands to this good work. But when Sanballat the Horonite, Tobiah the Ammonite official, and Geshem the Arab heard of it, they laughed at us and despised us, and said, "What is this thing that you are doing? Will you rebel against the king?"

So I answered them, and said to them, "The God of heaven Himself will prosper us; therefore we His servants will arise and build, but you have no heritage or right or memorial in Jerusalem."

Nehemiah was living comfortably as the king of Persia's cupbearer. A royal cupbearer had great access to the king and was in a position of honor. He carried the king's cup. The king trusted him, and part of his duty was to taste what was in the cup to make sure it was not poisoned. So, the king trusted him to a degree to where the king knew his cupbearer would not attempt to poison him. Nehemiah asked a brother of his how the Jews were doing in Jerusalem. The Jews in Jerusalem were those who returned home after being held in captivity by the Babylonians because of their sins. Ezra and a remnant had already returned and had rebuilt the temple. It was sixty-nine or seventy years after Ezra rebuilt the temple, and now Nehemiah heard that his people were still in great need.

This saddened Nehemiah because they were his people. He cried, prayed, and fasted for his people. He also asked the king for a leave of absence so he could go back. Instead of living comfortably where he was, he wanted to go back and rebuild the walls that had been destroyed. **You're looking for someone to fix it, but God will use you to help repair what has been torn down in the lives of people He assigns you to!** Nehemiah left his place of comfort to carry out the assignment God gave him. Sometimes you will have to leave a place of comfort or familiarity to go back home or to a specific location where you may not want to be because God has need of you to carry out an assignment. What you are familiar with is changing. God is taking you out of the familiar and leading you into something new! Nehemiah didn't know what he would face, but he knew God had shifted him to his next assignment. Some of you have been in denial and have allowed your flesh to drown out the pulling of the Holy Spirit. It's not about you; it's about doing God's will, which is always best for you. Don't stay stuck holding onto something old when God is trying to show you that He's doing something new.

Gates

Many other cities during that time were surrounded by high walls, like Jerusalem had been before its walls and gates were destroyed. The walls were used as a defense to protect against invading armies. Each city also had gates. A lot took place within these gates. The gates were the only way in or out of the city. Near the gate was like a marketplace where people bought and sold goods. Kings would sit at the gates and make judgments or feel the political climate of the people. The elders or wise men of the city would sit at the gates and would give their wisdom and also help settle disputes. Prophets would even prophecy near the gates. People would also gather at the gates to discuss local news and various topics. The gate was an all-access pass to the life of the city. Really, the gate was the pulse of the city.

The gate also represented power and authority in the city. Whoever possessed the gates ruled the city. This is why invading armies would always try to get control of the gate. At night, the gates were locked, closed, and guarded. Watchtowers were built at the top corners of the gates so that watchmen could work their shifts at night and be on the lookout for any incoming intruders and warn the people. You must stay on your post and watch and pray! You'll see the enemy coming when you stay on your post and will be ready to turn them around. Not only were the gates supposed to be guarded then, but the gates are supposed to be guarded now. Too many have fallen asleep on their watch and have allowed the enemy to come in and possess the gate. Too many have made prayer an option and not a mandate. When you don't pray, it means you aren't watching the gates of your life, home, community, church, etc., and the enemy can sneak in. Your life depends on prayer.

In verses 12-13 we see that Nehemiah had a few men with him. He took people with him he knew he could trust. It is so important that you are surrounded by people you can trust. However, trust is not enough. You need to be around people you are in covenant with, those who either are going where you're trying to go or have been where you're trying to get to. Just because they seem like good people doesn't mean you are supposed to be connected.

We see in verse 17 that the people were in great distress because the walls and gates were in shambles after the Babylonians had taken over the city, and they needed someone who would commit to rebuilding the wall. Your assignment may look like death, but by the time you're done with it, God will use you to bring things back to life.

As we continue to search Scripture, we see that Jesus talked about gates. The gates of hell cannot prevail against us when we walk in power and authority because Jesus told Peter that the gates of hell would not prevail against him in Matthew 16:18. Not only can the gates of hell not prevail against us as we walk in power and authority, but we have the ability to possess the gates of the enemy.

Genesis 22:15-17: *Then the Angel of the LORD called to Abraham a second time out of heaven, and said: "By Myself I have sworn, says the LORD, because you have done this thing, and have not withheld your son, your only son—blessing I will bless you, and multiplying I will multiply your descendants as the stars of the heaven and as the sand which is on the seashore; and your descendants shall possess the gate of their enemies."*

We see the promise God gave to Abraham after his faith was stretched and Abraham was willing to sacrifice his own son to God. However, it was just a stretching of his faith; God did not allow child sacrifice, that was what some people did when they worshipped idols. God just wanted to see if Abraham was willing to give up everything for God and to ensure that Abraham could be trusted with all God had for him. Take a step back and ask yourself how much you are willing to sacrifice to get more of God. Abraham's family would be blessed and all of his descendants. We are also descendants of Abraham. We also have the ability to possess the gates of our enemies. So, this again shows that Satan has gates. The enemy is trying to take your territory, but when you pray and war, you will possess your land while the enemy has to watch. When you're willing to put God first through your actions,

283

He will always reward you for it. You will be able to possess the gate of your enemies. Not only will you get what God released, but as you walk in authority, demons will have to pay you interest on what they held up.

Matthew 16:19: *"And I will give you the keys of the kingdom of heaven, and whatever you bind on earth will be bound in heaven, and whatever you loose on earth will be loosed in heaven."*

Jesus left us some keys with which we can access the kingdom of heaven (kingdom of God) right here on earth. Keys symbolize authority. God has given you keys in the spirit, and those keys will unlock many doors as you keep seeking Him in prayer! So, we see that we are able to operate in divine authority as followers of Christ to carry out the will of God. God gave you keys to unlock some doors in your life. It's time to use your keys. Some things have been locked up, but as you press into God, He will give you the right key to unlock the right door. The keys were used to unlock the kingdom of heaven.

We are here to carry out God's will on earth and do what He commands. God gave you the authority to bring heaven on earth. So, if it doesn't look heavenly, start using your authority more! To walk in the authority of Christ is to utilize that power and authority to accomplish God's will on earth. Some things you don't have to ask God for because He already released them. You just have to use your authority to take them back from the enemy!

Bind-To forbid something. To bind also meant to obligate.

Loose-To allow or permit something. To loose also meant to remove obligation.

So, we could also look at the passage as saying, "whatever you forbid on earth has already been forbidden in heaven, and whatever you allow on earth shall have already been allowed in heaven!" During this time, binding and loosing was authority given to disciples so they could apply discipline in the church. It was used

284

for leaders in the church to bind (forbid) or loose (allow) certain behaviors in the church. They had the right to banish or admit anyone into the community.

The terms binding and loosing are also often used in spiritual warfare. However, we must understand that binding in that context is like tying a demon up or arresting it to make it stop doing what it is doing for that moment. However, that is temporary. Casting out a demon is causing it to leave where it has taken refuge, whether that be in a person or in a place. You're forbidding the demonic spirits from doing what they are doing at that moment when you bind, but you must give them a command to leave after you've bound them.

Loosing in spiritual warfare deals directly with the person. It's loosing them from the hold of the enemy or trap of the enemy. It's like untying a person. However, for lasting results, that spirit must still be cast out and one must continue in faith and obedience to God. God gave you power over every work of the enemy, so you just have to accept your victory and fight back in the spirit. **You're an arresting officer in the spirit. God gave you the power and authority to arrest demons who have been messing with you.** Take back control of the gates in your life that demons took control of.

1 John 2:15-17: *Do not love the world or the things in the world. If anyone loves the world, the love of the Father is not in him. For all that is in the world—the lust of the flesh, the lust of the eyes, and the pride of life—is not of the Father but is of the world. And the world is passing away, and the lust of it; but he who does the will of God abides forever.*

We understand that we live in the world but are not of the world. This is why we should not love the world because if we do, the love of God is not in us. You cannot love the world and love God because it's a contradiction. However, you should love God who gives you power to rule in the world. Satan attempts to entice us through our flesh to indulge in things of the world. You're in

God's army, and that means you have the power and authority to defeat the enemy no matter how great the attack.

Lust of the flesh- Anything pertaining to outward senses like taste, touch, and smell; sensual pleasures. It could be anything dealing directly with desires of the flesh that go against God. We know flesh and spirit are complete opposites.

Lust of the eyes- Things our eyes see that can cause us to sin. One sees an attractive individual and may begin to fantasize in their mind. One sees riches and glamour and may do ungodly things to try to attain them.

Pride of life- Going after status, honor, notoriety, or anything producing arrogance.

We see this a lot in deliverance sessions. A demon or witch may manifest in a person, and they will talk about legal rights that they have to the person. They often mention oaths or pacts the person's ancestors, parent, grandparent, or spouse made with demons in exchange for power, status, notoriety, etc.

If you lose possession of your gate to the enemy, the enemy becomes the gatekeeper in your life. That strongman then gives commands to specific demons. So, if you lust, it gives the strongman in control an opening to invite adultery, masturbation, homosexuality, fornication, etc. You must protect your gates. It's possible that your gate was breached at childhood and you never got control of it. Some things from childhood may still give demons legal right to torment. It's time to confront and conquer what's been haunting you. You can take back possession of your gates through prayer and fasting. You can take back possession of your gates by identifying the areas you know the enemy has taken residence in. Those spirits must be evicted, and it goes back to praying and warring until you see the results.

Some simple ways to take back your gates are guarding what you watch on TV and what you listen to. There were some shows that

Donna and I really enjoyed, but it was best that we stopped watching them because of the content. It was feeding our flesh for entertainment, but it wasn't good entertainment. It was just becoming too much drama, ungodly content, etc. Some of it began to go too far. We had to guard our gates because if you're not feeding your spirit, you're feeding your flesh. Watching those shows was not sin, but remember, what you entertain is still a seed that is going into your soul. You have to have a standard and hold yourself to it. It was hard to give up some of those shows, but we didn't need any contamination.

Seeds grow if they are not uprooted. You can cleanse your gates with the blood of Jesus. Essentially, just be careful what you're entertaining because spiritual seeds are very real, and it's either healthy seeds or unhealthy seeds. It's either godly or ungodly seeds.

Chapter 21: Warfare Over Your Wealth

For every harvest coming due, there are always demons wanting to steal it. Harvest is not just financial. Harvest is any blessing from God that we can gather or accumulate. Keep your eyes on it by praying and warring so it will manifest. Your harvest belongs to you, but the enemy wants to rob you of it. They want you to be so weary that you just put your guard down and stop fighting. We all had a harvest stolen in the past, but you have learned the importance of spiritual warfare!

Command the enemy to return it with interest. In the world's economy, demons can play with your harvest. In God's economy, if they get in the way, there are consequences. God wants us all in a place where the enemy will have to think long and hard about trying to mess with our stuff because of how much they will have to pay back. As you grow in God's economy, you'll be too expensive for demons to mess with certain areas because they know it'll cost them more in the end. Your harvest will be too hot to handle. They may try to come at you after you get the harvest, but they will think long and hard about trying to take the harvest. Satan knows the legalities in the spirit realm and he hates losing, but he should get used to it because, as God's warriors, we keep on winning. Demons don't want you to get your harvest because they have an idea of what you'll do with it when it's to fund a vision God gave. It's about persistence and stamina. Demons hope they can outfight you so you'll give up. Don't give up because the power of the Holy Spirit in you is greater than any attack. Demons are trying to break you, but God has given you the power to break them. Your harvest isn't just for you. It will be used to bless others. The greater your harvest, the more God trusts you to manage properly! As an ambassador of heaven, you are to manage the parts of the earth you've been assigned effectively. God gave you jurisdiction and expects you to manage your territory well.

It may feel like you've been fighting for a long time, but you're not losing. All the enemy has delayed will result in more than you prayed for. God is simply making more room for you. There is plenty of room at the table for you. God is making room for you to have the capacity to handle your harvest. God's economy is different from the world's economy, and as children of God, we should be tied to God's economy, not the world's! It's easy to say that we operate in God's economy, but sometimes our actions show otherwise. God's economy is spiritual, yet it produces natural results. The world's economy is natural and can only produce natural results. The world's economy can be accessed by Satan, but God's economy can only be accessed by His children and angels. The world's economy has a huge deficit, but God's economy has never and will never experience any deficit. We are talking about two different economies: God's economy vs. the world's economy. Whichever economy you submit to is the economy that you're governed by.

If you live from the idea that you have to work for everything, you're already in a deficit because God's economy is marked by the miraculous! The concept of working for everything came from the world's economy. It's the world's system that attempted to train us to think a certain way contrary to the Word of God. The reason God sent you to a certain job is not first about making money; it's about the assignment He has given you. God may use it to provide resources, but it's less about making money. However, in the world's economy, that's how workers are trained to think. In God's economy, you don't work to gain because your works can't make transactions in God's economy. In God's economy, you sow seeds of faith. Money is only one form of seed. There are many types of seeds in Scripture. The world's economy can experience a recession, but God's economy is recession proof. So, you must begin to ask yourself which economy you put your trust in. There is no debt in God's economy because everything has already been arranged to be paid in full when we're governed by God's economy.

In order to begin to understand how God's economy works, you must first get money out of your head. Money is simply a tool on earth. Yes, we need to utilize money on earth, but it's not called money in God's economy. God calls it seed. The principle of sowing and reaping, sowing or planting seeds, seedtime and harvest, etc., are themes throughout Scripture. There is a reason for that. Everything in God's economy is a seed, and all those seeds are tied to a harvest. In the world's economy, you spend money, but that money does not always give you a positive return. There are things money buys that go to waste or depreciate in value. In God's economy, nothing goes down in value, but it only goes up. There is never a seed in God's economy that doesn't produce a greater harvest than what was planted. God's economy is the only one where the investment is guaranteed to produce 100% return or more every time. In the world's economy, you can choose what to invest into. In God's economy, you can't afford not to sow into it. The enemy has tried to blind the children of God to make us think it's all about money. Debt was created in the world's economy. America alone is in trillions of dollars of debt. Yet, countries need more people to get into debt for them to function because the world's economy needs consumers. God's economy just needs believers! God is looking for your faith. He gave it all to you and can give you more. Banks need your deposits to loan money to others. The world needs people to spend money because it boosts the world's economy. God gave you seeds to sow to boost your economy. You must ask yourself again: which economy am I submitted to?

The world's economy needs people in debt in order for it to grow. God's economy wants you debt-free so you can grow. If you have a house note, also known as a mortgage, it's no fault of your own; it's a part of the world's system for you to have that mortgage. In God's economy, it can be paid in full. According to Businessinsider.com, mortgage comes from two Latin words, "mort" and "gage." "Mort" means death, and "gage" means grip or pledge. So, mortgage means death grip or death pledge. So, if it's not free and clear, you don't own your home. That's why so many people lost homes during the last recession because they could no longer make payments. The more you owe, the more you have to work to pay it off. Of course, I'm not saying a mortgage is a bad thing. I'm just putting in perspective the difference between God's economy and the world's economy. God wants us delivered from the world's economy and to start living in His economy.

Look at how many got into student loan debts. It seemed like a necessity because we needed it to go to college. I, for one, amassed a big one in grad school. So many are in that debt that rapper Dee-1 released a popular song about paying back Sallie Mae, which is a major student loan lender. The artist received an advance on a new record deal, paid off his student loans, and made a song, "Sallie Mae Back," about it. Millions could obviously relate to the burden of student loans; paying them off is like a dream come true. For many, it seems like a lifelong thing. You toil to be rich in the world to make large purchases in cash, but you only need favor in God's economy to make it happen! That's simply God's favor upon your life. You already have it in accepting Christ because God's favor is His grace. You just need to work it through your faith.

John D. Rockefeller created the General Education Board in 1903 that was supposed to raise the level of education people received. However, as pointed out by G. Edward Griffin in the book about the Federal Reserve called *The Creature From Jekyll Island:*
The purpose of the foundation [the General Education Board] was to use the power of money, not to raise the level of education in America, as was widely believed at the time, but to influence the direction of education...The object was to use the classroom to teach attitudes that encourage people to be passive and submissive to their rulers. The goal was – and is – to create citizens who were educated enough for productive work under supervision but not enough to question authority or to seek to rise above their class. True education was to be restricted to the sons and daughters of the elite. For the rest it would be better to produce skilled workers with no particular aspirations other than to enjoy life.

Essentially, they wanted slaves in the economy. It was never created to make you wealthy. If you don't believe it, then name one job in the world that makes people wealthy other than some professional athletes. Yes, there are some six-figure jobs out there, but that's not wealth. I'm not talking about business ownership, but

I'm talking about hourly/salary jobs. Six figures is good money, but not wealth. Not only that, but how many of those jobs are available to the masses? Not many. We were always supposed to be dependent on the economy of God.

The same people who created the General Education Board also created the Federal Reserve, which essentially controls America's financing system. It was believed by some people who subscribe to the thoughts of Griffin that the education system was set up to keep people ignorant of financial education, which was considered real education, and the ultra-wealthy would teach it to their children. The standard education system essentially teaches: go to school, get a good education, so you can get a good job. The key things they left off are owning something, how to properly invest, etc. It wasn't created to teach true financial education. That would have to be sought out for yourself. I am not bashing the education system because there are many fantastic educators on every level, and I know there are still good things that come out of the standard education system, including training for professionals that we all utilize. The point is that the standard education was created with specific goals in mind, and true financial education was not one of them. The good news is that our true education system should begin at home with God's Word. Again, education is good, and there are many great educators who truly aim to teach not just education but life skills as well, just like there are great doctors and nurses who want to help people.

However, in God's economy, health and wealth have already been paid for. We just need to cash in and submit to God's economy. To thrive in God's economy, education is good, but you need revelation, which only comes with submitting to God. The moment you try to make it happen is the moment you step outside of God's economy, which says it already happened. You must seek God first in all things. He will execute His will on earth through you, but it's Him making it happen through you. Only prayer through faith in Christ can move the hand of God in our lives. Faith and prayer are our currencies for divine transactions. When you submit to the world's economy, you work to live. When you submit to God's economy, you just need to work His principles!

So, we must tackle debt so God's economy can work the way it's supposed to in our lives. The good news is what would take years to accomplish in the world's economy, you can accomplish quickly in God's economy. Everyone wants to be debt-free. In the world's economy, you spend your way into debt. In God's economy, you sow your way out of debt. It's a simple principle when you're in faith, but it's hard when you're in the flesh. You can't submit to both economies; you must submit to one, which should be God's economy. The world's economy is designed to take from you. God's economy is designed to give to you!

Galatians 5:1: *Stand fast therefore in the liberty by which Christ has made us free, and do not be entangled again with a yoke of bondage.*

We must begin from the premise that Christ already paid for us to be free: free from sin. He paid for the debt of our sin. He paid for our freedom by giving His life for us. He paid to put us back in right standing with God, placing us back in the place of rulership and power where Adam and Eve were before sin entered the world. Where have you ever heard of a broke king or queen? They don't even have to use much of their own money. Presidents don't use much of their money because of the favor that comes with the office. You're God's child, and favor comes with your office! When Adam and Eve were in the garden, they didn't work for anything because creation worked for them. Christ put us back on the level Adam and Eve were at in the garden and beyond. Christ paid the debt of our sin and came to free us from all types of debt. He died for you to be debt-free in every area of your life.

Apostle Paul did not want the Galatians to go back to being under the curse of the law. Christ came, and through Him we all have God's grace. The law did what it was supposed to do, but the law was never intended to bring salvation. Some of the Jews were tempted to go back to the law, but after Christ came, going back to the law brought about a religious spirit that kept people in bondage. The demonic religious spirit makes people self-righteous, and they are caught up in doing works and how good their works are compared to others. It's about how good their walk is compared to others, and they expect a reward for it. However, it's a demonic spirit that causes them to walk outside of God's love. Christ already set us free from the yoke of bondage. Christ already set you free, so don't go back to a place God freed you from. You will only find bondage there. The yoke Paul spoke of was like the yoke placed around the oxen's neck. They could not obtain righteousness through their works. It could only come through Christ. In God's economy, hard work doesn't get you paid, but it's your faith and obedience to God that allows you to make withdrawals from heaven. We were never supposed to have to war or work hard for our finances, but when sin entered the world, it all changed.

Genesis 3:17-19: *Then to Adam He said, "Because you have heeded the voice of your wife, and have eaten from the tree of which I commanded you, saying, 'You shall not eat of it':*
"Cursed is the ground for your sake;
In toil you shall eat of it
All the days of your life.
Both thorns and thistles it shall bring forth for you,
And you shall eat the herb of the field.
In the sweat of your face you shall eat bread
Till you return to the ground,
For out of it you were taken;
For dust you are,
And to dust you shall return."

Here we find God talking to Adam and Eve after they sinned in the Garden of Eden. God was now pronouncing the punishment on mankind for their disobedience. Before sin entered, man and woman had nothing to worry about. God had it all provided for them. There was no such thing as hard work. However, after sin, God said that in toil Adam was to eat of the herbs of the ground.

"In toil/sorrow" in this passage means painful labor. Man would be able to live off of what was planted, but it would now be with much painful labor. Fruit wouldn't just grow perfectly anymore; they now also had thorns and thistles, and pruning was now necessary, etc. This is what it was like until Christ came. Man was under the curse of the law and sin. In the Old Testament, there were many laws man had to abide by. It was by many works. God once did the work for them, but now they had to do more of the burdensome work. Provision used to work for man until sin entered. Then man had to work for provision.

Since Christ came, once again provision works for us. In the world's economy, you work to make gains from the world. This is different from a job assignment God gives. Some people just get a job to get a job for the sake of getting money. In God's economy, the world will have to work for you. Christ already completed the work, but when you think you have to work hard, you're going back to the curse of sin in the Garden of Eden. One of the curses put on mankind was hard work. Verse 19 even talks about the sweat of Adam's face/sweat of his brow from the hard work that man was not used to nor was ever intended to have to do. Hard work was a curse placed on man when sin entered the world. Now that Christ came, He redeemed us from the curse of hard work. In the world economy, hard work is glorified. In God's economy, hard work is frowned upon because Christ paid the price to lighten your burdens. You've been delivered from the curse of hard work, but we are constantly tempted to go back to that yoke of bondage. It's not that you won't do work, but it will be Christ doing the work in you through the power of the Holy Spirit. When Christ is at work in you, what is hard work to some becomes easy work to you because you will have God's grace to lighten the load. God is not looking for your hard work, but He's looking for you to work your faith. Too many are busy working hard in God's kingdom, but not busy praying and walking in faith. You must prioritize! Life is not about your job, career, businesses, etc. It's about the assignment God gave to you to complete on jobs, careers, and businesses. Your real job is to do God's will, which is really allowing Him to do a great work through you to bring His kingdom on earth.

Take the Enemy to Court

Proverbs 6:30-31: *People do not despise a thief*
If he steals to satisfy himself when he is starving.
Yet when he is found, he must restore sevenfold;
He may have to give up all the substance of his house.

This passage is a part of a longer teaching about what committing adultery will cause, but the principle here is found throughout the Old Testament. It was a law that if someone stole something that belonged to another, they had to repay double, four-fold, five-fold, and, in this case, seven-fold. Even when Cain killed Abel, God said that if anyone killed Cain, they would suffer vengeance seven times over (Genesis 4:24). So, we see those laws. It was a physical punishment and restitution then, but it still applies to Satan and his demons. If they steal from us, they must always repay more.
Use the law against demons! If they steal from you, they are required by the laws of God to restore seven times the amount they stole. They must pay restitution, which means they must give back or compensate you for what was stolen. Whether they snatched it before it manifested or used a person to steal from you or wound you, they must pay you back. The church has often said, "I'm going to the enemy's camp and taking back what the devil stole from me." However, when you know your rights, you don't just get back what they stole, but they must give back more than what they stole. Seven times is the minimum repayment. Take demons to God's court if they have stolen from you by commanding them to appear before the court of God and repay what they stole!
If demons stole money, they must pay back seven times what they stole. Seven is God's number of completion or perfection. You simply multiply to come up with the amount. A seven-fold return off $100 is $700. A seven-fold return off $1,000 is $7,000.

Imagine when you get into thirty-, sixty-, 100-, and even 1,000-fold returns. A thousand-fold return of $100 equals $100,000. If the enemy has to repay you more than what they stole, God will certainly give you far more than you asked. Keep in mind that it's not just money. It's whatever they steal; there should be restitution in some form. Don't let demons get off easily! If they robbed you, make sure they repay you.

You can call the enemy to God's court, and they are required by law to pay up. However, make sure you break those legal rights. When you pray, you simply ask God to call court into session. You repent of your sins, sins of ancestors, sins of family members, etc. Then you summon any demon, witch, warlock, or sorcerer who has stolen anything from you to the courts of heaven. You can bring charges against them. Whatever legal rights they may have, let them know that you're not under the curse of the law, but you're under God's grace. Declare that you're breaking every evil contract or covenant they brought you into and that you renounce it. You ask God as the Just Judge to rule in your favor as you state your case. State your case by saying what is going on, what has been stolen, and what you desire because of it. Ask God to punish those wicked enemies for what they have done to you. This could be a back-and-forth legal battle, where the enemy feels they have more accusations to bring against you, so you keep going back in prayer and taking it to court until you see the results. Remember, we pray and war until we see the results. It's about persistency and consistency.

Midianite Curse

Judges 6:1-6: *Then the children of Israel did evil in the sight of the LORD. So the LORD delivered them into the hand of Midian for seven years, and the hand of Midian prevailed against Israel. Because of the Midianites, the children of Israel made for themselves the dens, the caves, and the strongholds which are in the mountains. So it was, whenever Israel had sown, Midianites would come up; also Amalekites and the people of the East would come up against them. Then they would encamp against them and destroy the produce of the earth as far as Gaza, and leave no sustenance for Israel, neither sheep nor ox nor donkey. For they* *would come up with their livestock and their tents, coming in as numerous as locusts; both they and their camels were without number; and they would enter the land to destroy it. So Israel was greatly impoverished because of the Midianites, and the children of Israel cried out to the LORD.*

God delivered the Israelites into the hands of the evil Midianite army for seven years because of the continual sin and disobedience of Israel by serving false gods. They worshipped Baal. The Midianites stole from Israel. Every time the Israelites sowed, the Midianites, along with the Amalekites, watched and waited for when it was time for the harvest and destroyed it. It left the Israelites in poverty (v. 6). God did send Gideon to deliver the Israelites from the Midianites after the Israelites cried out to God, but it was after they came back to God.

Witches and warlocks attempt to put curses on your money, and they aim for the children of God. One curse they may send is the Midianite curse because it is a curse against your harvest. When you sow a financial seed and your harvest is en route, the enemy then comes in and steals your harvest. It causes frustration and can make some feel that it's pointless to sow because they don't see the harvest.

Another way this curse operates is that as soon as you are getting your finances in order and feel like you are getting ahead or on a good track, some major financial setback happens. It's a cycle. It aims to create a cycle of poverty, lack, and debt. It literally steals your harvest. The Midianite curse also works by causing people to have serious spending problems where they just have to buy things, almost like an addict. It also works with spirits of addiction like drugs, alcohol, gambling, etc., to cause people to spend all their money and neglect important matters.

You can break the Midianite curse. What the enemy has stolen from you for all these years must come to an end. Don't cry over it, but war over it. The curse doesn't necessarily come because of a sin you have committed, but it often comes from things some of your ancestors did in the past or a word curse spoken over you or your finances or over your bloodline. Any negative thing spoken about finances, like saying "I'm broke," gives witches and demons an opportunity to send the Midianite curse. Your words hold a lot of power, and you should use those words to speak life over you and your situation.

Not tithing is one of the easiest ways for this curse to be sent by the enemy because God said He would rebuke the devourer when we tithe (Malachi 3:11). So, if you are tithing and it still seems like your finances are being eaten up, cast down the Midianite curse. We must also look at our heart motive. We shouldn't sow seeds or tithe out of fear or solely because you expect something in return. It's supposed to be by faith. The enemy can also use wrong heart motives as a legal right to steal. You can break the Midianite curse by renouncing any sins you or your ancestors have committed regarding money, stealing, cheating, etc. You also can send the blood of Jesus to cancel the Midianite curse against your finances that has eaten up your harvest. Again, it still takes perseverance. It's not always immediate. We are in a real war. It takes us praying and warring until we see the results. Too much of our wealth has been stolen by the enemy on our watch. It's time to send the blood of Jesus to search for and break the curse. Don't back down.
The enemy is crafty, and this is why you shouldn't accept money from just anyone. Some witches will give money so that they can curse your money. The good news is we have power to cancel it all out, but we need to know the types of seeds the enemy has been sowing that we can't see with our natural eyes. Witches often work behind closed doors where we can't see what they're doing, but thank God for the Holy Spirit who can expose them! Since witches and warlocks are human agents working for Satan, we can also pray that they repent and be saved and begin serving Christ. Remember, you can send the warning in the spirit that they repent or die.

Demonic Banks

There are what's known as demonic banks. This is where witches store the wealth of Christians that they have stolen in the spirit. They intercept blessings that were en route to followers of Christ through whatever legal right they felt they had. These banks also help fund some of their evil plots. Satan can manufacture his own money, but they take more pleasure in stealing from the children of God to fund their evil projects on earth. These banks are often made out of cement in the spirit realm, and we can send the fire of God to destroy them.

I first learned about demonic banks when my wife and I were praying and targeting some things years ago. She had a vision of these demonic banks made out of cement. You can send an earthquake in the spirit to destroy them. You can send the heavenly host to destroy them. They will try to rebuild, so you should continue to war until your finances, or whatever was stolen, are returned to you.

Demonic banks are like big banks that are national/international, so witches can withdraw from all over. Regional demonic banks keep the church in debt. It's not God's will for any church to have debt. Demons have stolen from us, but we have the authority to force them to give it back plus interest! Demons can steal our wealth, and they don't always store it in demonic banks locally. They may take it across state lines because the laws governing that region are different from where you live. The good news is if they take our blessings across state lines or to any other jurisdiction, the setup is similar to how we have local, state, and federal laws. We have the ability to go straight to the Supreme Court in heaven and settle the matter no matter where they harbor our blessings. Remember, you can summon demons to court in prayer and bring charges against them.

This is not made to complicate things, but if we know how the enemy operates, it makes us more effective in spiritual warfare. It doesn't matter how elaborate Satan's plans are, his plans will never be able to hold up under the power of God when we use it!

Everything God creates, Satan tries to duplicate. There are some Christians who have had trips to heaven and have described a storehouse in heaven for things such as body parts when healing is needed on earth. An angel goes into the body parts room and brings it down to the person for the spiritual transfer. We also know in Scripture that there was a certain time when an angel came and stirred up the water in an area where a lot of sick people hung out, and whoever stepped in that water first was healed (John 5:4). So, Satan has demonic banks and storehouses, and his agents aim to fill them up with our stuff because they have nothing of their own. They make a living off of robbing us. That's why Scripture talks about Satan coming to steal, kill, and destroy. Christ came that we may have a more abundant life, but Satan sends his agents to try to stop us from living the abundant life on earth.

You can demand every demonic bank to be opened by the fire of God, and you must command all of it to be returned with interest. You can bankrupt these banks in your life, and that's why it's important to not try to do it all yourself. The key is that you cannot back down. It's not a one and done thing. These witches/warlocks have nothing else to do other than to try to plot against us. So, we need to make them very uncomfortable by maintaining a prayer life and warring in the spirit until we get the results. You have the mandate to fight in the spirit to get back everything God has already released that has been stolen by the enemy! It's your territory and inheritance to defend. God will do it through you, but you have to show up. You must go and cause havoc in the enemy's camp.

Matthew 12:29: *Or how can one enter a strong man's house and plunder his goods, unless he first binds the strong man? And then he will plunder his house.*

Here we find Jesus addressing the Pharisees, who were questioning His authority. They claimed He was casting out demons through the prince of demons. Jesus explained how a house divided against itself would not stand. He was also explaining that He was casting

301

out demons through God. He then gave insight on casting out demons. He shows that we must bind the strong man and then plunder. Bind the demons who have been causing problems in your life and then cast them out! There are demons who have sat on your harvest, but you have the power to evict them. Take what is yours plus extra. You are to operate in the economy of God as a child of God. Whatever rights demons felt they had to steal from you, they are still illegal because you're redeemed from the curse of the law through Jesus Christ. You must begin shifting completely into the economy of God. It's time to switch over from the world's economy. God's economy is superior to the world's economy, so you need to operate in God's economy full time. We can find another example of what it looks like to plunder the enemy's camp.

Exodus 12:35-36, 40-42: *Now the children of Israel had done according to the word of Moses, and they had asked from the Egyptians articles of silver, articles of gold, and clothing. And the LORD had given the people favor in the sight of the Egyptians, so that they granted them what they requested. Thus they plundered the Egyptians...*

Now the sojourn of the children of Israel who lived in Egypt was four hundred and thirty years. And it came to pass at the end of the four hundred and thirty years—on that very same day—it came to pass that all the armies of the LORD went out from the land of Egypt. It is a night of solemn observance to the LORD for bringing them out of the land of Egypt. This is that night of the LORD, a solemn observance for all the children of Israel throughout their generations.

After more than four centuries of bondage in Egypt, the children of Israel were finally free. This was a major transition: they had the mind-set of bondage since it's what they had known for so long. Worldly thinking keeps you in bondage; letting the mind of Christ think through you helps you walk in the freedom Christ came to give you. The mind-set of bondage of the Israelites was passed down from generation to generation. They complained in the wilderness at times and preferred to be back in bondage rather than to trust the same God who delivered them could also provide food and water. They were on their way to that blessed place, but their old mind-set kept them back in the old place.

You may physically be in a familiar place, but everything around you is changing for your good, and you will see a great harvest! The religious spirit has kept many in bondage, but God is renewing your mind to see it how He sees it and to live how He wants you to live. Don't allow what *was* prevent you from walking in what *will be* because what will be shall be greater than what was. God is bringing you out. You are being set free! It's never God's will for you to be in bondage. You will break through because freedom is your divine right. The shackles the enemy used to hold what's yours hostage will be the same shackles used to bind them. Christ came so you may have a more abundant life. If you don't see it yet, that's a clear sign that demons are in the way.

When God elevates you to a new place, don't allow an old mind-set to take you back to a place God already delivered you from. You're being ushered into the new, and what was once used to keep you in bondage is not invited to go with you. The enemy is desperate in an attempt to keep you from walking in destiny. Don't go back to what you've been delivered from. Regardless of words some may speak over you or how some may view you, you are not who you were back then. You are not where you were back then. Your mentality does not have to be defined by your locality. Where you are right now is not an indicator of where you're going. As you present heaven with your faith, God is going to trust you with more than you think you can handle, but He prepared you for it.

The Israelites also did not leave empty handed. They not only got set free, but they left with wealth! They plundered the Egyptians. They took silver, gold, and clothes. It really belonged to them anyway, but the Egyptians were living off of what belonged to the Israelites. Demons may have held you back for a little while, but you will win the battle and they will have to pay you for the hell they caused. If there ever was a divine opportunity for wealth to be created, this is the time, and the world will have to help fund it. The children of Israel became debt-free in one night when they came out of Egyptian captivity. God can do the same for you. You need to keep the faith. Faith is powerful! It's heaven's currency. God is looking for more faith because He wants to get more to you than you want to get to yourself.

Sometimes it can be a tough transition when you have not had something in a long time. It's hard at times to enjoy a great blessing because fear tries to haunt you and have you looking over your shoulders in fear that it's too good to be true. We are God's children, and He loves us more than any of our closest loved ones could love us. It is His divine pleasure to spoil you! It's God's will for you to shine because He said we are the light of the world. Start shining where God planted you. You're not some small light either. God said you cannot be hidden because you are light in this world, so let the world see just how far your light can shine. That in-between phase of the wilderness and the Promised Land may seem like too much. It's not as far away as it appears. Notice that in one day, God took an entire nation out of bondage. A great change can happen in your life in one day. You're in between the wilderness and the promise. Keep pushing because you are too close to the promise to quit in the wilderness! You're approaching the time when twenty-four-hour miracles won't happen every once in a while; they will happen often.

100-Fold Blessing

Genesis 26:1-3, 12-14: *There was a famine in the land, besides the first famine that was in the days of Abraham. And Isaac went to Abimelech king of the Philistines, in Gerar.*
Then the LORD appeared to him and said: "Do not go down to Egypt; live in the land of which I shall tell you. Dwell in this land, and I will be with you and bless you; for to you and your descendants I give all these lands, and I will perform the oath which I swore to Abraham your father…

304

Then Isaac sowed in that land, and reaped in the same year a hundredfold; and the LORD blessed him. The man began to prosper, and continued prospering until he became very prosperous; for he had possessions of flocks and possessions of herds and a great number of servants. So the Philistines envied him.

There are a number of lessons we can gather from this chapter. We see in verse 1 that there was a famine in the land. It was a dry season and things appeared hopeless. However, in the middle of a hopeless situation, God still speaks. He gave Isaac instructions in verse 2 to live in the land in which God told him to. Sometimes you have to go the uncommon way because God is using you to pave the path for others to go the same way. You're a trailblazer! God will surprise you with what you'll discover on the path, and you'll shock others who didn't take you seriously. Had Isaac gone down to Egypt, he would have missed God and His blessings. It is so vital to seek God about where He wants us to be because that is where the blessing is. God's favor can be on you and assigned to a particular place. Go where God is leading you because that's where more favor is! There's a guarantee that you'll flourish in the land God placed you in. Don't be fooled by the temporary because God's making permanent changes. Seek God for where He wants you to be, not where you or anyone else thinks you should be. Yes, it could even be in a dry place or an undesirable place for a season. Everywhere God sends you is a part of your assignment. Don't get caught up in how God will do it. Just know that He's more into details than we could ever be.

There was a famine in the land, but Isaac was still able to sow something in the land. He planted a seed in the ground, and in the same year he got a harvest. The favor of God not only places something in your hand to sow, but it also brings back a greater harvest. Not only will you get a return on the seeds you have sown in the lives of others, but God is going to give you unexpected harvests. God will send you instructions in any situation, but you have to be willing to trust Him when the instructions don't seem to make sense. It won't make sense as to how the favor of God on your life just keeps opening doors, but all you need to do is walk

305

through the door. Isaac got back way more than he planted in the same year he planted it. There have been many blessings attached to things that don't make natural sense, but when God says it, it always makes spiritual sense! Not to mention, Isaac sowed in dry ground during a famine. In normal circumstances, it would not make sense to sow during a famine because the seed would not grow. God has planted you, and you will grow where He has planted you. Others will be blessed because God sent you there. Isaac sowed and reaped a harvest. However, that was just the principle. The last part of the verse says, "and the Lord blessed him." So, the 100-fold return was not even the blessing; it was just the principle. Thirty- to sixty-fold returns were common and considered a good harvest. However, a 100-fold return was uncommon, not to mention seemingly impossible during a famine. God looks forward to making the impossible possible in your life because He knows you will give Him the glory. God looks forward to surprising you at times and in places you least expect.

After we see that the blessing was added in verse 12, we find in verse 13 that he began to prosper and continued to prosper until he became very prosperous. Now that is a lot of prospering, all because he got not just the principle, but he also got the blessing, and of course the enemy was upset because he prospered and continued to prosper in a famine. When you're in God, you'll prosper in any season, but when you're under an open heaven, you will prosper beyond your normal capacity. On top of that, God will add in just-because gifts for you!

Isaac's seed overturned the famine. The famine had to submit to the seed because the seed was attached to obedience to God. Your obedience to God will overturn any famine and lack that may be in your life. God can speed things up at any rate. What some say would take twenty years, you can get in twenty minutes. When God's favor is in acceleration in your life, everything goes at a rapid pace. Your life will shift suddenly for the better! You have to change your mind-set, and it begins with faith. Your faith is your proof that you're trusting God regardless of what is in front of you. Remember, faith is also a weapon in warfare. Isaac was obedient, but he also had to have faith. God already knows what you need, but He will give you far more than what you need. Your faith is a long-term investment that keeps bringing you a great return.

If you can do it yourself, the vision is far too small. God is pushing you beyond what you can comprehend because what He has is that big. You just have to make the choice to trust Him. You have to make the choice to ask Him and believe that it's already done. Isaac sowed in faith knowing a harvest was coming. He wasn't hoping, but he was expecting. Don't hope for a great harvest, but expect it because it's already done in heaven! Use your faith to bring it on earth. Acceleration is here, and it's up to you how fast you want it to go. God gave you the word ahead of time to prepare you. Ask God to make His will become your wants.

1,000-Fold Blessing

Deuteronomy 1:11: *May the LORD God of your fathers make you a thousand times more numerous than you are, and bless you as He has promised you!*

Moses was speaking to the Israelites, reminding them of the promise of God to go and possess the Promised Land. God promised them that they would get the land of Canaan. Moses spoke a very powerful blessing over the people. He spoke a 1,000-fold blessing over them. We are accustomed to hearing about thirty-, sixty-, and 100-fold, but this is a 1,000-fold return, and it's available to us. Don't just ask God for a 100-fold return, but ask Him for 1,000-fold because it's a blessing in Scripture that is available for us! Notice that Moses stated that God would bless them as He promised. The 1,000-fold blessing is an actual promise of God. There are some promises of God that God is ready to honor, but you need to search out the promises. This was a two-part blessing. Not only would the children of Israel multiply, but God would abundantly bless them. There's a harvest with your name on it that will far exceed what you prayed for. Call it forth to manifest in your life NOW!

Romans 13:8: *Owe no one anything except to love one another, for he who loves one another has fulfilled the law.*

This passage deals with being in debt to no one. The prior verse talks about paying what is due such as taxes, respect and honor, money owed, etc. Apostle Paul was saying that the only debt that we should owe is to love one another. God wants us free of all debt! Any debt outside of loving one another has already been paid for by Christ. Every other debt is a part of the world's economy. Debt is the world's way to keep us in bondage, so we will labor like a slave, even though we've been set free. Christ already set you free, but the enemy wants you to live on earth as though you aren't free. It's time to rule in your jurisdiction. It's in your jurisdiction where the seed will be released from heaven and the currency will be transferred into the world's currency of money so you can carry out your God-given assignment.

Of course, there is an enemy fighting to try to stop that, so you must enforce the laws of God in your assigned land. Christ freed us from all debt, so we just need to apply the principles of God's Word and fight against the enemy to get it to manifest. Laboring in the world's economy is like a rat race or running around on the hamster wheel going around and around but going nowhere. This is why although we're in the world, we don't need to submit to the world's system. When you're going on assignment for God daily, that's different from hard work. One you do with joy, but the other you do because you have to. There's no debt in God's economy. There's no debt in heaven, so there should be no debt in the lives of the children of God. I won't get into the details of what society considers good debt or bad debt when it comes to assets or liabilities. At the end of the day, money is supposed to work for us as God's children. Money doesn't rule you, but you rule money.

Matthew 6:24: *No one can serve two masters; for either he will hate the one and love the other, or else he will be loyal to the one and despise the other. You cannot serve God and mammon.*

Jesus made it clear that no one can serve two masters and be totally submitted to both, especially when it's two opposing kingdoms. When we are buried in debt, we're under the laws of the world's economy. It was never God's intent. So, He wants to get us out of debt, so we are not under the grip of the world's system. It's an Egyptian and Babylonian system. We've been set free from it, but we were influenced to go back under it. Debt is common and is a necessity in the world's economy, but supernatural debt cancellation is common in God's economy!

Satan's kingdom is not broke. There is a spirit called Mammon. Some translations will say money. The spirit of Mammon is in charge of Satan's treasury. He's the chief financial officer. This spirit is behind the money of the world's system. It causes love of money, which Scripture says is the root of all evil (1 Timothy 6:10). Not money itself, but the love of it. This spirit is worshipped by those who want to rule the world for selfish ambitions. The New World Order and other satanic organizations are funded by this spirit. You might have debt, but you don't have to stay in debt because, in God's economy, He can give you a clean slate. Don't love money because that is sin. Love and serve God, and God will make money love and serve you.

Chapter 22: One of Satan's Top Secrets to Delayed Manifestation Exposed

I cannot even begin to express how critical this chapter is. You won't get all of this book like you need to in one sitting, but this is a chapter that you won't fully grasp in one sitting. Read it over and over and allow the Holy Spirit to give you more revelation. Satan always has a plan B if the original plan doesn't work, but you have the power to cancel all of his plans! His secret is that if there is no room for demons to reside in a child of God, he will use wounds in the soul to gain access. In all actuality, it's his plan A and B because he can use soul wounds to gain legal access before or after deliverance. Soul wounds can cause you to reject revelation. They can cause so many delays in your life. Soul wounds can even be passed down through generations. A soul wound that a mother has can be passed on to a child in the womb. Your soul has been played with long enough by the enemy, and now it's time for it to be healed. What has been suppressed in your life must come to the surface. The enemy can no longer hide behind your hidden wounds. It's time to be free from demonic abuse. You can't have everything God has for you if your soul is wounded because the enemy can use those wounds to keep things from you. Satan may have plans, but you have power and authority to destroy his plans!

Let me make this abundantly clear: if you have never intentionally addressed the wounds in your soul, there are still wounds there. The goal of the enemy is that you never see the wounds in your soul so they can hide behind them, but I declare those hiding days are over! Your soul must be healed. You must always do a soul check to ensure nothing new has attached to it. God is doing some soul cleaning, and you are a perfect candidate for it. The enemy constantly plots against our lives, but with a healthy soul, we will be able to see much more. You have the weapons to overcome every attack and planned attack of the enemy, but you must use your weapons. Your body is world-conscious, and it's only concerned about the things of the world. Your soul is self-conscious, and it's only concerned about the things of itself. Your spirit is God-conscious, and it's only concerned with the things of God. Our spirit is perfect in itself, but our soul and body are not. Our soul must be saved and cleansed daily so it doesn't reject our spirit!

Soul

Man became a living soul, which is a living being. The soul is the seat of our mind, will, desire, emotions, as well as our ability to reason. It is our souls that can get saved. The soul is where one's personality is. Demons try to sit on a personality so the real you stays hidden! Those demons must be evicted. This is one reason why you may have noticed someone's personality completely change for the negative for an extended period of time. It's not always obvious. Sometimes a shy person is not really shy, but it could be a demon trying to alter their real personality. There is no such thing as a shy child of God because the Holy Spirit is bold in us.

The moment your spirit hit your body, your soul was formed. There's no life without your spirit. So, your spirit should run things! It's time to take back control from what has been secretly controlling things for too long. If your flesh is in control, your soul will always fall prey to the flesh. If your spirit is in control, your soul will submit to it. This is where the battle comes into play. Your spirit could not legally come to earth without a body, and that's why we had to have a physical body. However, the body was never meant to control things. Your soul was never meant to control things. Your soul was created to serve as a medium between your flesh and spirit. This is why we must be careful that we're not being moved by a soul experience as opposed to a true spirit experience.

The soul has many layers, and sometimes it picks up junk. It can carry a lot of waste, and our souls must be cleaned out. If your soul is wounded, it can cause so many additional problems. A wounded soul is unstable and cannot be trusted. It must be healed so that it will be led by the spirit all the time. This is why some of you have found yourselves doing or saying things over and over that you said you would stop. A wounded soul caves into the flesh more than it submits to the spirit. So, you must pray daily for God to send power into your soul. There are some things that you have carried around for years and you didn't know they had wounded your soul. Not only does sin wound our soul, but trauma, anger, negative words, ungodly images, certain music, etc., can all wound the soul. You may not feel sad or upset, but it doesn't mean your soul is not wounded. A wounded soul gives the enemy easy access to continue to inflict individuals legally. This is why we can't run from it. Don't run from things that happened, but confront them because you don't want to give demons a free shot to operate in the wounds in your soul.

Your soul can sometimes be a dumping ground for demonic waste, but you need to send the blood of Jesus in your soul to wipe it clean. Demonic waste that is not handled can build up and cause many problems in your life. Demonic waste can still be present even after someone is delivered because waste is what was left behind in your soul. This is why a person can be delivered when the demons who tormented them are forced to leave, but the waste left behind in the wounded soul gives those demons legal access to continue to cause issues at a distance or even enter again. Demons attempt to use our souls as wastelands for their waste and toxins. This is why our souls need to go through a spiritual detox fairly often. Our souls can receive spiritual deposits, whether good or bad. We must program them through prayer and God's Word to reject bad deposits. Demonic waste is the residue that can be left behind from unresolved issues and things that are suppressed. Demons look for the wound in the soul to send seeds in hopes that they will grow. Those demonic seeds create demonic waste stored in the soul. Those seeds that are not uprooted can be attached to a time-released curse scheduled to cause certain problems in someone's life at a certain time. If your soul is wounded, demonic waste remains there and demons swim in it. They feed off of it. They use it to keep certain issues going on in your life. For example, a person may be delivered from an addiction, but if their soul is not healed, demons can use the wound that the addiction caused to continue to torment the person. It may not be at the same level, but they hope it's enough to where the individual will cave in and they will be able to enter back in.

This is why deliverance and post-deliverance (renewing of the mind/healing of the soul) are equally important. A person can be delivered from a demon but still be tormented if the wounds in their soul are not healed. The death of a loved one can wound the soul if we don't grieve it properly. You may have grieved, but you still need your soul to be healed. The enemy can use a traumatic event that wounded our soul as an opportunity to sow a seed in our life. More demonic waste is accumulated in your soul as those seeds grow. So, even if the demon doesn't have enough room to enter to oppress a child of God, they can still use the demonic waste to access a child of God! This is again why it's important for our souls to be healed and whole.

We have walked many people through deliverance over the years, and there is not one person who has gone through the process who didn't discover they had hidden soul wounds. So often, many are convinced they have no wounds in their soul because many times they've been suppressed. It could have been something from childhood. Just because you move on from something physically doesn't mean it's moved on from you in your soul. It must be healed. Demonic waste is another crafty way demons use to try to attack God's children, but it is being exposed.

Your soul was created to serve your spirit, so you have the power to cancel whatever the enemy has done to try to change that. Demonic waste can also come through other openings such as the things you watch on TV or what you listen to. They can use those as opportunities to sow seeds that go into your soul, and that demonic waste will grow and grow if it is not dealt with. Many times, one would not even know they are there because of things they see as harmless. However, those little "harmless" things water that demonic seed and that seed grows, and all that demonic waste begins to build up inside a person until, all of a sudden, all hell breaks loose. Your soul is very sensitive, and you must guard it by guarding what you allow to enter into your life!

Words are very powerful and can be used for good or evil. The enemy can use anyone without them even knowing it. Something as simple as a doctor's report can be twisted if you receive the diagnosis. It may be good that it was brought to your attention, but if you receive it in your soul, the enemy can use it to cause more damage. The enemy can use the report to send stress, worry, anxiety, depression, etc. The enemy can use the diagnosis to send thoughts to your mind contrary to God. The doctor simply told you the problem, but you should already know that the solution is God. Yes, there are great doctors who mean well, but they're just giving you the enemy's report. You need to remind yourself of God's report! You are already healed. You just have to defend it.
A wounded soul is the enemy's secret playground because a wounded soul isn't always noticeable until things come to the surface. The enemy can use what someone said to you years ago to impact you when dealing with a new situation that has nothing to do with the past. That demonic waste in your wounded soul gave them access because of that seed that was never dealt with. You really must cast down word curses spoken over your life. You may have had an argument with that person or were upset at what that person did or said but never addressed the wound that situation caused to your soul. You may say you're over it because you aren't upset about it on the surface and have moved on, but if you didn't deal with the wound it caused, the enemy uses it to store their waste and filth. Those negative words spoken to you that you never cast down go into your soul as demonic waste. If it's never dealt with, it can legally stay there.

You must speak life into your soul. There are seeds the enemy tries to send in your soul, and you must command them to be uprooted! At least once a day, you need to send the blood of Jesus in your soul to rid it of anything ungodly that attached to it that day. I would highly suggest doing it far more than once. It's not just something to say, but it holds power and you need to use it daily.

The blood of Jesus works on your behalf when you send it to destroy demonic waste that has attached itself to your soul.

Genesis 2:7: *And the LORD God formed man of the dust of the ground, and breathed into his nostrils the breath of life; and man became a living being.*

Our physical body has no life without our spirit. According to Strong's Concordance, the Hebrew word is "Neshamah," which is translated as breath, breath of God, or spirit of man. We are spirit, from God, and God blew us (spirit) into a physical body. We are the BREATH OF GOD! **You are the breath of God, and God never wastes a breath.** Your real life is supposed to be in the spirit in Christ, and you simply use your body to drive you around. When your body or soul is in control, life lives you. When your spirit is in control, you live life. We must understand that humankind are triune beings. Human beings have a spirit, who lives in a body and possesses a soul. When a person dies, that soul will either be joined with the spirit and live forever with God or it will be eternally separated from God in hell.

Ecclesiastes 12:7 says, "Then the dust will return to the earth as it was, And the spirit will return to God who gave it." In heaven, you will have your personality. If you like to laugh, you will like to laugh in heaven. Your soul will be perfected in heaven when it joins with your spirit. However, on earth, it must be renewed daily. When you operate in the soulish realm, you are limited. When you operate in the spirit realm, there are no limits! We became a living soul when God blew our spirit into our body that was prepared on earth for our spirit. We're to be a living soul controlled by our spirit. God formed your physical body from dirt, but He pulled the real you, which is spirit, out of Him! Your soul is what makes you different from anyone else.

Proverbs 18:14: *The spirit of a man will sustain him in sickness, But who can bear a broken spirit?*

This passage talks about how the spirit of an individual in God can sustain or hold up against sickness, grief, pain, sorrow, weariness, etc., in the body. It can overcome those, but the physical body cannot withstand a broken spirit. It is not strong enough to do so, but your spirit is strong enough to bear any attack. Your spirit can hold it all together, but if it is broken, it seems unbearable. Your flesh is nowhere near the level of your spirit. So, take care of your spirit so it can hold up your body! Certainly, if the Holy Spirit can be grieved or quenched, our spirit can be grieved, starved, etc. Although our spirit is perfect in itself, it must still be fed. Your spirit needs to be fed daily so that your soul won't receive and act upon any bad advice from the flesh.

According to Strong's Concordance, the Hebrew word translated spirit in this passage is "ruach," and it means breath, wind, or spirit. In this passage, it speaks of a broken, wounded, crushed, or afflicted spirit. This comes from the result of a wounded soul. If the soul was healthy, the spirit wouldn't be impacted. If a wounded soul is in control, it can cause your spirit to become weary and grieved. Feed your soul and spirit with things of God. The soul is very unique in that it can take on things of the flesh or the spirit. Your spirit could not and would never receive anything from the flesh. Your soul is really the middleman between your body and your spirit. Your spirit is perfect in itself because it is literally the breath of God. It is the DNA of God because we came out of God. It is the real you, but your spirit can be starved and silenced. It is clear that it can be impacted because when one dies, their soul and spirit join together and either go to heaven or to hell.

Every aspect of you has a will. Your body/flesh has a will. Your soul has a will, and your spirit has a will. Your body/flesh wants things of the world. Your soul wants whatever it wants that makes it most happy. Your spirit wants the things of God. God has a will. Jesus has a will. The Holy Spirit has a will because Scripture says that the Holy Spirit gives gifts to individuals as He wills (1 Corinthians 12:11). The key for us is that we submit to the will of God through our spirit, and our spirit communicates it to the soul and the soul to the flesh. This is why our spirit must be in charge as it is submitted to God. The real you is your spirit, and you must chase after God daily to make sure you're submitting to His will, not the will of the flesh. Satan can't touch your spirit, but he tries to get to your body and soul in an attempt to quiet your spirit.

1 Corinthians 3:9-11: *For we are God's fellow workers; you are God's field, you are God's building. According to the grace of God which was given to me, as a wise master builder I have laid the foundation, and another builds on it. But let each one take heed how he builds on it. For no other foundation can anyone lay than that which is laid, which is Jesus Christ.*

Apostle Paul made it clear that there is no other foundation that will be recognized by God than the foundation laid by Christ. Therefore, any foundation laid that is not of Christ can only be from Satan. It can be something believed to be a nice foundation. It can sound good and feel good, but if the foundation is not the foundation of Christ, it is not of God. There is also no such thing as a good witch, even though they have been led astray to believe so. Keep Christ as your foundation and the storms the enemy sends will not be able to break you.

We are God's field because we grow in Him. He plants us as seeds that take root on earth that His will shall come to pass through us. You are God's building that is built upon the foundation of Christ. God planted you here, and He is going to make sure that you flourish here if you keep the faith. You are God's field, and you must command every demon that is trying to play in your field to leave in Jesus's name! The apostle Paul referred to himself as a wise master builder because through the power of God at work in him, he taught the people about Christ. He laid that foundation and built upon it with God's Word. You build up your spiritual armor by sharpening it with God's Word and prayer through faith. Your soul needs to be influenced daily by your spirit, which is why your spirit must be fed daily. Your soul is actually easily influenced because it's familiar with both your body and your spirit. The more you feed your spirit, the louder it is. The louder your spirit, the less your soul can hear what the flesh has to say.

You too are a wise master builder. You can build others up with God's Word. You build others up with your testimony of what God has done in your life. You can laugh at the enemy because what they used to try to break you made you stronger and now you can bless others. We must first understand the true foundation and know it so that we can then identify the wrong foundation. With Christ as your foundation, you have the remedy to all of life's challenges. You just need to let God keep building on the foundation. As you move forward on the journey, you must understand that God wants you to prosper, and it begins with your soul.

3 John 1:2: *Beloved, I pray that you may prosper in all things and be in health, just as your soul prospers.*

Apostle John spoke of prosperity of the soul. The soul must also be in health in order to prosper. Soul wounds can cause us to not walk in all God has for us. Apostle John tied prospering and being in health to our soul prospering. There is a connection. Your soul must be healed from past wounds or trauma so that you can prosper the way God intended. If one's soul is wounded, it's not prospering and that impacts other areas in life. A healthy soul produces a healthy life. God wants you to prosper in all things because He loves you and you represent Him. There is no lack in His kingdom. Your spirit is already prosperous, but your soul must be healed so that it can prosper. Your soul must prosper so you can prosper in the natural. The enemy wants to block your soul from prospering to avoid manifestation. This is why you must fight back. A wounded soul is bound to mess things up. Send the blood of Jesus in your soul to repair it!

This is why it is important to also ask the Lord to order our steps. He will lead us. The enemy wants God's children sick because we make the enemy sick every time we do God's will. You aren't supposed to prosper in just one area of your life; Christ came for you to prosper in all to live the more abundant life He promised. God wants you to wake up to the healing power He placed in you so you can deliver healing to others. You cannot shrink back in fear of doing God's will. Jesus wasn't afraid to die on the cross for us, so we shouldn't be afraid to go and do God's will, even if it seems uncomfortable. Your soul was made to serve your spirit, not the other way around. Submit to the spirit so you can flourish on earth like God intended! You must pay close attention to your soul.

1 Peter 1:22: *Since you have purified your souls in obeying the truth through the Spirit in sincere love of the brethren, love one another fervently with a pure heart.*

Apostle Peter wrote this letter to followers of Christ who were in various countries. He was letting them know that their souls were purified. Your soul can be healed and cleansed with a healthy dose of the Word of God daily! Simply declaring some Scriptures over your soul daily can bring healing to it. It will bring things to the surface that may have been buried.

Peter also told them to love one another with a pure heart. You can't have a pure heart if it is wounded. You can mean well, but if it's wounded, it's not pure. It's not in good shape. Submit your heart in as-is condition to God for complete healing. It must be trusted in His hand before it can be trusted anywhere else. He mentioned that they should love one another fervently, which meant fully, without slack, and completely. True love can only be sustained through God because God Himself is love! A wounded soul can reject true love because the enemy uses the wounds as a wall against the things of God. You must pray for a renewed soul.

How to Heal the Wounded Soul

Ephesians 3:16, 20 (emphasis mine): *That He would grant you, according to the riches of His glory, **to be strengthened with might through His Spirit in the inner man...***

*Now to Him who is able to do exceedingly abundantly above all that we ask or think, **according to the power that works in us.***

Here we find the apostle Paul addressing the church and concluding his prayer for the saints, and in that conclusion he made it known that even after all that he prayed and thought to pray, God is still able to do far above what he asked or even thought. God never does just enough because He is the God of more than enough. Don't get comfortable or even satisfied with where you are because God always has more! According to Strong's Concordance, the Greek word translated might in verse 16 and power in verse 20 is "dunamis" (pronounced doo-nam-is).

Verse 16 talks about God strengthening our inner man, which is our soul, with power through the Holy Spirit. Since God is so rich in mercy and grace, He can grant us an unlimited amount of this power into our souls. A wounded soul can block so much because it gives demons a license to steal and to cause delays in your life. I declare no more delays in your life, and I send the dunamis power of God to heal wounds in your soul that demons used to cause the delay!

I suggest you look up Katie Souza as a great resource on the topic of soul healing. She is a great woman of God who heavily teaches on how to heal wounds in your soul. She is the one who received revelation from the Holy Spirit on sending the dunamis power into our souls to heal them so that we can be excellent of soul. We need the dunamis power in our soul. Thayer's Greek Lexicon says dunamis also means inherent power, the ability to perform miracles, moral power, and excellence of soul. The dunamis power in you through the Holy Spirit not only allows you to perform miracles through His power, but also makes your soul excellent and whole. Again, look up Katie Souza, who goes into great detail about soul healing. Send dunamis power, which is the power of the Holy Spirit, into your soul daily to heal any wounds in your soul. We also see in verse 20 that we need this power in our souls because God is able to do above and beyond what we could ask or think, but He does it according to how much power is at work in us. So, the less power operating in our lives, the less we will see the abundance of the things God actually has for us. If you feel you have just enough of what you prayed for, brace yourself because God promised to do more than enough, but your wounded soul needs healing. Notice that the key was "according to the power" at work in us. We must put our will down and pick up God's will so the Holy Spirit can flow freely in our lives! A wounded soul is nothing to take lightly because it's a part of Satan's plan to steal, kill, and destroy.

God is opening your eyes so you can target the wounds in your soul. God is taking you from the back to the front, and He is doing it at an accelerated pace. It's according to the power at work in us. We have the Holy Spirit the moment we accept Christ. However, having the Holy Spirit living in you is not the same as the Holy Spirit working through you. Ask the Holy Spirit to go to work in your life!

The Blood of Jesus

The blood of Jesus has more uses than cleansing sin. The blood of Jesus can be used to heal wounds in the soul. Our soul needs the blood of Jesus daily. A wounded soul doesn't heal itself, but it needs you to inject healing power into it through the blood of Jesus. The blood of Jesus heals and cleanses our soul from wounds caused by sin and wounds caused by anything else. The blood of Jesus is ointment to wounds in your soul! Your soul is a storage house that can keep memories you want and those you don't want. So, you must do your part to make sure it is restored in order to receive all that God has for you.

Jesus was wounded once so that we don't have to carry around wounds in our soul. Send the blood of Jesus to flow in your soul. As I have already mentioned before, the blood of Jesus is a weapon. It is not just something we say. The blood of Jesus has the ability to bring life to anything that is dead in your life! There are some things that have been dead and stagnant that need to come back to life, but they have been buried and inactive in your soul. God is bringing back to life some things that appeared dead in your life, and He will get the glory out of it.

Sometimes the soul tries to protect itself from more wounds, but your soul is not equipped to heal itself. It needs help from your spirit. You may have prayed about something and God sent the answer, but if your soul is wounded, it can reject it without you being fully aware of it! Sending the blood of Jesus will begin to heal your soul. There are some things you were supposed to have some time ago, but your wounded soul rejected them. Thank God for redeeming the time! The blood of Jesus can be applied to any wound in your soul or any situation that arises, but it won't flow until you send for it. When you send the blood of Jesus in your soul, it cleanses it of demonic waste so your soul can be renewed. The blood of Jesus doesn't take long to go to work in your life when you send it, but keep sending it until that job is completed.

Part IV. Assassins' Strategy to Maintain the Victory

Chapter 23: The Need for Deliverance

This could be an entire book alone because there is so much that can be said. This isn't a book solely about deliverance, but a chapter is necessary when discussing spiritual warfare. My wife and I walk individuals through deliverance on a consistent basis. People who say they do deliverance don't always have a full understanding of deliverance. Truly, it's an ongoing learning process. And we say often that post-deliverance is just as important as pre-deliverance.

Please hear me and hear me well. If you have never officially gone through deliverance, you need deliverance. It doesn't matter your title. You can be the apostle, prophet, evangelist, pastor, or teacher. If you've never gone through deliverance (**thorough** deliverance), you need to go through it. Yes, I had to go through deliverance as a preacher. My wife had to go through deliverance as a pastor. Yes, our son too went through deliverance, when demons manifested and were cast out. Sometimes, going through deliverance more than once is necessary. Soul healing is also a very important part of the deliverance process. You can think you have a normal life, but you don't know what demons are on your bloodline that still have legal access to you. Wherever there's demonic activity in your life, a form of deliverance is needed. Demons are looking for any legal right to gain entry.

One legal right they often use is the bloodline. There are demons on bloodlines that have had sex with every member on that bloodline. There are demons who have caused the same pattern of sickness and disease on a bloodline. There are demons who have caused the same vicious cycles on the same bloodline for centuries. As I already mentioned, you are one of the curse breakers God sent to your bloodline. We have had deliverance sessions where demons manifested in a person and stated that they had a right to be there because of pledges and pacts the individual's ancestors made with them, unknown to the individual going through deliverance.

This is real, and you have a responsibility to help set your bloodline free. Typically, in deliverance sessions when we are casting out demons, we command the demons to remove the curses off of the individual and their children. They hate having to remove the curses before they are evicted, but they really hate lifting the curses they have on the children. I'm reminded of one particular deliverance session when I was in the process of casting a demon out, and the demon was very upset that I told it to lift the curse off the child. It moaned and groaned and complained. It put up a big fight because it said it knew the child was going to be great. It already saw it. It practically begged to not have to lift the curse off the child. It was more concerned about the child than the parent in that case.

Even Herod tried to find out about Jesus because he wanted to kill Jesus as a child (Matthew 2:13). The enemy doesn't look to attack just when a child is born, but they look to attack the moment we are conceived. They try to attack in the womb because there are certain things they can already see about a child in the realm of the spirit. Yes, the enemy knew about your greatness before you were even aware of it. This is why we also have a responsibility to defend our bloodline through prayer.

Repeat after me, "I need deliverance, too." I encourage you to contact the ministry at info@doquoigreen.org to be a part of our deliverance and soul healing class or find a strong ministry that can also walk you through deliverance. You can also begin doing some deliverance on yourself as you gain more understanding. My deliverance from the spirit wife I talked about earlier in the book was a result of self-deliverance. Yet, I still needed more because that spirit wife was not the strongman in my life.

If the strongman is not identified and cast out, it doesn't matter if some lower-ranking demon was cast out because the strongman is there. The strongman is the ruling spirit attached to that person in need of deliverance. It's the spirit controlling all the other demons. It's the chief demon, also known as the ancestral demon. Just because someone says they cast out a demon of lust, for example, doesn't mean that's the strongman, or ruling spirit. More often than not, it's not.

Deliverance is simply being freed from demonic influence! Deliverance does not just deal with demonic possession, but it also deals with demonic oppression. A child of God cannot be possessed, but they can be oppressed. Witches and warlocks who know they work for Satan are demonically possessed because they invite demons in. Demons give them certain powers. Demons function in them freely. Demonic oppression is when demons impact the life of another and influence them in certain ways. Yet, they don't have full control.

One deliverance you'll need to get in life is to be delivered from opinions of people who give opinions contrary to God's will for you. Deliverance is not just for casting demons out from you, but it also entails evicting demons from a place where God has assigned you. However, one thing that is for certain is that wherever there is a demon, deliverance will always be needed. Deliverance comes into play when demons are hindering what God has called you to or what He has sent to you. This again is why spiritual warfare is important. Spiritual warfare isn't an option, but it's mandate. If you can't war for what's yours, you're saying you don't care if you get it or not.

There is nothing spooky about deliverance because deliverance is necessary in order to effectively carry out the will of God in your life. It is a must have. The great thing is that you have the power and authority not only to bring deliverance in your life, but in the lives of others. While it's wonderful that there are many great leaders in the body of Christ who have powerful healing and deliverance ministries, it doesn't take an extra-special anointing because once we have Christ, we all have the same power of the Holy Spirit and authority of Christ that we can operate in. Christ gave us power to cast out demons. Since Jesus gave us power to cast out demons, if deliverance is needed, you need to locate and activate the power that's already been given. There are people in your family, on your job, etc., who need your prayers and you warring in the spirit to set them free from bondage.

We must also be aware of the tricks of the enemy. Demons want you to get used to something that opposes God's will so you don't think deliverance is needed. Be delivered in Jesus's name. Again, demons don't want to be seen or exposed. They simply want their works to manifest. You have the power and the duty to cast them out. You always have an assignment! Everywhere you go, someone needs deliverance. You are the light of the world, and you shine in dark places. So, there is no reason to ever really get bored. I assure you that someone needs deliverance, and the power is in you. This is why understanding your power/authority and warfare is so important. It's not just good information. It's what you need to do your job for God.

Any time you don't deny your flesh, a level of deliverance is needed because you just became captive to something that opposes God. Sure, this is not the same thing as a continual cycle that you need to be delivered from. The simplest form of deliverance begins with deliverance from sin. You either give yourself to sin or give yourself to Christ. Let me be abundantly clear: Contrary to popular belief, you're not delivered just because you're saved. That is a form of deliverance, but it's not total deliverance. Salvation is the beginning where we get a fresh start to life. It helps us get back to heaven, but salvation doesn't automatically mean that demons just leave. Some deliverance is immediate, and some deliverance occurs over a period of time. Make sure you remain persistent in attacking it in prayer.

There are too many things God's children have gotten comfortable with that are contrary to God's will. No form of sickness is in God's will because Christ not only died for our sins, but He died so we might be healed! Healing is also a part of deliverance. Demons attempt to attack our bodies with sickness. When you accept any type of sickness as a normal part of you, you're daily renewing a contract for demons to attack your body. Reject it! Some people don't even pray against it anymore because they're used to it. Diabetes, high blood pressure, constant migraines, chronic pain, depression, etc., are some things too many have accepted as normal as opposed to cancer, AIDS, heart disease, lung disease, etc. God does not characterize one sickness as greater than another. He sees it all as an attack of the enemy against His will for you. This is no different than how He doesn't see one sin as greater than another. Sin is sin to Him, and sickness is sickness. They all oppose God. Sickness and pain oppose God. In all these things, a form of deliverance is needed. You simply need deliverance from what has attacked you. You don't have to pray, "Lord, if it's your will" in cases like this because sin and sickness are never in God's will.

Also, sickness is not necessarily a result of sin. Some have made an erroneous doctrine around this. Sickness is simply an attack of the enemy on your mind, body, or soul. Sin is not even always the main cause. The main cause is that the enemy will do whatever they can to try to slow you down. If sin was the sole cause of sickness, then the whole world would have a sickness. Deliverance is necessary on this journey because there's always an enemy who wants to trap you and always a Savior who wants to set you free.

Galatians 1:3-5: *Grace to you and peace from God the Father and our Lord Jesus Christ, who gave Himself for our sins, that He might deliver us from this present evil age, according to the will of our God and Father, to whom be glory forever and ever. Amen.*

We see here that apostle Paul opens the letter to the church of Galatia reminding them that Christ died for our sins and to deliver us. If we're in Christ, although we live in the world, we all must be delivered from the world in order to bring God's kingdom on earth. When you begin to accept the world's opinion of you and allow it to determine your status, you need to be delivered from the world. Demons work in the world to try to get you to forget your royal status. Disorder is in the world, but in Christ, you have peace in you that you can bring to those in the world and restore order. So, we see that simply being in this world requires deliverance so we don't get caught up in the world! If we slip back into the ways of the world, deliverance will be needed. Your deliverance from your past will help you deliver someone from the pain of their present.

Romans 6:16-18: *Do you not know that to whom you present yourselves slaves to obey, you are that one's slaves whom you obey, whether of sin leading to death, or of obedience leading to righteousness? But God be thanked that though you were slaves of sin, yet you obeyed from the heart that form of doctrine to which you were delivered. And having been set free from sin, you became slaves of righteousness.*

Apostle Paul made a clear point that whomever we present ourselves to obey are who we are slaves to. If you submit to Satan's plan, you become a slave to him and must be delivered. If you submit to God's plan, you become a slave to His will. We must be reminded that our lives no longer belong to us when we accept Christ. His life becomes our life. He lives in us and through us on earth. Satan employs his demons to try to cause us to disobey God. To continually cave in to demonic influence to sin only leads to more and more problems. Walking in obedience to God brings freedom! It doesn't mean problems won't come, but it's a guarantee that they won't stay. They won't be able to live with you.

There's a difference between demons trying to get to you and demons who live with you. Moving in requires more room. Check yourself in prayer. The apostle Paul talks about our transformation in Christ. We all were once slave to sin, yet God's Word is what allows us to see the alternative. We have already been set free from sin because of Christ's sacrifice, but we must daily die to self and come alive in Christ to stay free. If our heart is not healed, it can open a door for the enemy. Keep in mind that your heart is a part of your soul. So, if your soul is not healed, your heart isn't, no matter how much we may think it is. That's why it's one of Satan's top secrets.

Jeremiah 17:5-10: *Thus says the L*ORD*:*
"Cursed is the man who trusts in man
And makes flesh his strength,
*Whose heart departs from the L*ORD*.*
For he shall be like a shrub in the desert,
And shall not see when good comes,
But shall inhabit the parched places in the wilderness,
In a salt land which is not inhabited.

*"Blessed is the man who trusts in the L*ORD*,*
*And whose hope is the L*ORD*.*
For he shall be like a tree planted by the waters,
Which spreads out its roots by the river,
And will not fear when heat comes;
But its leaf will be green,
And will not be anxious in the year of drought,
Nor will cease from yielding fruit.

"The heart is deceitful above all things,
And desperately wicked;
Who can know it?
*I, the L*ORD*, search the heart,*
I test the mind,
Even to give every man according to his ways,
According to the fruit of his doings."

At this time, Jeremiah had to bring an unpopular message to a rebellious people. To make matters worse, false prophets and priests were misleading the people to have them believe everything was ok. God had sent other prophets continuously to the houses of Israel and Judah, but the people would not listen. Even Jeremiah's own family tried to get him to stop prophesying. But Jeremiah knew who called him. Sometimes those God sends you out to deliver may reject you. It's not them, but it's the demonic influence, and they are angry that you showed up!

In verse 5, God means that someone who makes their flesh their strength will be cursed. Your flesh can't be your strength because your flesh is what the enemy preys on. Scripture says that our flesh is weak. So, a person who claims to be strong but trusts in themselves alone is really a weak person and they need deliverance. There was a drought because the people believed in other gods and mere humans. When disobedience is at work, we are like a bush in the desert that cannot sense good coming along; it is scorched in the desert. Disobedience to God scrambles your senses and makes you blind to what God is actually doing and causes you to accept a lie. Obey God!

In verses 7-9, we see the rewards of obedience to God. You are blessed simply by trusting in God. Faith is the ability to trust God in all things! You will be like a tree planted by the water. You won't fear when the heat hits. Keep the faith in God and you won't fear when challenges come. You won't fear because faith gives no room to fear. If fear tries to pop up, your faith will attack it. If someone lives in fear, deliverance is needed because fear is a demonic spirit sent to keep you living below who you are to be in God.

Verse 9 lets us know that our heart is deceitful above all things. You can't live off of your feelings because they blow with the wind. They can be honest one day and lie to you the next. Yes, your feelings matter, but God never intended for you to be led by your feelings; He said we are to be led by the Holy Spirit! God searches the heart, and only He truly knows it. This is why we are never to be led by our heart, but by our spirit. It's a shame if the very thing we try to cast out of someone else is in us and we don't know it. This is why we need the Holy Spirit to reveal things to us. The Holy Spirit not only reveals the secret things of God, but He will also reveal the secret plans the enemy is plotting against you.

1 Corinthians 10:13: *No temptation has overtaken you except such as is common to man; but God is faithful, who will not allow you to be tempted beyond what you are able, but with the temptation will also make the way of escape, that you may be able to bear it.*

The temptation you may face in the world is not uncommon. The enemy may tempt you, but God will rescue you if you call on Him. God is faithful because when you are tempted beyond what you can handle, He will provide a way of escape for you so that you can handle it and overcome it. God provides a way for you out of any situation, but you must be willing to take His way out. The flesh and spirit are always at war with each other because they are two complete opposites, but there is no temptation we could ever face where God does not allow for us to have a way out. It's impossible for problems to be bigger or stronger than you because the Holy Spirit in you is bigger and stronger than any problem you face! So, the flesh may very well be weak, but we are more than able to overcome giving into lustful desires or anything the enemy tempts us with because the Spirit is strong, which makes us strong. You are not mere flesh, but you are living power being escorted by flesh.

Spirit of Python

Acts 16:16: *Now it happened, as we went to prayer, that a certain slave girl possessed with a spirit of divination met us, who brought her masters much profit by fortune-telling.*

We see that this girl was a fortune teller. She operated in witchcraft. In Strong's Concordance, the Greek word translated divination is "puthón," which means Python. The name Python was sometimes used in reference to a prophetic demon and was also used of soothsayers. Python was another name for the false Greek god Apollo. Greek mythology said that Python was a huge serpent that predicted future events and Apollo destroyed it and was thus called Python. There were some who worshipped this false god and were influenced by this spirit in predicting future events (fortune tellers). This was the spirit of divination, which is what we see in this text.

Notice when this spirit tried to present itself. It presented itself while apostle Paul and others were on the way to prayer. Demons will do everything in their power to try to prevent you from praying because they know the damage your prayer causes! The spirit in this passage was a spirit of divination. Divination means using witchcraft to try to discover future events or cause future events to happen by supernatural means. When you see the spirit of divination (Python) operating, you will also see false prophesying and a profit motive. Money will often be attached just as it was here. This is why fortune tellers/psychics charge to release information. Going to a fortune teller is literally paying to curse yourself. People are paying for a demonic attack and don't know it. If a person goes to a soothsayer or witch, they legally give Satan power over their soul through curses. There is also a written record of the interaction, which Satan uses to bring accusations against us. The curse is then released to follow the person who went to the fortune teller and their family. Those curses must be broken. Again, some demons legally attack because of what someone in your bloodline did, and you have the authority of Christ to break that curse!

Those written records are kept under the sea, which is a demonic world known as the marine kingdom. Satan has agents on land, the air, and the sea. Many types of demons fall under this marine kingdom. There are entire demonic cities under the sea where Satan trains those who work for him. Everything that is supposed to be kid friendly isn't necessarily so, and that's why these demons are being exposed: so that you know. Mermaids are not fictional characters; they are actually demons. Their real name is Merfolk. One way demons gain access is through the media. They're not trying to be discovered, but that's why they're being exposed. Don't take your responsibility lightly. Your prayers literally save lives! The sorcery world is very organized; it even has its own government. As I mentioned already, women hold the highest position in the sorcery system. This is why when you've seen psychics advertising on TV, they were mainly women. This is similar to how there are many male witch doctors.

The spirit of Python is a principality/ruling spirit that has demons of lower rank answering to it. This type of spirit is very mature. You don't directly engage a principality unless they engage you.

We have more power than them, but there are just rules in the heavens. Principalities will face final judgment when Christ returns. So, they still operate in the second heaven. Demons can be cast out of a person or place. Principalities' works can be stopped, but they still operate from the second heaven. When you deal with principalities, send the heavenly host to fight them in the second heaven.

The ruling spirit of Python will many times hide behind demons, but it is controlling their actions. Generals in an army don't expose themselves. Python usually has several spirits closely aligned that it controls. The principality Python can transfer some of its power into demons. This is why a demon can carry the name Python and have characteristics of the principality Python, but it's just like an offspring. It carries the persona of Python, but it's just a demon carrying out the commands given to it by the principality Python. So, casting out the python spirit is not casting out the principality Python because principalities don't need a body. They have a body. Demons are disembodied spirits, and they need a body to dwell in or blood sacrifices to survive. Essentially, the demons are soldiers working for principalities. There are ranks of demons, but all demons work for principalities. Demons can work for witches and warlocks as well, but principalities have the highest rank in Satan's kingdom with Satan being in charge of them all. The demons work for fallen angels such as Python. When you deal with Python, you will often find beguiling spirits. To beguile means to deceive, allure, and entice. They work to cause division in the body of Christ. Certain demons bring division between you and loved ones. Go straight to the root of the issue and command those spirits to leave in Jesus's name.

A python is a powerful snake that constricts and squeezes its prey to death slowly. Just like the snake, the spirit of Python gets around its victim, which can be a person, family, church, or area, and it slowly squeezes the life out of them. Its manifestations may be weariness, fatigue, confusion, and frustration. Its actions in churches, ministry, finances, or a home are felt as it begins to tighten its grip on people. People leave their circumstances because it manifests heaviness, depression, oppression, and pressure. Depression is not just a mental illness. It's a spiritual attack. You can't simply treat a demon, or it will come back. It must be cast out! Mind-attacking spirits want to get you out of your right mind so that they can try to convince you to do things outside of God's will. With Python, there will be manipulation involved and people will not be completely open to correction. They will try to control every situation. Customs and traditions may be strong and have to be torn down. Visions and creativity will be choked. Python will cause people to become fearful, weak, and weary. People will start questioning their own vision, position, and calling. It tries to squeeze out of you everything God has called you to do. There are demons trying to steal the vision God placed in you because they know if you keep going forward, the vision will destroy their plan. This is what Python will do. It impacts groups of people at once. It's greedy because it's not coming for one, but it's coming for all because it deals with regions. That's why the same attack and pattern can be found in families. That's why you see a history of certain illnesses and other attacks in families.

There are other slick things Satan will do to try to deceive. Python loves to wrap around churches. One of the biggest functions of Python is to squeeze out your prayer life. Python attacks your prayer life. I remember a deliverance session we had when the python spirit manifested and said it was trying to choke out the prayer life of the individual going through deliverance. It said it always made them sleepy during prayer. Thank God the individual was set free from the python spirit, who also happened to be the strongman in the life of that individual. Python loves to attack prayer because it knows the power of prayer. Again, we know the importance and necessity of prayer and to pray on the level of your promotion. In other words, pray at the level you've been elevated to. More responsibility requires more prayer. In all honesty, prayer is your greatest responsibility!

What's Wrong with Yoga?

Yoga is very dangerous. Christians shouldn't do it even if they try to say it's Christian yoga. Just because the name is changed doesn't mean the positions do. Just because someone puts "Christian" on something doesn't necessarily mean it's Christian. The enemy is not trying to be exposed! Yoga means union with god, but it's the Hindu god. Some who open the fifth chakra in yoga literally go insane. The fifth chakra is located at base of the neck and where the end of your tongue connects. When you open the fifth chakra, you will begin making sounds you don't know. Those are demonic tongues, not tongues from being baptized in the Holy Spirit.

So, if you have done yoga, renounce it and command any spirit attached to it to leave in Jesus's name. Every position in yoga is a prayer position to different demonic gods. It calls those demons down when the position is made. All the positions are animal positions representing certain animals that call those spirits down. Of course, animals aren't evil in nature, but again, everything God creates, Satan tries to duplicate with his twisted version.

Spirit of Leviathan

Job 41:1-5, 34: *"Can you draw out Leviathan with a hook,*
Or snare his tongue with a line which you lower?
Can you put a reed through his nose,
Or pierce his jaw with a hook?
Will he make many supplications to you?
Will he speak softly to you?
Will he make a covenant with you?
Will you take him as a servant forever?
Will you play with him as with a bird,
Or will you leash him for your maidens?...

"He beholds every high thing;
He is king over all the children of pride."

Here, God was describing Leviathan to show Job how powerful this Leviathan spirit was and that Job could not fight it in his own strength; he needed God. Leviathan is a principality. Job developed pride and thought he could approach God in any manner and assume he was so sure of what God was doing. The problem was that Job was wrong, and God had to correct him. Don't get mad with God when you don't even have all the details. Don't blame Him for things He gave you power to change. Walk in power! Leviathan is known as the king of the sea in the demonic world. Leviathan has a couple of different meanings. Its description in Job points to a type of sea monster more associated with a crocodile. It is also referenced as a serpent or dragon. A dragon or sea monster is sometimes referred to as a serpent. God calls it the "fleeing serpent" and "twisted serpent" in Isaiah 27:1. God told Job that Job could not draw Leviathan out with a hook, as it is an evil spirit that cannot be detected through the natural eyes. It's hidden under the surface. It tries to hide. Again, just like Python, there is a principality named Leviathan, and Leviathan can have demons take on its characteristics. Demons are always trying to hide so they aren't exposed, but when you show up, they must present themselves and bow to your authority. It is very true, as found in Scripture, that they tremble at the thought of God (James 2:19). The spirit of Leviathan is rooted in pride and tries to promote pride and self-righteousness. It deals with much more than just pride, but pride is one that it's known for. This spirit tries to hide revelation from us and twist the Word of God. It causes miscommunication and uses lower-ranking demons who are a part of Satan's marine kingdom to destroy marriages, family, friendships, business partnerships, ministries, etc. It also twists the truth in an attempt to destroy relationships. You may speak something and mean well by it, but the other person may become angry and misinterpret what you said. This is similar to what a crocodile does. It twists its prey until it kills it. The enemy may try to twist your words, but the truth of God's Word will always prevail! Also, this spirit attacks and then tries to go back into hiding.

Again, principalities control demons who report directly to them. Again, it is rooted in pride. We know pride comes before the fall. Pride causes one to be easily offended. This spirit rules over the children of pride. According to Job 41:34, this spirit becomes the king over everyone who is full of arrogance and pride just as every creature in the water fears it. Pride isn't from God! Don't just swallow your pride, but cast the spirit of pride out of your life and tell it not to return in Jesus's name. Leviathan is overcome through the Word of God and repentance of pride.

Shape Shifting, Astral Projection, and Charms

Ezekiel 13:18-23: *"And say, 'Thus says the Lord GOD: "Woe to the women who sew magic charms on their sleeves and make veils for the heads of people of every height to hunt souls! Will you hunt the souls of My people, and keep yourselves alive? And will you profane Me among My people for handfuls of barley and for pieces of bread, killing people who should not die, and keeping people alive who should not* live, *by your lying to My people who listen to lies?"*

'Therefore thus says the Lord GOD: "Behold, I am against your magic charms by which you hunt souls there like birds. I will tear them from your arms, and let the souls go, the souls you hunt like birds. I will also tear off your veils and deliver My people out of your hand, and they shall no longer be as prey in your hand. Then you shall know that I am the LORD.

"Because with lies you have made the heart of the righteous sad, whom I have not made sad; and you have strengthened the hands of the wicked, so that he does not turn from his wicked way to save his life. Therefore you shall no longer envision futility nor practice divination; for I will deliver My people out of your hand, and you shall know that I am the LORD."'"

Prophet Ezekiel was delivering a prophetic word to the false prophets, sorcerers, and witches in the city. There were some people so desperate for a word that they would believe anyone who appeared to offer hope. That was an easy trap of the enemy. Don't be so desperate for a word that you listen to anyone who has a mouth! Don't ignore the discernment given to you by the Holy

Spirit. You will leave with much more than just a word if it's demonic. Seeking a witch doctor or some other demonic practice is simply inviting demons in your life personally. Things may appear to be good momentarily, but you just legally invited demons in to keep the party going. The enemy doesn't want you free, but when you're in Christ, freedom is the only choice.

When this passage talks about the charms used by those false prophets, it's the same types of charms used by those who practice divination today. They are demonic and are usually tied to spells. That's also why, to ensure you completely sever a soul tie, it's good to get rid of possessions given to you by someone you had an unhealthy soul tie with—clothes, jewelry, shoes, paintings, household items, etc. This is important because just as demons can oppress or possess a person, they can also possess a house or object. This is what people call ghosts when they say a house is haunted. They're not ghosts of dead people. They are demons, and demons can take on the appearance of people as well. As I addressed earlier in the book, they can also turn into different animals, and that demonic ability is known as shape shifting. Also, calling on or communicating with the dead is demonic.
This passage also speaks of hunting souls in verses 18 and 20. Human witches and wizards who get to a certain level in the demonic world can literally "soul travel," also known as "astral projection." This is when the soul leaves the body, and a demonic spirit takes over their body so they can travel. Witches use this to spy on people they're trying to cast a demonic spell on or to see why something isn't working according to their plan. In the midst of it all, this passage still lets us know that God is a deliverer. God can deliver us out of any trap of the enemy! It doesn't matter how deep you feel you have fallen; God can deliver you with one word.

Baal and Jezebel Spirits

1 Kings 18:38-40: *Then the fire of the LORD fell and consumed the burnt sacrifice, and the wood and the stones and the dust, and it licked up the water that was in the trench. Now when all the people* *saw it, they fell on their faces; and they said, "The LORD, He is God! The LORD, He is God!"*

And Elijah said to them, "Seize the prophets of Baal! Do not let one of them escape!" So they seized them; and Elijah brought them down to the Brook Kishon and executed them there.

Here we find Elijah, who was a true prophet of God, in a battle of the gods between God the creator and the false god Baal. Of course, God proved Himself to be God. No matter what demon tries to go toe to toe with you, it will be outmatched by the power of the Holy Spirit in you! Jezebel was the wife of King Ahab, who was a king in Israel. She also wanted to have Elijah killed (1 Kings 19:2). We see from this passage that Elijah had the false prophets of Baal killed. Of course, this enraged Jezebel because she helped establish worship unto the false god Baal. The spirit of Jezebel often controls other demons. Jezebel is the puppeteer. Jezebel is a principality. Jezebel is not a fallen angel, but Jezebel is now a principality. One spirit can leave a person and go and get seven stronger spirits. The spirit of Jezebel can control lower-ranking demonic spirits until there is room enough for it to take full residence in a place, and this is why some people influenced by this spirit seem to progressively get worse over time. Jezebel is more concerned with a group than with one individual. If you know something is out of order in the spirit, make sure you pray that it gets in order!

Although Jezebel was a woman in the Bible, the spirit is not gender specific. It can manifest in men as well as women. The spirit of Jezebel loves to attach itself to leadership and aims to control and manipulate others. When it is fully manifested, it is not necessarily obvious because it tries to create soul ties to have the individual feel they need to be dependent on the leader who's under its control. It tries to get others to believe that they cannot survive without being under that leader or connected to a person. It creates a co-dependency to continue to have control. It's very manipulative. You see some symptoms manifested in abusive relationships. This spirit uses spiritual authority and authority in general to seduce.

All three of Jezebel and Ahab's children mentioned in the Bible did evil. This spirit tries to create a lineage of evil in the church, businesses, family, etc. It wants to be transferred from one generation and one leader to another. You have the power to ensure certain demonic spirits won't have the opportunity to reach the next generation. This spirit tries to get one to worship a church/religious spirit and not the true spirit of God. This spirit also tries to kill and silence the true prophets of God or to gain influence with them. This spirit can also try to get the church to reject prophets of God and say they don't exist anymore. Once someone or an institution is under this spirit's control, it disguises itself as the spirit of God to fool others. When one tries to expose it, that spirit may prophecy and be accurate because of demonic activity; it imitates the power of God but can't imitate purification. Hence, we cannot worship gifts, but we must pray for discernment. This spirit tries to pervert true praise and worship and bring in a spirit of idolatry. We see some leaders abuse authority in the church because they are under the influence of this spirit among other spirits working with it.

Every person not in their place leaves room for Jezebel. One way to get Jezebel to flee is through getting in your position and through obedience. You can't afford to be out of your position in God because Satan will try to fill the space with his agenda! Jezebel can actually enter in many ways. Quite often, Jezebel is the spirit behind molestation and usually automatically comes with some other high-ranking demons. Jezebel can enter through nothing the individual did, but it can be through a demonic legal right to the bloodline, which is often the case. This spirit can manifest in many ways outside of what the church typically talks about as far as control and trying to get at the leader and prophet.

Baal is a principality as well. Baal is assigned a region just like every other principality, and whatever the dominating sin is, that is what the city is known for. Whatever the dominating sin in the

340

church is, that is what the church is known for. Baal names the territory. Jezebel worshipped Baal. Those who worshipped Baal believed that this spirit gave them prosperity because it was the god of nature and fertility. Oftentimes, whatever the weakness of the leader is will dominate the church or organization.

This spirit also promotes sexual immorality in the church through lower-ranking spirits of lust, perversion, etc., under its control. Hence, we discussed the sexual orgies where male priests used women to get men to convert (Jeremiah 3:6-9). This is a principality, so it truly will take a remnant of people to get it to take its grip off a city, region, etc. It must be expelled from a region. We have all of heaven backing us to handle this, but we can't afford not to pray. We can't afford to let the enemy come on our territory and take over. We were sent to take over. Deliverance is necessary.

Chapter 24: Defending Against Demonic Retaliation

For every blow you make against Satan's kingdom, you can expect the spirit of retaliation to try to come. The good news is we will win and keep winning! It's our job as warriors to respond with holy retaliation against our wicked enemies and show them no mercy. There is nothing to be fearful of, but it helps to know how to remain prepared for what's to come. You should always cover your family, friends, and those you're connected to. That helps us stay on the offensive. If the enemy is upset at you and can't quite get at you, they will always try to retaliate against family. Make sure you are covering your family in prayer and warring for them on a consistent basis. We're in spiritual warfare, but it's a war that we win when Christ is the general. When Jesus is your captain, the only way you can sink and not come back up is if He's no longer the anchor.

Retaliation comes as a response from Satan's camp to the damage we have caused. It's Satan's kingdom striking back at God's kingdom. Satan knows that he's no match for God, so he sends attacks against God's people. However, he and his demons are no match for the God in us! Demons tremble at the power and authority of Jesus, but they flee when the person calling the name of Jesus knows Jesus. The relationship must always be growing. You should never get complacent with Christ. You are a part of God's army, and you have been authorized to use the authority of Jesus Christ! Since you have this authority, you must use it. Agents of Satan's kingdom terrorize God's children with hate, but agents of God's kingdom terrorize them with holy retaliation. Demons may attack, but your counterattack in the spirit will cause much more damage than they think they caused. However, you must counterattack. Christians don't run from a demonic attack, but we face it head on with the power and authority of Christ. There is no reason to fear. The moment you feel fear, that's an indication that it's the enemy because fear is an enemy of God. Christians don't walk in fear; we walk in faith. Faith is a far superior assassin when compared to fear. The enemy will try to force fear on you, but don't accept it. Fear must be your enemy as a child of God, and faith must be your friend!

Every time you're closer to something God has for you, you can expect an attempted demonic attack. Counterattack with your praise unto God. Praise is a spiritual weapon to use against the enemy. When you praise God during a demonic attack, you confuse the enemy and mess up their plans to try to get you to react in your flesh. Demons are always planning to try to stop God's will. While they're planning, Christians should always be planning to keep doing God's will. You must keep your focus on why God sent you here. Don't lose focus by focusing on demonic distractions, but focus on God's plan, because His plan always triumphs. Don't put stock in what the enemy is doing; put stock in what God is going to do through you to spoil the plans of the enemy.

Some of you have gotten frustrated with what appears to be one attack after another, but you must recognize that the attack is coming because of how much damage you've caused and because you're a threat. Demons try to attack you so much because your threat level against Satan's kingdom has increased! They're not fighting you just because of you. They're fighting you because you're carrying generations. So what if a bigger target is on your back? Get used to it. Get used to winning. Some are afraid of demons, and that's why they might try to talk you down from dealing with them. We are supposed to cast them out. We are supposed to confront them when they get in our way. Just because you don't talk about demons doesn't mean you're not a target. Yes, there will be a bigger target when you confront them and spoil their plans. If you're not a target, then you're not a threat. If you're not a threat, you're not truly bringing God's kingdom. The enemy targeted Jesus, so they will target you. It's a compliment when they want to come after you because of your threat level. We aren't to be afraid of them. They will back down before we do. They know you will set many free, including your bloodline. You're carrying more of God's glory! The more of God's glory on your life, the greater the threat. The more of God's glory you carry, the more damage you cause to Satan's kingdom. Ask God to enlarge your capacity for more of His glory.

Demonic familiar spirits create a report on you and take it back to their headquarters so higher-ranking demons can form a plan to attack you. You must fight back! This is again why you must understand that your life is to be taken seriously. You should take your life very seriously because you're important enough that angels and demons fight over you. Demonic retaliation is something every child of God should expect to have to fight against, but the key is that you're equipped for the fight. The enemy may wage war against the church, but the mistake they continue to make is being ignorant of the fact that we can never lose as long as we fight back. You were born to win. God didn't tell you to negotiate with demons, but He told you to do His will. If demons get in the way, you have power to cast them out! The enemy may attempt to retaliate, but you have the weapons to defend against retaliation. They may try to kill you, but you get them before they get you. You assassinate them before they can get you because you're a holy assassin.

1 Samuel 30:3-8, 18-19: *So David and his men came to the city, and there it was, burned with fire; and their wives, their sons, and their daughters had been taken captive. Then David and the people who were with him lifted up their voices and wept, until they had no more power to weep. And David's two wives, Ahinoam the Jezreelitess, and Abigail the widow of Nabal the Carmelite, had been taken captive. Now David was greatly distressed, for the people spoke of stoning him, because the soul of all the people was grieved, every man for his sons and his daughters. But David strengthened himself in the LORD his God.*

Then David said to Abiathar the priest, Ahimelech's son, "Please bring the ephod here to me." And Abiathar brought the ephod to David. So David inquired of the LORD, saying, "Shall I pursue this troop? Shall I overtake them?"

And He answered him, "Pursue, for you shall surely overtake them and without fail recover all."...

So David recovered all that the Amalekites had carried away, and David rescued his two wives. And nothing of theirs was lacking, either small or great, sons or daughters, spoil or anything which they had taken from them; David recovered all.

At this point, David was with the Philistines because King Saul had caused David to flee, and the king of Gath, who was a Philistine named Achish, showed favor to David and gave him the city of Ziklag. We find here that David and his men are returning back to Ziklag because the Philistine army did not want David and his men going with them to war, for fear David might turn on them when fighting Israel. Although the Philistine king liked David, his men did not want him going with them to war. Some don't want you around for reasons they can't explain. If they knew how much your presence slowed the enemy down, they'd be grateful! It matters greatly that we seek God to carry more of His glory.

When David and his men returned home, the Amalekites had retaliated against them because David and his men had raided their territory. The Amalekites knew David and his army were not there, so they knew they could capture their families without any resistance. While David and his men were working and fighting, the enemy was sneaking into their camp to destroy. What we see at work here is a spirit of retaliation. You will find that when you are doing the things of the Lord and carrying out your assignment, the enemy may plan some retaliation against you because of the damage you've caused to Satan's kingdom. The spirit of retaliation is the enemy trying to pay you back for the losses you caused to their kingdom. This is another reason why we must open our mouths and tell the blood of Jesus to cover us and our families and those connected to us daily. The enemy may have bullied you in the past, but you're not that same person anymore because you've been awakened to your true power!

The Amalekites set the city on fire and took their wives and children. David and his men were so hurt, they cried until they had no more strength to cry. They were in deep anguish. David's army followed David, and now that their families were taken, some of them went from sadness to anger and blamed David. Some of the people who celebrate you today may be some of the same ones who try to bury you tomorrow. Thank God you have resurrection power! David knew he was in God and encouraged himself. His mind was on recovering what was stolen. Don't get caught up in people because people are not your enemy; people are just sometimes used by your real enemy, Satan and his workers. David didn't act out of emotion. We must be careful not to allow feelings to lead us. You don't want to make emotional decisions. It made sense that they should go after the enemy because the enemy took their families, but David knew he had to seek God for strategy on how to get back what was stolen. The enemy wants you to react to the problem, but God wants you to respond to His instructions. He prayed to God and asked if he should pursue, and if he was to pursue the enemy, would he be able to overtake the enemy? God's response was, "Pursue, for you shall surely overtake them and without fail recover all."

David left with 600 men, but 200 were too weary to continue going. You would think that they would do whatever they had to do to go and get their families and what belonged to them. However, God will sometimes trim the fat. There are some people who don't have the strength to fight, but God will trust you with the battle strategy to go in and set them all free. He will remove some people from around you who were once good to you, but in the place He has you now, they have become weight that will pull you down. It may have hurt because you all were once very close, but if you go into this war with that type of backup, not only will you be fighting the enemy, but you will also be fighting these people. It's not personal. They couldn't cross the brook with you because that season has passed. When you come back, you can still bless them, but some just can't go into battle with you. Don't take people with you in battle who will just get in the way. You need warriors whose mind-set is that victory is the only option! So, God can use a few to accomplish a lot rather than have you go into hostile territory with a lot of people who just make a lot noise but haven't tapped into a lot of power. The problem wasn't the person, but it was the spirit behind the person. Your battle is never flesh and blood. It's spiritual. When you go into battle, you should take it personally. However, don't take it personally with people; take it personally against the demons.

2 Corinthians 2:10-11: *Now whom you forgive anything, I also forgive. For if indeed I have forgiven anything, I have forgiven that one for your sakes in the presence of Christ, lest Satan should take advantage of us; for we are not ignorant of his devices.*

Someone had sinned, and Paul was stressing the importance of forgiveness to the church community. The power of forgiveness takes power from the sin and gives it back to the person who was sinned against! The sinner was very sorrowful for what they had done. Some obviously were trying to make the person who had sinned feel even worse. He warned them of the dangers of doing this because Satan would use it to his advantage. He would try to use those in the church to make the church look bad through their actions and unforgiveness, and to try to make the person who sinned feel even worse in an attempt to make them leave the church and faith all together. We must demonstrate Christ's love no matter what because we represent Him on earth. Our lights must shine.

This also lets us know that we don't want to be ignorant to Satan's schemes. He sends his demons to look for any opportunity to attack. He doesn't care if you're ignorant to his plots because ignorance won't stop them from taking advantage of it. Demons try to take advantage of our ignorance, and that's why we must never stop praying, studying, and seeking God for more revelation. Demons want you to be ignorant to the true power of your prayer by trying to get you to buy into the lie that your prayers aren't producing. They know that if you slack in prayer, they can find an easier way to set traps. Demons know that if we lack in prayer, we will lack in the demonstration of God's power in our lives!

347

This passage makes it clear that one way Satan can take advantage of us is through unforgiveness. Unforgiveness gives power to what Satan did, but forgiveness gives power to what Christ did! It doesn't mean you will be friends with the person, but it means that what they were influenced to do will no longer have power in your life. Apostle Paul knew what the enemy was trying to do, and that's why he said that they were not ignorant to Satan's devices. Demons look for every opportunity to take advantage of us, but we should look for every opportunity to demonstrate the power of God.

Acts 17:5-6: *But the Jews who were not persuaded, becoming envious, took some of the evil men from the marketplace, and gathering a mob, set all the city in an uproar and attacked the house of Jason, and sought to bring them out to the people. But when they did not find them, they dragged Jason and some brethren to the rulers of the city, crying out, "These who have turned the world upside down have come here too."*

Paul and Silas traveled on this mission together. They were spreading the good news about Jesus Christ to the Jews and Gentiles. They went from city to city. They traveled in groups. There were teams who went into regions proclaiming the word of God and removing demonic spirits in the places they entered. They were changing the world one city at a time. They were uprooting what Satan's kingdom had established and establishing God's kingdom. They proclaimed God's word, healed the sick, and raised the dead. They did exactly what God commissioned the disciples to do. They were turning the world upside down. They had power over ALL demons, power to heal ALL sickness, and power to raise the dead. We still have ALL this power today because the Holy Spirit dwells in us. When you boldly engage the enemy in warfare and fight for what's yours, you turn Satan's camp upside down!

Some of the Jews didn't believe, but instead of walking away, they became angry and plotted against Paul and Silas. Notice that it said they attacked the house of one of Paul and Silas's friends, named Jason, in an attempt to impact Paul and Silas. People aren't trying to destroy you. It's demonic spirits influencing the people. Don't fight the people; fight the spirit behind the people. Even if it's a witch or warlock, we are still dealing with their tactics in the spirit, and they will suffer the physical consequence from what took place in the spirit.

Demonic spirits will look for your physical weakness in an attempt to attack you in different ways. They will try to slow down your progress and what you are trying to accomplish for God. If they can't get to you directly, they try to get to someone who can get to you in some way. However, you must recognize what is happening to know how to counterattack when Satan tries to get at you. Accept the fact that not everyone will agree with you, like what you do, or even like you. It doesn't matter how nice of a person you are—Satan will always try to find a way to bring you down. God didn't send you here to win a popularity contest, but He sent you here to do His will whether it's popular or not. The enemy can try to attack, and even if they get in some shots, our retaliation will be far greater and cause much more damage. We will win and keep on winning.

Chapter 25: The Hostile Takeover

It's a fact that the enemy is a thief, but you have been given the power and authority to strip them of what belongs to you. You must go and recover what's yours. Some things that you're waiting for have already been released, but you just need to fight in the spirit and snatch them from the enemy! In other words, it's a recovery mission. Some answers to your prayers have been held up by demons who think they own rights to you, and you must remind them that you belong to God. It's a recovery mission that you're more than capable of handling in the spirit. Don't spend time trying to figure it out yourself. God's already worked it out, but you just need to walk it out.

It's your fight to win, but frustration sometimes makes us feel like nothing is changing. It's a guarantee that every time you pray, something changes. The key to effective prayer is found in the power of consistent prayer. The enemy is fully aware that you will pray at least sometimes, but their goal is to try to get you to be inconsistent because they know God doesn't want you to be lukewarm. Being lukewarm is being neither hot nor cold, but it's like playing on both sides. Power is found in consistent prayer, and frustration is found in inconsistent prayer. You must put in the work, but it's not burdensome.

Scripture clearly tells us that faith without works is dead. When you pray, God sends an angel at a set time with the answer. Demons are always trying to stop them from reaching you. Therefore, you must keep praying until your angels break through. The angels aren't weak, but they work for God on your behalf and your lack of prayer slows them down. A lack of prayer impacts the workflow of the angels God sends to you on His behalf. Don't make their job more difficult. A child of God who prays to God has absolutely nothing to worry about because God has a perfect record. If you want to recover what's been stolen, you need to pray more. Pray and war until you see the results!

God gave you jurisdiction over your assigned territory, and He has equipped you with all the power you need to rule there. You are on active duty in God's army, and this mission requires you to destroy the enemy's camp and leave no trace that it was ever there. You accomplish this through consistent praying and warring against the enemy. Not every battle requires us to fight, but we need to seek God for the strategy. It doesn't change the fact that we are in a war. Every battle may just look different. Some things you have been waiting on for a long time, and it's not because God didn't send them. It's because you were robbed by the enemy. Take them back! There must be a hostile takeover in the spirit. Some things will require a greater fight than others, but the key is that you have all the spiritual tools necessary to win every fight. God's army is not an army where you just take up space and never use your weapons. There is an assignment for you daily in God's army, and what you do or don't do always matters. Your presence matters. Your existence matters. God would not have sent you on earth if you didn't matter.

Don't believe the words of people, but believe the Word of God! It's a proven blueprint to get you exactly where you need to be. This is a season when you must apply all that you know in God to do all He's telling you to do. All your training in God has prepared you for this season in your life. It's time for a hostile takeover. You don't engage the enemy in warfare and be nice. Nice stays home and the nasty wakes up when you fight the enemy. Demons know who you are, and they know that you're on the rise. You're powerful in God, and they can't touch your power. God made you a leader in whatever area He has assigned to you, and it's time for you to come forward. People are depending on you. The baton is in your hand. Whatever has been asleep in you, it's time for it to wake up! This is the season that you come alive. The excuses have gone on long enough. The procrastination has gone on long enough. The enemy has tried to stop you long enough, and it didn't work.

God sent you to earth on assignment, and it's time for you to wake up to who you are in Him. Your status, bank account, degrees, etc., do not define who you are in God. They may define you to certain people, but not to God! God didn't send you here to be like people, but He sent you here to be like Him and change the lives of people. That is a significant difference. Your life is not insignificant. Your life is very relevant because God sent you here with assignments that He gave to no one else except you. If you go just by what you see in the physical, the enemy can use that to set you back. You must look through the lens of faith. When you wake up, you will no longer be focusing on people, but you will focus on God and what God wants you to do for the people.

Leadership comes with responsibility, and if God thought you couldn't handle the assignment, He would not have sent you on earth. You cannot allow yourself to get caught up in what others are doing or what others have, but you must get caught up in what you are to be doing. God has more than enough work for you to do on earth, so you don't have time to give to what makes you lose focus. You are needed here on earth, and just in case you forgot why you were sent, let me remind you that God sent you to fulfill a need on earth. You are part of a new generation of leaders who are emerging. You don't have to try to fit in because, with what God placed in you, there's not enough room to fit in. It's going to stand out!

We have the opportunity to be the remnant of the remnant, the set apart among the set apart. It all goes back to how badly we want it. Creation is looking for manifested sons and daughter of God. What separates regular sons and daughters of God from manifested children of God is our pursuit of God. It's all in how badly you want it. Every child of God should be a warrior, but all haven't stepped up to that position. So, it's on you. You can be a spiritual assassin. You are what others have been praying for. You are who you have been looking for. It's time to manifest.

Perhaps you are waiting for the next move, assignment, manifestation, etc. It's already here. It's already at the door. You've waited for what seems like a long time for certain things to manifest, but the wait was not in vain. God always exceeds expectations! You are seated in Christ. You came out of God, and God let you borrow the power of the Holy Spirit. Losing is supposed to be impossible in your life. God is simply reminding us. He is waking us up to get back to what He sent us to do. You may still be waiting for the next assignment from God, but make sure that you are handling the one right in front of you. You have a family assignment, career assignment, community assignment, etc. We sometimes get so caught up in the next thing that we miss the thing God placed right in front of us. Open your eyes! Let's get our houses in order, and keep them in order.

You were born to lead in some capacity. God has given and will give you assignments that require you to lead. So many children of God say they just want to be behind the scenes. As a child of God, your light is far too bright to hide behind any scene! What are you hiding for and who are you hiding from? Demons recognize you, so it would make sense that you recognize God's power in you. They study you. They know who you are. They know the threat that you present. It would be a shame for demons to know you better than you know yourself. Wake up to who you are in Christ. You must stop shrinking back and start speaking up. Demons want to shut you up so the power of the Holy Spirit in you will stay shut up. You are a leader, and you must lead in the area God assigned for you to lead in. You are on the rise.

The problem is that the world tries to tell us what assignment is important and what is not. Every role God gives you throughout life is important to God, and it's important to the advancement of His kingdom on earth. Your earthly position is no match for your heavenly position. Where you are doesn't define who you are. Complete the assignment God gave! There is work for you to be doing. There is always kingdom work. You have been looking for the next big thing, but you are the next big thing. You have to work it. God is expecting you to aggressively move forward in the assignments He has given you and for you to flourish in the place He has planted you.

Romans 8:31-32, 35-37: *What then shall we say to these things? If God is for us, who can be against us? He who did not spare His own Son, but delivered Him up for us all, how shall He not with Him also freely give us all things?...Who shall separate us from the love of Christ? Shall tribulation, or distress, or persecution, or famine, or nakedness, or peril, or sword? As it is written:*
"For Your sake we are killed all day long;
We are accounted as sheep for the slaughter."
Yet in all these things we are more than conquerors through Him who loved us.

You must know that God is for you! God is on your side, and because He is, it's impossible for problems to stay around long. We must look at wherever we are through a different lens from what we see in the physical. In spiritual warfare, in the midst of the battle, you must see the victory in advance.

With God in our lives, all things we face will work together for our good. The good mixed with the bad will work out for our good as long as we get on track and remain obedient. We have been called by God to do something in this army of God. Everyone has a calling from God, and it's according to what He chooses that to be. What God called you to do is just as important as anyone else's calling because all require an invitation from God. Regardless of what it looks like, there is a confidence and sobriety in the spirit knowing that if God is for us, no one can be against us because it won't work. Death couldn't stop Jesus, and fear of some type of death in our situations cannot stop us.

God gave up His only son because of His love for us. It is impossible to love ourselves or anyone else more than God does. Tough times will come in all of our lives in various seasons, but we are more than conquerors. That's beyond just a normal conqueror. We know we win because the Holy Spirit is in us. God didn't send you on earth to share space with the enemy. He sent you to bring His kingdom and conquer the enemy on earth.

Exodus 1:8-12: *Now there arose a new king over Egypt, who did not know Joseph. And he said to his people, "Look, the people of the children of Israel are more and mightier than we; come, let us deal shrewdly with them, lest they multiply, and it happen, in the event of war, that they also join our enemies and fight against us, and so go up out of the land." Therefore they set taskmasters over them to afflict them with their burdens. And they built for Pharaoh supply cities, Pithom and Raamses. But the more they afflicted them, the more they multiplied and grew. And they were in dread of the children of Israel.*

There was a king, or Pharaoh, who came to power in Egypt who did not know the works Joseph had done for the children of Israel in Egypt. Joseph had become second in command right under a previous king in Egypt. So, this new king either did not know what Joseph had established or didn't care. All he saw was that the children of Israel were mightier than the Egyptians. Don't be discouraged by how the enemy has tried to stop you. They may have formed a wall, but God loves to break down walls through you. Pharaoh's insecurity and fear caused him to place the Israelites in bondage so they could not rebel against him and so they could stop multiplying in numbers. Satan knows that God's army is stronger, so he sends his demons to try to stop you. You confuse the enemy because you don't know how to quit!

The taskmasters put hard labor on the Israelites and also had them build two cities to serve as fortified places against enemy attack and to store the king's money, goods, etc. However, no matter how much the Israelites were afflicted by the Egyptians, Pharaoh's plans backfired because the Israelites multiplied and grew the more they were afflicted. When you're in Christ, the more the enemy tries to pull you down, the higher you will rise because all you know how to do is shine! We know that God gave Moses the vision to lead the people out of bondage, even though it was not an easy assignment. The joke is on the enemy because God does math differently. The more the enemy tries to steal, the more God will multiply in your life. The enemy gets confused and frustrated when you face challenges as a child of God and continue moving forward. He gets frustrated when it doesn't break you but only makes you stronger and your faith in God stronger. You don't have to know the demon's name, but they know your name because you've been causing a lot of hell lately in their kingdom!

1 Corinthians 15:31-34: *I affirm, by the boasting in you which I have in Christ Jesus our Lord, I die daily. If, in the manner of men, I have fought with beasts at Ephesus, what advantage is it to me? If the dead do not rise, "Let us eat and drink, for tomorrow we die!" Do not be deceived: "Evil company corrupts good habits." Awake to righteousness, and do not sin; for some do not have the knowledge of God. I speak this to your shame.*

Apostle Paul was talking about the resurrection of the dead in Christ. In other words, some thought there was no life after death. Paul was defending the fact that there is life after death. Paul spoke of how he died daily. Not only to sin, but he was experiencing persecution and ridicule daily for preaching about Christ. The life you live for Christ will attract attacks, but those attacks can't bury you because they will only attract more of God's glory to you!
The apostle Paul spoke of how he fought with beasts at Ephesus. He was referring to demons. He was saying that his fight was not in vain, but it would have seemed to be so if there was no promise or reward after death. He was saying, why risk death daily for no reward? However, he knew he did have a greater reward than just what he got on earth. When you fight against the enemy here on earth, not only will you walk in victory here, but your ultimate reward will be in heaven.

The apostle Paul was telling the people not to entertain those who didn't believe in the resurrection. It would only cause confusion. The enemy tries to connect you with the wrong people because they don't want you to get to the right people, so you must pray for discernment! There are just some people you can't hang with or associate with a lot. Sure, you are to let your light shine and spread the gospel of Christ. Either they will sway you with their ways or you will sway them. Obviously, we should sway them, and that's why we keep sowing seeds in their lives. However, everyone can't have the same type of access. Sometimes we have put people in the wrong places in our lives. So, you need to understand the assignment when it's an assignment. God sends you on assignment, but you should be careful not to make a part-time assignment have a full-time place in your life. You know the difference between someone who is trying to change your mind about the truth and someone who just doesn't know the truth and is curious to learn more. We are to bring the influence, but also be mindful of when your time is being wasted, or if you're being taken advantage of. Keep praying for them. Prayer travels.

The enemy knows your weakness, and he will send distractions to try to keep you from getting to what God has for you. Cancel every distraction! In verse 34, apostle Paul was telling the people to wake up from their drunken sleep. They were drunk in sin, and they had fallen into the trap of the enemy to believe the false doctrines. The problem was that it was going on in the church community. So, Paul was saying that it shouldn't be among them because they should know better than to entertain such foolish talk. They had experienced the grace of God. They had no reason to entertain the foolish talk of those who did not believe in the resurrection of the body and life after death in heaven. Don't get into debates with people over God's Word. You just sow seeds, but you don't have to go back and forth with them trying to convince you, and you trying to convince them. You simply deliver the mail, and it's up to them if they choose to open and read it or not. When you know the truth of God, the enemy can't steal it. When you don't know, they have more lies to use. Study God's Word!

2 Chronicles 16:7-9: *And at that time Hanani the seer came to Asa king of Judah, and said to him: "Because you have relied on the king of Syria, and have not relied on the LORD your God, therefore the army of the king of Syria has escaped from your hand. Were the Ethiopians and the Lubim not a huge army with very many chariots and horsemen? Yet, because you relied on the LORD, He delivered them into your hand. For the eyes of the LORD run to and fro throughout the whole earth, to show Himself strong on behalf of those whose heart is loyal to Him. In this you have done foolishly; therefore from now on you shall have wars."*

Here we find King Asa of Judah having a conversation with the prophet Hanani. Asa was afraid because the king of Israel was going to war with him. So, Asa sent gold and silver to the king of Syria to try to form a covenant with him to help fight against the army of Israel. The king of Syria accepted, and Israel backed off. The prophet told Asa that because he relied on the king of Syria instead of God, not only did he lose an opportunity to conquer both armies through the help of God, but now he would have many wars. Reject fear because fear will convince you to do things that offend your faith in God. Asa took matters into his own hands and was reminded that God had already delivered him from large armies in the past. Don't let the loud noise of the enemy fool you. This isn't the first battle you've seen. You conquered in the past, and you will conquer again.

God's eyes run all throughout the earth to show Himself strong in our lives through anything we face if we are loyal to Him. There's nothing the enemy tries to do in your life that God doesn't see. That's why God gave you permission to use His power to handle it! We must seek God in all things and not try to take matters into our own hands because God may have a better way. This was an act of distrust by Asa. God is looking for an opportunity to show up big in your life if you walk in faith not by sight. Asa went by what he saw. Don't look at how big the problem appears until it makes you forget who God is. No problem looks big when you're in Christ! If it does look big, that's an indicator that you're in the flesh and need to get in the spirit. Some people may try to magnify the problem or think you are crazy for believing God the way you do, but that's why you must be reminded that you're not from the world. You live by faith. Get used to it.

John 15:18-19: *"If the world hates you, you know that it hated Me before it hated you. If you were of the world, the world would love its own. Yet because you are not of the world, but I chose you out of the world, therefore the world hates you."*

The kingdom of this world is not the kingdom of God. Satan tries to operate in the world system. We are not of the world's system or government. We are of the government of God. God didn't send you to be ordinary. He sent you because you would do the extraordinary on earth through His power in you. So, the world sees us as intruders trying to overthrow their system. You don't adapt to the system the enemy has set up around you, but you overthrow it and bring the kingdom of God. Jesus was crucified because the people did not accept Him, even when He did so many great things. You can already expect to not fit in or to be normal in this world because God chose us. You shouldn't be concerned with fitting in, but you should be concerned with standing out for God! We've established that God has a kingdom and Satan has a kingdom. The earth belongs to God, but Satan tries to operate within the system of the world. God wants us to carry out our heavenly assignment on earth, but Satan wants us to carry out his evil assignment on earth. Again, with this battle going on, we must pray. Satan and his demons are haters, but they hate because we have what they can no longer have and that's the power of God. You weren't meant to be normal. The world is normal. If you're looking for normal, you forgot who God is.

Exodus 5:15-23: *Then the officers of the children of Israel came and cried out to Pharaoh, saying, "Why are you dealing thus with your servants? There is no straw given to your servants, and they say to us, 'Make brick!' And indeed your servants are beaten, but the fault is in your own people."*

But he said, "You are idle! Idle! Therefore you say, 'Let us go and sacrifice to the LORD.' Therefore go now and work; for no straw shall be given you, yet you shall deliver the quota of bricks." And the officers of the children of Israel saw that they were in trouble after it was said, "You shall not reduce any bricks from your daily quota."

Then, as they came out from Pharaoh, they met Moses and Aaron who stood there to meet them. And they said to them, "Let the LORD look on you and judge, because you have made us abhorrent in the sight of Pharaoh and in the sight of his servants, to put a sword in their hand to kill us."

So Moses returned to the LORD and said, "Lord, why have You brought trouble on this people? Why is it You have sent me? For since I came to Pharaoh to speak in Your name, he has done evil to this people; neither have You delivered Your people at all."

Here, we find Moses and Aaron, who were called by God to lead the people of Israel out of bondage in Egypt. They were emerging leaders. This was after Moses's first attempt to deliver the word to Pharaoh that God had told him to say. It would be perfect for us if everything we were told by God to do worked perfectly the first time in our eyes. The plan did not go as Moses thought. Pharaoh thought Moses was crazy. First Moses said that this God who Pharaoh knew nothing about wanted him to let the Israelites go. After he said no, Moses then had the nerve to ask for time off for the Israelites to go and worship God, who Pharaoh didn't have a relationship with or even know. Some folks may think you're crazy for doing what you're doing because it doesn't make sense. You are crazy, but you're crazy about Christ!

Pharaoh became upset and thought the people were being lazy, so he said that they would now have to go and find their own straw to make bricks. It would no longer be given to them. So, now their workload became a lot more difficult: they still had to meet the same quota given to them when the straw had been provided. Of course, the people were not pleased about this. The leaders of the Israelites were also beaten because their production was slowing down. The Israelites became angry with Moses and Aaron. Sometimes the people God sent you to bless may reject you! They don't know they need you yet, but they will. This is why you can't listen to opinions or critiques of others when God gave you a snapshot of what is to come. The Israelites blamed Moses for their pain. Some people take things out on you because they feel you're the easy target. Just as Jesus prayed, pray for them because they know not what they do!

Moses felt like he was under a lot of pressure and went to God about it. You are a leader, so don't panic under pressure, but pray under pressure. Moses was basically saying that God told him to do this, but things had not changed. Things had actually gotten worse. Moses didn't understand why God had not delivered the people as He said He would. Yet, he knew he needed answers from God. You may not see all the answers right now, but what is certain is you have access to God, who has all the answers. Just pray! Sometimes your situation may appear to get worse, but keep the faith. The key word is it "appears" to have gotten worse. We must look through the lens of faith. The joy in your victory is always better than the agony in your pain.

We can imagine how frustrated Moses was. He showed up by carrying out his God-given assignment, and now he not only found opposition from Pharaoh but also opposition from the very people he was sent to help. Sometimes those who you are to help as a part of your assignment may reject you because what you said does not appear to work. However, remain consistent and patient because God is still at work. You must realize that when God gives you an assignment, all the pieces will not come together overnight all the time. It is part of a bigger plan. Just because everything does not fall into place the moment you act on the vision does not mean God is not still at work in the vision. You trusted God when He showed you a snapshot of what was to come, so continue to trust Him when challenges come! This situation was also building Moses's character and ability as a leader. God never wastes time or space. He accomplishes multiple things in your life through each assignment regardless of what the enemy tries to do. God will get glory out of it. So, don't become discouraged because it seems everything is not going at a fast pace or if you don't see the full manifestation yet. It's here. It's done in the spirit. There are some things you prayed for that have manifested on earth, but it's a matter of you being in the right place at God's divine time. What God promised will take care of itself, but you must make sure that you take care of your part of the agreement.

God is so strategic that He will sometimes allow it to appear to Satan that he has won in your life only to literally change everything overnight! We saw it with Jesus. Satan thought he won when Jesus was buried, but God turned it around. Satan thought he won when you were buried, but resurrection is here. You may feel like you're buried in certain areas of your life, but God has already planned your resurrection.

You are an emerging leader, and it's time for you to rise. It's time to know how to fight the enemy. It's one thing to talk about it, but it's another to know how to do it effectively. You've been given tools and insight in this book to help you tremendously. It's time to be the spiritual assassin and warrior God is raising you up to be. You are a good kind of different. You don't back down. You don't shut down or shut up when it comes to spiritual warfare. God is calling you. Answer the call. Rule and reign on earth as the kings, queens, and priests that you are. I declare war against the enemy! The good news is you can't lose because you've already won in Christ. There is no time to roll over; now it's time for you to take over. Let the church say, "Amen!"

Warfare Declarations

Prayer targets help you focus in on a specific thing in warfare or in prayer. In prayer, you can write out a list of things you want to cover in prayer. If you want to pray for thirty minutes, it's not that hard. All you need is six things on your list, and you can pray on those for five minutes each. If you want to get to an hour, write out six things to cover and pray on them for ten minutes each. You can come up with your own way of doing it.

I have included some sample warfare prayer targets. You can declare these as often as necessary as you engage the enemy in warfare and come up with your own.

Prayer Targets

Every demonic spirit assigned to block manifestation in my life, I send the fire of God to destroy you in Jesus's name!

Every curse spoken against my future, I override it and overturn it in Jesus's name!

Every demonic spirit assigned to block me from getting married, die by fire, die by fire in Jesus's name!

I declare that every counterfeit the enemy has assigned to come my way to be canceled now, now in Jesus's name!

Every demon assigned to attack my mind, I send Holy Ghost fire to destroy you in Jesus's name!

I dispatch the heavenly host to do war on behalf of me, my family, and my community. Do war, do war, do war in Jesus's name!

Every evil report sent out against me, my family, church, and community, I override and overturn it in Jesus's name.

Every death covenant and death assignment sent out against me and my family, I break it. I break it in Jesus's name.

Every evil pot that witches and warlocks have stirred up against me, I break it! I break it in Jesus's name!

I send Holy Ghost fire to locate every evil altar erected against me and my family! Be destroyed by fire, by fire, by fire in Jesus's name!

Every witches' coven in my community, be destroyed by fire, by fire, by fire in Jesus's name!

Every demonic spiritual assassin sent to take me out, I release the arrows of God to locate you and strike you down in Jesus's name!

Every spiritual robber and hijacker sent to rob me of my finances, I cut off your hands with the sword of the Lord in the name of Jesus!

Every curse of sickness and disease sent out against me and my family, shrivel up and die, die in Jesus's name!

Every demonic spirit sent to swallow up my blessings, cough it up, spit it out, vomit it up in Jesus's name!

Every strongman assigned to weaken my faith, die by fire, die by fire in the name of Jesus!

Every curse sent against me, I send it back to the sender in Jesus's name.

All demonic chains preventing my advancement be broken in the name of Jesus!

Every marine spirit sent to attack my life, I dry up your waters, I dry up your waters in the name of Jesus!

Every demonic tree harboring my blessings from the Lord, I send the blood of Jesus to destroy your roots! Shrivel up and die, die, die in Jesus's name!

Writing Legislation

You are an ambassador of heaven. That's a political position. It's a position of power. Scripture says that, "You will also declare a thing/And it will be established for you;/So light will shine on your ways" (Job 22:28). You can literally create laws to be carried out in the spirit that will manifest in the natural. All countries have laws that were written and executed within a government. You have that same right and responsibility as a part of God's government here on earth. Making laws in the spirit also gives the heavenly host definitive dates to complete the missions you give them. So, you need to start writing legislation.

2 Corinthians 5:20-21: *Now then, we are ambassadors for Christ, as though God were pleading through us: we implore you on Christ's behalf, be reconciled to God. For He made Him who knew no sin to be sin for us, that we might become the righteousness of God in Him.*

Paul was speaking to those at the church in Corinth, but this also applies to us. We are ambassadors for Christ. In other words, we represent Him. We speak on His behalf within God's government. You become a great leader when you follow the leadership of Christ! As an ambassador of Christ, you are also a legislator. You have the ability to make laws. You can make legislation that will go into effect where you live. **You can make laws in the realm of the spirit to be instituted on earth that will be backed by heaven because God told you to rule here!** There are some things you are asking God for that He is telling you to put in the atmosphere. He already handled them, but you need to make sure they're enforced.

This passage shows us that it's as though God is pleading through us that others would come back to Him and get in right relationship with Him (be righteous). Your life matters because it is a light that God can use to help others navigate through a dark place! So, how can we be ambassadors of Christ if we don't know what He wants? How can we know what He wants if we don't pray?

I have included some examples below so that you can write your own legislation:

I hereby declare that Robert's and Emma's hearts will be changed, and that they will accept Jesus Christ as their Savior by December 1, 2020. Any demonic violators will be prosecuted to the full extent of the law of God. This legislation goes into effect on

Thursday, August 20, 2020, and is hereby sealed in the blood of Jesus.

I hereby declare that Laura Smith will have complete soul healing and be delivered by September 23, 2021. Any demonic violators will be prosecuted to the full extent of the law of God. This legislation goes into effect on Monday, August 16, 2021, and is hereby sealed in the blood of Jesus.

It is hereby declared that my new home is under contract in the spirit. It belongs to Jane Smith. It will be in my possession by December 28, 2020. Any other contract in the natural or the spirit is illegal. Any demonic violators will be prosecuted to the full extent of the law of God. This legislation goes into effect on Monday, June 1, 2020, and is hereby sealed in the blood of Jesus.

I hereby declare that the negative soul-ties my daughter Susan has with Ted and whoever else is a counterfeit and negative influence will be severed with evidence in the natural by November 30, 2021. Any demonic violators who try to delay or block or do anything to hinder these soul-ties from being severed will be prosecuted to the full extent of the law of God.
This legislation goes into effect on Sunday, October 3, 2021, and is hereby sealed in the blood of Jesus.

I hereby declare that every demon, witch, warlock, or demonic stronghold that is hindering my finances be destroyed and that my finances are released with evidence in the natural by September 1, 2022. Any demonic violators who try to delay or block or do anything to hinder it will be prosecuted to the full extent of the law of God. This legislation goes into effect on Thursday, May 19, 2022, and is hereby sealed in the blood of Jesus.

Works Cited

Biblestudytools.com. "Shekinah."
https://www.biblestudytools.com/dictionary/shekinah/.

Accessed November 1, 2019.

Biblestudytools.com. "Inheritance."
https://www.biblestudytools.com/dictionary/inheritance/.

Accessed November 1, 2019.

Brown-Driver-Briggs Hebrew Lexicon, Eden means "pleasure."
https://www.bibletools.org/index.cfm/fuseaction/Lexicon.show/ID/
H5731/%60Eden.htm.

Accessed November 1, 2019.

"Cartoons Are No Laughing Matter." The Parents Television

Council, August 16, 2011,

http://www.parentstv.org/PTC/news/release/2011/0816.asp.

Accessed April 3, 2019.

Dictionary.com. "Self-abuse."

https://www.dictionary.com/browse/self-abuse?s=t. Accessed

November 1, 2019.

Douglas-Gabriel, Danielle. "Dee-1, who rapped about paying off

his student loans, joins financial literacy campaign." *The*

Washington Post, September 28, 2016,

https://www.washingtonpost.com/news/grade-

point/wp/2016/09/28/dee-1-who-rapped-about-paying-off-his-

student-loans-joins-financial-literacy-campaign/. Accessed

November 18, 2019.

Etymonline.com. "Self-abuse."

https://www.etymonline.com/word/self-

abuse#etymonline_v_23135. Accessed December 8, 2019.

Griffin, G. Edward. *The Creature from Jekyll Island: A Second

Look at the Federal Reserve.* Westlake Village: American Media,

2010.

Kane, Libby. "The origin of the word mortgage will make you

think twice about buying a house." Businessinsider.com, March

16, 2016, https://www.businessinsider.com/mortgage-means-

death-pledge-2016-3. Accessed November 13, 2019.

Langley, Noel, Judy Garland, Frank Morgan, Mervyn LeRoy,

Florence Ryerson, Jack Haley, Ray Bolger, et al. *The Wizard of

Oz.* 1939; Hollywood, CA: Metro Goldwyn Mayer.

Strong, James. *Strong's Exhaustive Concordance of the Bible*. New York: Abingdon Press, 1890.

Thayer, Joseph Henry, Carl Ludwig Wilibald Grimm, and Christian Gottlob Wilke. *A Greek-English Lexicon of the New Testament: Being Grimm's Wilke's Clavis Novi Testamenti*. New York: American Book Co., 1889.

Printed in Great Britain
by Amazon

56006815R00216